HEIDEGGER'S HERMENEUTICS

Egor Falyov

Translated by Jafe Arnold

2025

PRAV Publishing
www.pravpublishing.com
prav@pravpublishing.com

Translation copyright © 2025 PRAV Publishing

Copy-edited by John Stachelski

Originally published in Russian by Aleteia (Saint Petersburg, Russian Federation) under the title *Germenevtika Martina Khaideggera*, copyright © 2008 E.V. Falyov, Izdatel'stvo «Aleteia» (SPb.), «Aleteia. Istoricheskaia kniga»; 2nd edition © 2018 E.V. Falyov, Izdatel'stvo «Aleteia» (SPb.).

All rights reserved. No part of this book may be reproduced or distributed in any form or by any means, electronic or mechanical, including photocopying, recording, or by any information storage and retrieval, without permission in writing from the publisher.

ISBN 978-1-952671-54-8 (Hardcover)
ISBN 978-1-952671-55-5 (Paperback)
ISBN 978-1-952671-56-2 (Ebook)

TABLE OF CONTENTS

Preface to the English Edition   7

Methodological Introduction:
A Few Principles of Martin Heidegger's
Historico-Philosophical Method   15

I. HEIDEGGER'S EARLY HERMENEUTICS (1919-1924)   33

§1. The Sources that Directly Influenced Heidegger's
Hermeneutic Philosophy   33

§2. The Role of Husserl's Phenomenology
in the Formation of Heidegger's Hermeneutics   43

§3. The Interpretation of Actuality
in Heidegger's Early Hermeneutics   65

§4. Heidegger's "Discovery" of the Principle
of "Temporality" (Historicity)   84

II. HERMENEUTICS IN THE PERIOD OF *BEING AND TIME* (1925-1929)   89

§1. *Prolegomena to the History of the Concept of Time* (1925):
Posing the Question of Being   89

§2. Working out the Question of Being by Hermeneutic Means   101

§3. The Analytic of Dasein in its Temporality (Historicity)   110

§4. "Projecting" as the Basic Structure of the Being of Dasein   120

§5. "Hermeneutic Ontology" or "Phenomenological Hermeneutics
of Dasein" in *Being and Time*   130

§6. The Hermeneutic Solution to the Problem of Grounding
Metaphysics in *Kant and the Problem of Metaphysics* — 146

§7. The Existential Hermeneutics of Nothing in the Works of 1929
("What is Metaphysics?" and *The Fundamental Concepts of Metaphysics*) — 167

III. HEIDEGGER'S PHILOSOPHY OF LANGUAGE — 173

§1. The Essence of the "Turn" in Heidegger's Philosophy:
Prerequisites and Consequences — 173

§2. Heidegger's Hermeneutics after the "Turn":
Creating a "Non-Conceptual" Language — 192

§3. Language and Being — 200

§4. The Relation of Thing and Word
in Heidegger's Later Hermeneutics — 208

§5. "Interpreting Actuality" after the Turn — 223

§6. Heidegger on the "Neighborhood" of Thinking and Poetry — 227

§7. The "Hermeneutics of Language" — 233

IV. HEIDEGGER'S PHILOSOPHY OF HISTORY — 243

§1. The Problem of Time in Heidegger's Philosophy
and his Philosophy of History — 243

§2. Event and Meaning — 246

§3. The Emergence of Metaphysics and the Meaning of History — 253

§4. The Events of the History of Being
and their Corresponding Epochs — 257

§5. Interpreting Hölderlin's Poetry — 278

Conclusion: The Outcomes of Heidegger's Hermeneutics — 293

BIBLIOGRAPHY — 300

HEIDEGGER'S HERMENEUTICS

Preface to the English Edition

This book was written in the early 2000s with the aim of acquainting Russian readers with what are, in my view, the most important and interesting ideas of Martin Heidegger's philosophical hermeneutics. The book was relevant at that time because there were not many translations and studies on the topic in Russian. Even after the removal of the ideological restrictions of Soviet times, the difficulties of translating and understanding Heidegger's language continued to severely limit the possibility of studying and popularizing Heidegger's ideas. The situation in the West at the time was much better: even though English-language readers encountered the same difficulties, efforts to overcome them had already begun. In fact, even in Germany itself, where one might expect no language barrier to hinder the understanding of Heidegger's ideas, there remains the problem of translating "from German into German," i.e., from Heidegger's specific language into more intelligible and customary German philosophical language.

In Russia nowadays, not to mention in the West, there are already many valuable studies that have advanced the deciphering of Heidegger's language and the intricacies of his thinking, which means that this book, published back in 2008, might be more of historical interest. If I were writing this book today, I would write it differently and would have much to add, especially given the many new volumes of Heidegger's *Gesamtausgabe* and many wonderful studies that have come out since 2008, not to mention the sharp polemics surrounding Heidegger's *Black Notebooks*. Thus, I was pleasantly surprised when Jafe Arnold reached out to me with the proposal to translate this work into English. Despite my doubts, he insisted that this work would be of interest to English-language readers even today.

What distinguishes great philosophers is that their thinking and reflections are read in new ways in each epoch, in new historical circumstances, and are found to reveal aspects which are relevant precisely for the current epoch. The situation in the world today is one such background, against which some of the ideas of Heidegger's "History of Being" stand out especially vividly.

Heidegger spent his entire life thinking of the fate of Europe and the West as a whole, yet he was far from the first to have seen signs of a deep crisis of Europe as a spiritual phenomenon. Among those German thinkers in temporal proximity to Heidegger, it is sufficient to mention Nietzsche, Spengler, and Husserl. Among the latter, I think that it was namely Nietzsche and his sharp critique of contemporary Western humanity that inspired many subsequent philosophers to reflect on the "crisis of Europe." This critique features the figure of the "last man," the exposure of "slave morality" and *ressentiment*, and the famous pronouncement that "God is dead." Both Spengler in his *The Decline of the West* and Husserl in his "Crises"[1] attempted to present a philosophical conceptualization of the problems of the West, their historical precedents, and their semantic sources. In fact, even if we take only the history of Western philosophy into account, not even they were the first to bear witness to a crisis of the West. If we look back to Ancient Greece, we might conclude that Europe has been in a state of crisis since its inception — or even that crisis is inherent to Europe's very essence. Heraclitus was called "the weeping philosopher" because he mourned the decline of the morals and piety of his contemporaries[2], and Pythagoras fully concurred.[3]

---

1   This refers to Husserl's "Philosophy and the Crisis of European Man" and his *The Crisis of the European Sciences and Transcendental Phenomenology*.

2   "The Ephesians deserve to be hanged, every last one of them, for casting out Hermodorus, the best man among them, and saying: 'let there be no best among us; if there is, let him go to a foreign land and be with others!'" [105 (DK121)] in A.V. Lebedev (ed.), *Fragmenty rannikh grecheskikh filosofov* (Moscow: Nauka, 1989), 247.

3   Ibid., 489: "'What is the truest saying?' 'That people are vile.' Thus they say that Pythagoras praised the poet Hippodamanta of Salamis for composing [the following lines]:
    Gods! Where are you from, whence were you born such?
    Men! Where are you from, whence were you born so wicked?"

The civilization of Europe is Christian civilization, but Christianity itself has gone through several crises over its long history, each of them endangering the very fate of Europe as a spiritual whole. For instance, the crisis of the 16th century, which led to the Reformation and Counter-Reformation, gave Giordano Bruno the occasion to say that "the world cannot go on like this."[4]

In this line, Heidegger appears to be a representative of a typically European self-critique, such as when he sympathetically quoted the words of Count Yorck von Wartenburg in his letter to Wilhelm Dilthey dated 21 August 1889:

> It seems to me that the oscillations brought about by the principle of eccentricity, which led to a new era more than four hundred years ago, have now become extremely broad and flat. Knowledge has progressed to the point where it annuls itself and human beings are so removed from themselves that they can no longer

---

[4] "'The procedure which the Church uses today is not that which the Apostles used: for they converted the people with preaching and the example of a good life, but now whoever does not wish to be a Catholic must endure punishment and pain, for force is used and not love; the world cannot go on like this, for there is nothing but ignorance and no religion which is good; the Catholic religion pleases him more than any other, but this too has need of great reform; it is not good as it is now, but *soon the world will see a general reform of itself, for it is impossible that such corruptions should endure...*' So Mocenigo reported, in one of his delations to the Venetian Inquisition (May, 1592), what he had heard Bruno say." Frances A. Yates, *Giordano Bruno and the Hermetic Tradition* (London: Routledge and Kegan Paul, 1964), 340; idem, *Dzhordano Bruno i germeticheskaia traditsiia* (Moscow: Novoe literaturnoe obozrenie, 2000), 208. [My italics]. Of course, according to the published materials of his trial, Bruno denied Mocenigo's accusations: "Question: 'Did you say that as a result of the immoral living of monks, the current state of the world cannot go on, that no religion can be considered good, that all religions need great reforms, especially the Catholic religion, and therefore imply that everyone will soon see general reform?' Response: 'I did not say and did not think anything of the sort on this matter.'" See *"Dokumenty venetsianskoi inkvizitsii"* in V.D. Bonch-Bruevich (ed.), *Voprosy istorii religii i ateizma. Sbornik statei* (Moscow: Academy of Sciences of the USSR, 1950), 352.

see themselves. 'Modern man,' i.e., man since the Renaissance, is ready for burial.⁵

In this vein, however, Heidegger, like Husserl, is not playing the role of yet another herald of the "decline of Europe"; rather, it is the living spirit of Europe that "takes the floor" to "have a word" in their philosophies, and this spirit is, in the opinion of both of these philosophers, much deeper and more powerful than the historical form it has obtained over the course of the epoch of Modernity since the 17th century.

The religious dimension of Heidegger's philosophy is well-studied today, including in Russia — thanks to the works of Svetlana Alexandrovna Konacheva and Natalya Zinovyevna Brosova.⁶ It can now be stated with confidence that Heidegger was engaged in carrying out a critique of the Christian civilization of the West, but his aim was not to overcome or destroy this civilization, but rather a "critique" in the Kantian understanding of the word, i.e., to search for the grounds and conditions of possibility in order to ground anew and acquire — through self-overcoming — the impetus for a new round of development. Heidegger, like Husserl in his "Crises," saw Europe's only path to salvation in turning to the sources, i.e., to the

---

5   Wilhelm Dilthey, *Briefwechsel zwischen Wilhelm Dilthey und dem Grafen Paul Yorck von Wartenburg: 1877-1897* (Hildesheim: Niemeyer, 1974), 83. Quoted in Martin Heidegger, "Wilhelm Dilthey's Research and the Current Struggle for a Historical Worldview," trans. Theodore Kisiel, in Theodore Kisiel and Thomas Sheehan (eds.), *Becoming Heidegger: On the Trail of his Early Occasional Writings, 1910-1927*, 2nd ed. (London: Routledge, 2014), 273; idem, "Issledovatel'skaia rabota Vil'gel'ma Dil'teia i bor'ba za istoricheskoe mirovozzrenie v nashi dni. Desiat' dokladov, prochitannykh v Kassele (1925 g.)" in G.G. Shpet and M. Khaidegger [Heidegger], *Dva teksta o Vil'gel'me Dil'tee* (Moscow: Gnozis, 1995), 182-183.

6   S.A. Konacheva, *Khaidegger i filosofskaia teologiia XX veka*. Doctoral dissertation (Moscow: Russian State University for the Humanities, 2010); idem, *Bog posle Boga. Puti postmetafizicheskogo myshleniia* (Moscow: Russian State University for the Humanities, 2019); N.Z. Brosova, *Teologicheskie aspekty filozofii istorii M. Khaideggera*. Doctoral dissertation (Moscow: Institute of Philosophy of the Russian Academy of Sciences, 2008).

very emergence of the idea of Europe in Ancient Greece in the 6th-5th centuries BCE. Husserl defined the nature of Europe's crisis in terms of "naturalism" and saw its cause in the "mathematization of nature" by Galileo, Descartes, and Newton, whereby mathematical models replaced real things in scientific cognition. Heidegger spoke of the "oblivion of Being" (*Seinsvergessenheit*), the "abandonment of Being" (*Seinsverlassenheit*), and the dominance of *Machenschaft*. But both philosophers were generally calling for one and the same thing: Heidegger called for returning to the "soil of Being" and the "originary experience of Being," while Husserl called for returning to "the things themselves" and to the "lifeworld." Would the West remain "the West" following such a return? Husserl was sure of this, whereas Heidegger was doubtful[7], but both were in agreement that without such a return, it would be difficult to speak of any future horizon for the Western type of thinking and living.[8]

---

7 "*What is now happening* is the *ending* of the history of the great beginning of Western humanity; in this beginning, the human being was called to the stewardship of beyng, although this calling was immediately transformed into the claim of representing beings in their machinational distorted essence." Martin Heidegger, *Ponderings VII-XI: Black Notebooks 1938-1939*, trans. Richard Rojcewicz (Bloomington: Indiana University Press, 2017), 75; idem, *Razmyshleniia VII-XI. Chernyie tetradi 1938-1939*, trans. Aleksei Grigoryev, ed. Mikhail Maiatskii (Moscow: Izdatel'stvo Instituta Gaidara, 2018), 115. "'Europe› is the actualization of the *decline of the West*. There is no longer the least inducement to take the field against the 'pen pusher' Oswald Spengler." Martin Heidegger, *Ponderings XII-XV: Black Notebooks 1939-1941*, trans. Richard Rojcewicz (Bloomington: Indiana University Press, 2017), 217; idem, *Razmyshleniia XII-XV. Chernyie tetradi 1939-1941* (Moscow: Izdatel'stvo Instituta Gaidara, 2020), 322. However, Heidegger does not deny the spirit of Europe one last hope to be saved again: "If the history of the West is to be rescued once again in an essentially inceptual configuration, then needed is a transformation which surpasses all the previous revolutions that concerned beings alone: the change in beyng and the concomitant decision against beings and their supremacy designate the 'place' of the beginning of another history." *Ponderings XII-XV*, 99; *Razmyshleniia XII-XV*, 151.

8 "If we do not succeed in actually doing something again with the beginning of Western philosophy, then the end is inevitable." Martin Heidegger, *Ponderings II-VI: Black Notebooks 1931-1938*, trans. Richard Rojcewicz (Bloomington: Indiana University Press, 2016), 39; idem, *Razmyshleniia II-VI. Chernyie tetradi 1931-1938* (Moscow: Izdatel'stvo Instituta Gaidara, 2016), 62-63.

Hermeneutics is not as much a science as it is the art of understanding and interpreting signs and texts. In Heidegger, of course, this art is not directed towards understanding other people, but rather towards understanding Being (as event, *Ereignis*). However, I posit that Heidegger would agree that genuine understanding is possible only between people who understand Being, who stand in a "re-lation" to Being, and for whom the "abandonment of Being," so to speak, "hits a nerve." To draw an analogy with religious disputes over God and true faith, the greatest disagreements and hostility arise between those who stick to the established forms of beliefs and cult. Those who are really engaged in spiritual practice, such as monks, ascetics, yogis, hermits, and saints — in other words, those who have real experience of putting themselves out in the open in the face of the Divine — always manage to find a common language proceeding from their own experience. Even if this does not succeed, they still maintain respect for others' real experience earned by the sweat and blood of the spirit, because every practitioner knows that his path is not the only possible one and that any path requires sacrifice. The same applies to the real experience of thinking: genuine thinkers, questioners of Being, representing all countries, peoples, and languages, will always be capable of finding a common language in the soil of the real experience of thinking and approaching the experience of others with respect.

Heidegger did not address only European or Western man alone. In the era of the ultimate "oblivion of Being" and the desolation of beings, he addressed all thinking people, drawing them into the laborious and painstaking work of thinking. Today, this call is even more relevant than it was in Heidegger's lifetime, as technology and *Machenschaft* have achieved much greater sophistication in manipulating the consciousness of masses and are now demanding ever greater human sacrifices, pitting whole countries and peoples against each other in pointless hostility and blinding them with hatred for one another. When the world is balancing on the edge of self-destruction, every voice in favor of healthy common sense and responsibility before Being and all beings might turn out to be decisive. Heidegger believed that if we succeed in ridding ourselves of the blindness imbued by *Machenschaft*, then the "originary affiliation of nationalities"[9] shall open up.

To conclude, I would like to express my thankfulness and admiration for the translator, who has carried out the immense work of translation, verifying sources, and correcting more than a few typos and inaccuracies, which makes the English edition of this book superior to the original. I hope that his labor will not have been in vain, and that this translation will be to the benefit of at least a few readers.

— Egor Falyov
Moscow
14 April 2025

---

9   Heidegger, *Ponderings XII-XV*, 38; idem, *Razmyshleniia XII-XV*, 64. Heidegger here is speaking of the existential closeness of the Russian and German peoples, but I believe that this is equally true of many other peoples.

Methodological Introduction: A Few Principles of Martin Heidegger's Historico-Philosophical Method

Posing the Problem

In turning to such a complex, difficult, and ambiguous figure as Martin Heidegger, the historian of philosophy finds himself facing a very complex methodological problem. On the one hand, the old Marxist paradigm of historico-philosophical research lost its "legitimacy" around the end of the 20th century; on the other hand, when it comes to discussing Heidegger, there is the strong temptation to use his own methods, techniques, and even language. Heidegger's works demonstrate a developed historico-philosophical method, although it is hardly anywhere formulated in an explicit manner. Therefore, to take the opportunity to establish clear boundaries between my own scholarly approach and Heidegger's own methods, I consider it appropriate and expedient to offer some preliminary indications of the principles of the method of historico-philosophical research that can be found in this philosopher's works.

To determine the starting "system of coordinates" in evaluating Heidegger's method, we shall employ Vyacheslav Stepin's distinction, which in my view is very productive, between "three types of rationality": classical, non-classical, and post-non-classical.[10] The principle of such a tripartite division of the history of thinking is, of course, provisional. It can be interpreted as an individual incident within a certain universal system through whose prism we perceive the past in different epochs as well as different countries: (1) the

---
10 V. S. Stepin, *Teoreticheskoe znanie* (Moscow: Progress-Traditsiia, 1999).

distant past, which does not directly affect us; (2) the recent past, which we still face but which is supposed to yield to the future; and (3) the present giving birth to the future, to a desired becoming. Comte divided history in a similar manner into theological, metaphysical, and positive stages, and Joachim of Fiore divided history into the era of the Father (the era of the Law), the Son, and the Holy Spirit (the era of Grace). Nevertheless, despite the provisional character of such a division, it is quite effective insofar as it allows for distinguishing within the present both the remnants and vestiges of the past as well as the beginnings of the future.

In my view, historico-philosophical methods can be classified according to this division into three "types of rationality." While the shift in types of rationality might not always chronologically coincide in the natural sciences and in the history of philosophy, this can be explained in terms of "contingent causes," such as the relatively late formation of the history of philosophy as a science. Also important is that all three types of rationality *coexist* among natural scientists as well as scholars in the humanities. A type of rationality is like a characteristic of a certain mentality, one which can be shared by "naturalists," historians of philosophy, philosophers themselves, as well as ordinary people. Philosophers themselves, however, do not simply share these types of rationality, but rather are the ones who establish them.

This general schema can, with some qualifications, be applied to history in general and to the history of philosophy in particular, wherein these three types will signify approximately the following.

1. The first type, the "classical attitude," corresponds to classical natural science and classical philosophy. Characteristic of this type is belief in "objective" truth, which is to say that any given philosophical system's genuine meaning and real significance for mankind *can be known as such*, as long as the scholar manages to attain *"absolute clarity and precision"* in expounding and analyzing the material. From this point of view, the historian of philosophy should not harbor any sympathy for one or another philosophical system, i.e., he should *not be a philosopher*, in the very least during his historico-philosophical research work. Such research should be, to speak the language of Husserl, "presuppositionless." The maximal degree of "objectivity" is also attained by means of drawing upon the largest possible scale of information that is not only philosophical in character, but also historical, psychological, biographical, and any other. In my view, Kuno Fischer's series of works on modern philosophy can be read as one example of this type of historico-philosophical research.

2. The beginning of the second type is conventionally dated to the 1830s and is connected with the decomposition of the Hegelian school and the emergence of positivism. This type of research emerged in parallel in the natural ("positive") sciences, history, and philosophy. This attitude is characterized by a critique and "removal" of any faith in "objective" knowledge. The *active quality* of human cognition is taken into conscious account, as is the recognition that obtaining knowledge about any object necessitates the exertion of effort — the greater the effort, the greater the sum of acquired knowledge. This method of cognition is extremely pronounced in the natural sciences, such as in the case of particle accelerators, where the cognized system is supposed to be subjected to complete destruction. In philosophy, an analogous method is vividly expressed in Nietzsche's "philosophizing with a hammer."

In general history, this attitude corresponds to "partisan" historiography, where the "party's" values serve as the foundation for conceptualizing an event as a historical fact. The most striking example of this type of historiography (or rather project) is Karl Marx and Friedrich Engels' theory of socio-economic formations. In the history of philosophy, this approach also finds expression in Marxist science (if any Marxist history of philosophy ever existed) as well as the systems of the positivists (e.g., Comte's "law of three stages"), particularly in their relation to their predecessors, Hegel, Schopenhauer, and Nietzsche. This approach is most often typified by its philosophers' arrogant attitude towards their philosophical predecessors and opponents, whose doctrines they evaluate exclusively through the prism of their own "paradigm." Generally speaking, at the core of such an approach lies the "principle of relativity," which was known in philosophy long before it was discovered as the "theory of relativity." This principle maintains that any thesis has meaning only *relative* to the researcher's attitude, i.e., there is no *absolutely* "objective" meaning, and hence there is no need to strive for such. In the meanwhile, the criteria of the *relative* objectivity that is accessible to man are built into the research paradigm itself. From this point of view, the historian of philosophy is obliged to be a philosopher, and at that a "partisan" philosopher who is loyal to the starting principles of his "party."

3. The third type, as prescribed in a dialectical triad, is a certain synthesis of the first two. In the natural sciences, it is expressed thusly: (a.) the degree of the cognizing person's influence on the cognized system is to be strictly accounted for and, as far as such is possible, reduced to a minimum (but not, of course, to zero), so that (b.) the event of cognition does not lead to the destruction and death of the cognized system and, as far as such is possible, does not take it out of the framework of its natural homoeostasis. This could be called the method of "non-destructive" cognition: the cognized system is supposed to have the possibility to continue in its life activity after the act of cognition, deviating as little as possible from the natural balance in which the system existed before the encounter with the cognizing subject. In the natural sciences, this approach is most manifest in certain fields of biology — biochemistry, electrobiochemistry, ethology, ecology, etc. It could be said that the principle of relativity is preserved here, but in a preconceived form: while the subject alone gives meaning to an object, it does not follow that the object should be "reduced" to the subject; to the contrary, both the subject and object should "adapt" to or "accommodate" each other. The research attitude at work here does not figure in the form of a "party dogma" from which one should not stray, but rather a working hypothesis which one must always be ready to give up.

In my view, Heidegger's philosophical evolution, both in his philosophical ideas and in his historico-philosophical excursions, illustrates the transition from the second type of rationality" to the third. The turning point of these excursions, as in the philosopher's work as a whole, was the "Turn" (*Kehre*) in the 1930s. Before the "Turn," Heidegger set the task (as presented in *Being and Time*) of a "destruction of the history of ontology," as he accused (in the "best traditions" of "philosophizing with a hammer") all preceding philosophy of an "oblivion of Being" and submersion into beings. In his historico-philosophical studies, Heidegger professed the principle of "thinking with a philosopher further than he himself thought." Although it is true that Heidegger applied this principle in his later period, its employment differs strongly up to and after the Turn. Before the Turn, Heidegger altogether boldly drew conclusions on the "authentic meaning" of various philosophers' doctrines, thereby insinuating that these philosophers themselves did not understand their real meaning. It is in this spirit that Heidegger evaluated Husserl's preface to the second volume of *Logical Investigations* in his Kassel lectures (1925), and the same kind of judgment was pronounced on the meaning of the Dilthey's works (i..e, this meaning was not even understood by Dilthey himself, not to mention his scholars and followers like Rickert). In the Kassel lectures, Heidegger developed his interpretation of Dilthey's "work" in such a way that the principles characteristic of Heidegger's own "phenomenological hermeneutics" came to "shine through" Dilthey. In his *Kant and the Problem of*

Metaphysics lectures (1925-1926), Kant was subjected to the same judgment: "Whether Kant himself achieves the full clarification of this problem [the relation of ontic and ontological knowledge] remains a subordinate question."[11] In his work "Overcoming Metaphysics," written after the Turn, Heidegger admitted that he had tried to "read out" of Kant more than Kant himself would have wished to say:

> At first the overcoming of metaphysics can only be represented in terms of metaphysics itself, so to speak, in the manner of a heightening of itself through itself. In this case the talk about the metaphysics of metaphysics, which is touched upon in the book *Kant and the Problem of Metaphysics*, is justified in that it attempts to interpret the Kantian idea from this perspective, which still stems from the mere critique of rationalist metaphysics. However, *more is thus attributed to Kant's thinking than he himself was able to think within the limits of his philosophy*.[12]

Heidegger's own hermeneutic philosophy, in which all philosophical problems are to be resolved on the basis of proceeding from certain hermeneutic principles, began to take shape after the Turn. *Interpreting* as such is understood as an ontological category, and life itself as existence practically boils down to interpreting. Heidegger treated history in general and the history of philosophy in particular as *interpreting*. In the following, we will present a brief exposition of this hermeneutic philosophy's own view and understanding of the tasks and methodological principles of history in general and the history of philosophy in particular. Of course, Heidegger himself did not formulate these principles, but in analyzing and expounding these principles I have striven to not "think up" anything that is not already implied in Heidegger's historico-philosophical research.

---

11 Martin Heidegger, *Kant and the Problem of Metaphysics*, trans. Richard Taft (Bloomington: Indiana University Press, 1997), 8; idem, *Kant und das Problem der Metaphysik* (Frankfurt am Main: Gerhard Schulte-Bulmke, 1934), 11.

12 Martin Heidegger, "Overcoming Metaphysics" in idem, *The End of Philosophy*, trans. Joan Stambaugh (New York: Harper & Row, 1973), 92. My italics.

History as Interpreting

1. From Heidegger's point of view, any historical research is creative *interpreting*, which is always the *self-interpreting* of the researcher. Historical research is *interpreting* because it presupposes the procedure of *establishing* (constituting) the *meaning* of an event (past or present) as *historical*. It is none other than the historical research itself that establishes the meaning of an event as "historical." To say that research "imparts" such meaning to an event would be inaccurate, since there is no "event" as such before the "imparting" of meaning.

Let us attempt to offer some working definitions of the main concepts which Heidegger applies to historical phenomenon.

a.) *Meaning* is the capacity of a phenomenon to affect the *being* of the subject — namely *being*, not the *consciousness* of the subject, since meanings are by and large established unconsciously, and not even the *essence* (the *ontic*, empirical subject which itself is a totality of established meanings). However, the subject-object duality loses its force in *being*, hence it would be more accurate to say: "Meaning is the capacity of the interaction between a phenomenon and a subject to affect the *being* of both."

b.) *Event* is the "atom of meaning," the unit of the being of meaning. "Atom" here does not mean that an event is absolutely indivisible and cannot consist of other events, for the sum of individual events does not constitute the event as a whole; rather, this means that dividing an event destroys its meaning and thereby generates a multiplicity of new ones.

c.) *Historicity*, or "historicality," is a special kind of meaning. An event is regarded as "historical" if its *meaning* (understood according to the first definition) does not diminish but grows over time, i.e., an increasing number of people feel its consequences regardless of whether they themselves are aware of it and its significance at all. An event has its historical character at the very outset by virtue of the fact that it touches sufficiently deep layers of human and world *being*. But for the researching *consciousness*, the historical character of an event might become accessible, as a general rule, only with the passage of time, due to the fact that the human being can never have direct access to Being and is always "thrown" among beings.

Just as meaning is always meaning for someone, so is an event always an event for someone and thus presupposes being-with (*Mit-Sein*), or the being together of a certain manifestation of duality and the consciousness engaged in interpreting. An *historical* event is established as the "joint" being of the immense circle of the phenomena of the past and the "interpreting life" of the historian. The historian therefore bears full responsibility for the picture of history that he established through his interpreting, and he ought to possess an immense "historical instinct," i.e., a capacity to feel the *movement of meaning* in the onto-history of mankind.

Strictly speaking, history is the past as we have interpreted it. Hence the heterogenous, multilayered, and multilevel character of history. Many events might for centuries remain unintelligible and not enter into history, and if they are not forgotten altogether, then this is only because they have been imprinted in texts and monuments (hence the significance of libraries, archives, and the preservation of monuments, especially during armed conflicts). With the onset of a new epoch and the arrival of new historian-interpreters, such events can be extracted out of the "storages" of history and acquire the status of being historical.[13]

2. Insofar as historical research is always interpreting, to it are applicable the main rules of the *interpretive*

---

13 The example of the Egyptian pyramids shows how whole eras can remain unintelligible to us, like gaps in history, partially due to insufficient texts and other records that could establish the *context* of interpretation, but to a greater extent due to the fact that the feelings, aspirations, thoughts, and prejudices of such eras are too remote from us.

method (hermeneutic method): (a.) congeniality and (b.) the hermeneutic circle.

(a.) *Congeniality:*

The requirement of congeniality means that the historian of philosophy, in order to be able to understand, evaluate, and interpret philosophical ideas, must be, *in the very least*, a philosopher; *moreover*, in order to establish their historical meaning, he must be an historian. Of course, this does not mean that a historian of philosophy should be an *historical philosopher*, nor that historical philosophers will be the best historians of philosophy.

In order to be an historian of painting or music, it is not necessary to be an artist or musician (and perhaps such is even undesirable), but in order to be a historian of philosophy, it is necessary to also be a philosopher. This is bound up with the fact that historical interpreting in the history of philosophy presupposes the art of wielding the word and depth needed to penetrate the thought of a philosopher in its past as well as the present, which only a philosopher can do (properly speaking, it is the possession of these abilities that makes a person a philosopher). Of course, to repeat, it is not necessary for an historian of philosophy to be a philosopher of such a magnitude that defines an historical epoch, but it is the case that historical research which will be of the greatest value (in the strictly scientific sense) will be that produced by philosophers, not least by those who wield an "historic scale." There are, in the very least, two reasons for this: (1) such philosophers wield the best access to the "historical layer" in the depth of the being of mankind; (2) their position as researchers is the most distinctly delineated, i.e., although their position is, as a general rule, not "objective" in the ordinary sense of the term and is often openly premeditated, this premeditatedness can easily be taken into account in analysis insofar as it proceeds from the articulated provisions of the philosopher's doctrine.

The position of the ordinary historian of philosophy is no less conditioned by a definite philosophical standpoint, but this standpoint is not articulated and is therefore more difficult to factor into consideration.

The history of philosophy is inseparable from philosophy because, among other reasons, philosophy is the *doctrine of the human spirit's movement from non-truth to truth*, and the history of philosophy is a testimony to, and conceptualization of, how this movement has come to be in actuality. This is not, of course, tantamount to recognizing some kind of uninterrupted progress in philosophy, but as a general rule it is the case that grand historical epochs begin with a significant breakthrough by the efforts of one or a few *geniuses*, wisemen, and enlightened ones. The essence of philosophy lies in the process and method of such "changes in attitudes," in the path of the spirit that creates and goes through the birth pangs of generating Itself, and this essence most fully manifests itself and unfolds in the historico-philosophical process, and even in the lives of individual philosophers, as if in "holographic fragments." Thus, the genuine *subject* of philosophical development turns out to be *humanity* as a whole, as an *historical subject*. Therefore, no philosophy can be complete (after Hegel and especially after Dilthey and Heidegger) that is not historical, and there can be no genuine history of philosophy that would not itself be a determinate *philosophy*.

(b.) *The hermeneutic circle:*

The hermeneutic circle is the most general structure of interpreting. Historical interpreting, moving around this circle, entails:

i) *understanding* — the passive, "receptive" side;

ii) historical *critique* — the active, creative activity of the interpreting subject.

According to Heidegger, *understanding* is not as much a *result* of interpreting as it is the necessary condition for any interpreting. Understanding is the starting point of the hermeneutic circle, and interpreting, going through the cycle of critique, returns to this starting point (and is checked with it while it moves around the circle). As a result, understanding becomes truer, fuller, deeper, and clearer.

Understanding entails *learning the language* of the original *text* or monument, whereby "text" and "language" are to be understood in the broadest possible sense, ranging from the "natural" language of linguistics to the language of allegories, symbols, as well as that which remains unsaid, as employed by the author in a given text. Ultimately, understanding should lead to *full identification*, insofar as such is possible, between the research standpoint of the historian and the attitude taken up by the author when they wrote the text.

In the act of understanding, the researcher approaches the text *directly*, "uncritically," as the direct expression of the author's thought. Understanding requires the ability to attain a maximal "presuppositionlessness," which involves excluding and bracketing contemporary elements, all personal positions, prejudices, and preferences. It is a sign that understanding has been reached to a significant degree when one is unable to *say* anything about the text, and instead reposes in a state of "silent thought" — because only in silent thought can one hear what the text itself bears. The process of expressing understanding in words is very difficult, complex, and demands the enormous, additional work that constitutes *historical critique*.

Historical critique, properly speaking, constitutes the *visible* part of what is called historical research (whereas understanding is its invisible and inexpressible basis). On the whole, the aim of critique coincides with the aim of interpreting to the extent that the understanding achieved by the historian in battling the "spirit of oblivion" can express a given thought in words and render it accessible to his contemporaries. Critique is carried out in two aspects, *synchronic* and *diachronic*. The first includes a number of altogether complex and subtle tasks, such as:

(1) reconstructing the distance between the author and the text: defining the meaning that the author *intended* to inlay in their texts;

(2) comparing and demarcating the latter from the meaning that the author *actually* inlaid in their texts;

(3) logical analysis: determining the extent to which the author is consistent in the development of his thought. For the historian of philosophy, in the very least as an historian, instances of inconsistency are not simply shortcomings but are of the greatest interest; after all, it is precisely in such cases that rational logic yields to the antinomian mind and the supra-rational dictates of the heart which most fully reflect the *existential meaning* of philosophizing, as the philosopher feels an "event of the onto-history of mankind" and bears it out through his thought. For example, in his book *Kant and the Problem of Metaphysics*, Heidegger advances the thought that Kant, in the revisions to the second edition of his *Critique of Pure Reason*, deviated from the consistent development of thought that had in the first edition led him (according to Heidegger) to the "productive power of the imagination" as the ultimate ground of both of the main cognitive faculties, sensibility and reason. Heidegger sees in this inconsistency not simply a "logical defect" in Kant's system but, to the contrary, its substantive outcome: the "groundlessness" of metaphysics, the indication that metaphysics cannot be grounded within the limits of its own attitude and therefore has to overcome and "remove" itself.

(4) assessing the authenticity and expediency of terminology. This task includes, firstly, the *strict* (as far as possible) *definition of the signification* (the logical content) of the *concepts* employed by the philosopher, and the comparison of these concepts to the particular terms of the philosopher's natural language and other natural languages (above all the

language of the interpreter). Thus, this task is particularly concerned with analyzing the boundaries of the possibility of translation, which in distant cultural areas determines the entirety of historico-philosophical research.

Secondly, this entails properly *terminological critique*, that is, determining the authenticity and expediency of the *terms* used by the philosopher to express his *concepts* in language. The degree of expediency might be minor, for example, when the connotations of a term in natural and philosophical language do not align with the primary meaning attributed to the term within the context of the given philosopher's thought. For example, in his later works (such as *On the Way to Language*) Heidegger came to regard the term "being" in *Being and Time* as inadequate for the matter he wanted to express, because the long tradition of using this term in "metaphysics" had imparted it with a whole range of connotations which are irrelevant within the context of Heidegger's thinking. In this instance, Heidegger acted like an historian of philosophy towards himself. The philosopher is not the only one capable of successfully carrying out this task. The historian of philosophy can also judge the adequacy of terms on the basis of reconstructing the main course of a philosopher's thought, although this does not mean that these terms ought to be replaced with more adequate ones — it is usually enough to qualify the sense in which a certain term is used in certain contexts.

(5) highlighting and clearly formulating the *problems* and *questions* facing a philosopher. This work should, of course, take as its point of departure the philosopher's own formulation of the problems, if such a formulation exists. However, the problem should be formulated such that its significance becomes obvious *beyond* the confines of the given philosophical doctrine and in its connection to the historical life of humanity in a given epoch.

Besides *synchronic* analysis, *critique* obviously includes *diachronic* analysis. This means:

1. Defining the preconditions and "roots" of a philosophical doctrine in:

    a) philosophical prehistory, i.e.:

        — how the philosopher himself came to be aware of it;

        — how it can be reconstructed from an historical point of view

    b) the "civilian" prehistory, i.e., the totality of factors and motives of a social character.

It is here that the philosopher's most important quality is manifested: being an expression of the "objective spirit of the time." Philosophy does not only *reflect* the determinate state of the *being* of humanity in a given epoch, but itself composes the *event* that forms the epoch. For example, according to Heidegger's thought, Plato's philosophy was the event that formed the entire epoch of European metaphysics lasting at least until Hegel. The role of the philosopher here lies in expressing a certain reality influencing the deep layers of the being of humanity, one that has only vaguely been felt by many others, and to express this not in the form of poetic insight, but in the form of a precise and substantiated *logos*-word. Philosophy comes very close to poetry on this matter, but poetry appears to be more of an expression of the "spirit of the times" within categories of the eternal through insight into the eternal meaning at play in temporal and transient phenomena, whereas philosophy, conversely, gives the eternal expression in the word, in language, and thereby envelops it in the flesh of the time. Hence, studying the history of philosophy, rather than the history of poetry, allows for a deeper penetration of the "spirit of the times" in a specific historical era.[14]

---

14 On the relation between philosophy and poetry in Heidegger, see Chapter III, §6 below.

2. Determining a given doctrine's consequences and paths of development, including those which:

a) have actually materialized;

b) are logically and historically possible, but have not been realized.

It is very often the case that the potency of a philosophical doctrine is fully realized only long after the doctrine becomes known. Such was the fate of the works of Aristotle, Nicholas Cusanus, and Spinoza. Such is the current fate of the majority of Russian philosophers. The role of the historian of philosophy is especially important here, as he can restore to humanity an achievement and inheritance of immense value by giving a doctrine from the past a second birth and life.

Now that we have outlined the work of historico-philosophical critique in general contours, we need to return, in accordance with the method of the hermeneutic circle, to understanding. It really is the case that understanding imposes substantial limitations on the work of critique. Critiquing terminology and the substitution of terms, for instance, is generally only applicable to contemporary or recent philosophical doctrines. There are two reasons for this: firstly, past philosophers largely determined the connotations of terms in natural and philosophical language themselves (Parmenides' "being," Plato's "idea," Descartes' "subject," etc.); secondly, the living fabric of language in which philosophical texts are written "dries up" over time, and language becomes, to one degree or another, "dead" (such, for example, is the case with Hegel's language, even though the German language is still alive), while replacements can be made only in living, developing language. Moreover, the actual word-usage of a philosopher can offer material for etymological critique, for bringing into relief the "inner form of a word" (Potebnya) and the resounding of the atomic meanings in the roots of words, even when these meanings cannot be derived from etymology (cf. Plato's pseudo-etymologies in the *Cratylus*).

The situation with terminology and the exterior "dressing" of thought is even more severe when it comes to ideas, i.e., *concepts*: in no case whatsoever should the concepts used by a philosopher (no matter how he might have terminologically designated them) be replaced by other concepts, whether concepts from contemporary thinking or simply other philosophical "styles." Concepts which are "transcendent" in relation to a given philosophical language need to be used extremely cautiously when it comes to generally characterizing and evaluating a philosophical doctrine. Hence the general methodological requirement of *conceptual authenticity*: in historico-philosophical interpretation, as a rule, one can use and reconstruct only those concepts (not *terms*) which were actually present in the language and thinking of the era in question.

In particular, this presupposes "archaeological excavations" in the multidimensional significations of terms (since we only have access to concepts through terms) and distinguishing the older layers of meaning from later ones by way of philosophical and linguistic critique. Heidegger himself carried out such work with respect to the Greek notions of *logos, aletheia, physis,* etc., thereby liberating them from "metaphysical overlayerings."

One example of historical-philosophical research that fails to be scientifically rigorous would be that of Hegel, who projected onto the past his own concept of dialectic, itself a cutting-edge philosophical doctrine of his time, and his own conceptual apparatus, which could not provide any authentic concepts for historico-philosophical research. Conversely, Aristotle's historico-philosophical views would be more scientific, because even though Aristotle examined past philosophy through the prism of his own concepts, these concepts were not entirely alien to the language and thinking of the philosophers he interpreted (e.g., the concept of matter, the prime mover, forms and ends).

The outcome of such an "understanding critique" should, according to Heidegger, be new philosophical content that creatively develops the essential kernel of the interpreted text. This expresses the historicality of philosophy, which is rooted in thinking through the history of philosophy and grows out of this thinking. In Heidegger's words:

> Every exposition must of course not only draw upon the substance of the text; it must also, without presuming, imperceptibly give to the text something out of its own substance. This part that is added is what the layman, judging on the basis of what he holds to be the content of the text, constantly perceives as a meaning read in, and with the right that he claims for himself criticizes as an arbitrary imposition. Still, while a right elucidation never understands the text better than the author understood it, it does surely understand it differently. Yet this difference must be of such a kind as to touch upon the Same toward which the elucidated text is thinking.[15]

---

15 Martin Heidegger, "The Word of Nietzsche: 'God is Dead'" in idem, *The Question Concerning Technology and Other Essays*, trans. William Lovitt (New York: Harper Perennial, 2013), 58; idem, *Raboty i razmyshleniia raznykh let*, trans. A.V. Mikhailov (Moscow: Gnozis, 1993), 171-172.

I
HEIDEGGER'S EARLY HERMENEUTICS (1919-1924)

§1. The Sources that Directly Influenced Heidegger's Hermeneutic Philosophy

Heidegger himself, as is well known, sparingly cited sources that influenced him in one way or another. Yet, it is only natural that there were many such sources, and we can highlight at least three that exerted a direct influence on the formation of Heidegger's hermeneutics. Perhaps it is the case, however, that none of them can be deemed predominant or definitive. For example, Edmund Husserl wrote to Roman Ingarden: "I, unfortunately, did not determine his philosophical formation — it was obvious that he was already original by the time he studied my works."[16] The same could be said of Heidegger's relation to the works of Dilthey, Nietzsche, and Plato, or the poetry of Hölderlin and George. It appears to be the case that Heidegger is one of those philosophers of whom Plato said in the *Cratylus* (having Heraclitus in mind) that they are "born themselves." Speaking of the "phenomenological period" in Heidegger's philosophy, Igor Mikhailov poses the task of "pointing out, as far as such is possible, the originality of his philosophizing, which calls into question whether the philosopher himself belongs to any school of thought (in the traditionally understood sense of the word)."[17] Indeed, it is the originality and independence in Heidegger's interpretation of the works of his most prominent predecessors that allows us to immediately, *a priori*, issue a judgment on the question, "Was Heidegger a phenomenologist?" Phenomenology was only

---

16 From a letter dated 19 November 1927 (*Briefe III*, 234), quoted in the translator's commentary in Martin Heidegger, "*Moi put' v fenomenologiiu*," trans. Igor Mikhailov, *Logos* 6 (1994), 283.

17 Ibid., 284.

one of the sources on which Heidegger drew. Therefore, we can regard as uncontroversial the thesis, long discussed and demonstrated in Heidegger studies, that "Heidegger's path to *Being and Time*, a work that reinterpreted phenomenology in a completely new way, began back in 1919,"[18] which means back at the very beginning of the decade (1919-1929) to which, as Richardson has established[19], Heidegger's use of the term "phenomenology" (with respect to his own works) was confined. Even though the originality of Heidegger's philosophy as a whole became manifest only in *Being and Time*, a work finished in Spring 1926, the formation of his philosophy followed a definite internal logic from the very beginning, and this logic left its imprint on all other exterior influences.

Thus, in speaking of the sources that directly influenced the formation of Heidegger's hermeneutic philosophy, we find ourselves before the task of tracing and revealing the internal logic of the development of Heidegger's ideas first and foremost. In other words, in accordance with Dilthey's understanding of the method of the human sciences, the point is not to explain the formation of Heidegger's hermeneutics in terms of various exterior influences, but to endeavor to better understand this formation by tracing how his hermeneutics "assimilated" or "appropriated" other sources.

On the list of sources that exerted an essential influence on Heidegger's hermeneutics, Dilthey can be put in first place at the very outset, as the very method of hermeneutics, along with some of the main problems that arise therein and the intentions to resolve them that clearly emerge in Heidegger, have much in common with Dilthey's posing of the question. Dilthey was the first to expand the traditional understanding of hermeneutics as the science or art of interpreting texts to encompass the understanding of "manifestations of life"

---

18 Ibid., 285.

19 William J. Richardson, S.J., *Heidegger: Through Phenomenology to Thought* (The Hague: Nijhoff, 1963).

through which one must pass in order to reach the "life of the other." With Dilthey, hermeneutics was transformed from an auxiliary discipline of historical critique into the foundational method of the sciences of the spirit (*Geisteswissenschaften*). As we will see below in our examination of Heidegger's 1923 lectures, *Ontology — The Hermeneutics of Facticity*, it is precisely from Dilthey's understanding of hermeneutics that Heidegger proceeded to develop his own hermeneutic philosophy. Mikhailov speaks of Dilthey's influence on Heidegger thusly:

> Already in Heidegger's lectures of the 1919-20 winter semester, the influence of Dilthey is felt no less strongly than that of Husserl: to the greatest extent this pertains to the problem of the 'hermeneutic facticity' of human existence (Dasein)."[20] Scholars even consider it possible to speak of a "philosophy of life" period in Heidegger's development in 1919-1923, which presumes that if Heidegger would have been compelled to write a book at the time, then it most likely would have been titled *Life and Time*, not *Being and Time*.[21]

The previously unpublished Kassel lectures that appeared in the 1980s, which are devoted to the "research work [*Arbeit*] of Dilthey," shed new light on this period of the formation of Heidegger's original philosophy and Dilthey's role in particular. These 10 lectures, entitled *Wilhelm Dilthey's Research Work and the Present Struggle for a Historical Worldview*, were delivered in 1925 at the Kurhessen Society for Art and Science. In these lectures, Heidegger developed his interpretation of Dilthey's "*Arbeit*" in such a way that Dilthey himself "sheds light" on the fundamental principles that would be characteristic of Heidegger's own "phenomenological hermeneutics." This is yet another testimony to Heidegger's use of the above-described principles of historico-philosophical interpretation before the Turn.

---

20 Martin Heidegger, *Sein und Zeit*, 16th ed. (Tübingen: Max Niemeyer, 1986), 72.
21 Igor Mikhailov in Heidegger, "*Moi put' v fenomenologiiu*," 283.

Heidegger was particularly concerned with distancing himself from the traditional treatment of Dilthey, as expressed, for example, in Eduard Spranger's article on the occasion of Rickert's 60th birthday.

> All of us — Rickert, the phenomenologists, the movement connected with Dilthey — we all find ourselves in the great struggle {imagine: the great struggle!} for the timeless in the historical, for the realm of sense and of its historical expression in a developed, concrete culture, for a theory of values that leads beyond the subjective to the objective and valid.[22]

Heidegger remarked: "Dilthey's authentic tendency is not at all the one designated here, and I'd ask the phenomenologists to remove me from their list."[23] This utterance, which testifies to a special interpretation of Dilthey, is supposedly from 1923, and it was at the end of that year that Heidegger received the correspondence between Dilthey and Count Yorck von Wartenburg from Rothacker, which for Heidegger turned out to be a real discovery and revelation. Although the new material mainly confirmed Heidegger's existing interpretation of Dilthey's philosophy, the correspondence originated the new stage of interpretation that would be reflected in the Kassel lectures. Heidegger wrote:

> What was surprising for me was Count Yorck's superiority on all principal philosophical questions; his instinct was ahead of his time by half a century. The direction in which he prompted Dilthey to go is the same one that I worked out in my lecture course on Dilthey, where I remarked that Dilthey had not achieved his goal along this path. Nevertheless, Yorck did not lack conceptual possibilities and the way to work through them. Expressions in the likes of "philosophizing is historical thinking" are in their very nature more instinctive and require due insight, but here is where the real problems begin… From the correspondence I have taken

---

22 Eduard Spranger, "Rickerts System," *Logos* 12 (1923/24), 198, quoted in Heidegger, *Logic: The Question of Truth*, trans. Thomas Sheehan (Bloomington: Indiana University Press, 2010), 76.

23 Quoted in Frithjof Rodi, *Erkenntnis des Erkannten. Zur Hermeneutik des 19 und 20 Jahrhundert* (Frankfurt am Main: Suhrkamp, 1990), quoted by Mikhailov in Heidegger, "*Moi put' v fenomenologiiu.*"

the central question of "historicity," and I am attempting to make it more intelligible over the course of substantive discussion.²⁴

Speaking of his interpretation of Dilthey's *Arbeit* in his Kassel lectures, it is noticeable that Heidegger is not striving for a literal interpretation of Dilthey's texts, just as he does not consider it necessary to follow Dilthey's self-interpretation of his own philosophy.

> Dilthey was open to all suggestions. It thus came to pass that even Windelband's and Rickert's philosophy of history, which he himself had influenced, could then have a retroactive effect on him such that he in the end misconstrued the directions of his own work. Thus his most proper intentions were still left unrealized.²⁵

In what, according to Heidegger, did Dilthey's authentic intention lay? We will return to this question in greater detail, as well as to the content of the Kassel lectures themselves, in our examination of Heidegger's own hermeneutic philosophy. In the meanwhile, in speaking of Dilthey's influence on Heidegger, here we shall only point to the fundamental "principle of historicity" which, according to Heidegger himself, he took from the Dilthey-Yorck correspondence. Reference to Yorck is also present in the Kassel lectures:

> The cultivation of a historical worldview is grounded in historical research. (Yorck: "Our common interest is to understand historicality."²⁶). It is a matter of elaborating the being of the historical, i.e., historicality and not the historical, being and not beings, reality and not the real. It is therefore not a question

---

24 Frithjof Rodi (ed.), *Dilthey-Jahrbuch für Philosophie und Geschichte der Geisteswissenschaften* (Göttingen: Vandenhoeck & Ruprecht, 1988), 202-203, 207.

25 Martin Heidegger, "Wilhelm Dilthey's Research and the Current Struggle for a Historical Worldview," trans. Theodore Kisiel, in Theodore Kisiel and Thomas Sheehan (eds.), *Becoming Heidegger: On the Trail of his Early Occasional Writings, 1910-1927*, 2nd ed. (London: Routledge, 2014), 251; idem, "*Issledovatel'skaia rabota Vil'gel'ma Dil'teia i bor'ba za istoricheskoe mirovozzrenie v nashi dni. Desiat' dokladov, prochitannykh v Kassele (1925 g.)*" in G.G. Shpet and M. Heidegger, *Dva teksta o Vil'gel'me Dil'tee* (Moscow: Gnozis, 1995), 151.

26 Wilhelm Dilthey, *Briefwechsel zwischen Wilhelm Dilthey und dem Grafen Paul Yorck von Wartenburg: 1877-1897* (Hildesheim: Niemeyer, 1974), 185.

of empirical research upon history. Even a universal history still would not deal with historicality. *Dilthey made his way to the reality which is properly historical and possesses the sense of being historical; in short, he made his way to human Dasein.*[27]

Subsequently, Heidegger speaks of the limitation of the Diltheyan point of view and the need for phenomenology to further unpack the question of "historicality itself, the question of the sense of be-ing, the question of the be-ing of beings."[28] The latter three formulations of Dilthey's main question and his "proper intentions" are given simply by way of commas, as if synonymous designations of one and the same conceptual meaning. It is obvious that Heidegger here has not yet found a suitable conceptual form for expressing the very same idea of Yorck's that had stimulated Dilthey. In the subsequent development of Heidegger's thought, it becomes clear that Yorck's idea was incorporated into Heidegger's hermeneutic philosophy and later into the fundamental ontology of *Being and Time* as the fundamental category of Dasein.[29] The use of this term in Heidegger's texts is ambiguous and has its own history, which will be discussed below. But the primordial initiation, in my opinion, was Yorck's and Dilthey's principle of historicality as the foundation for the methodology of the sciences of the spirit. In German, the term *Dasein* means "life," the "existence" of man, i.e., something historical, a specific interval of time from birth to death. At the same time — and this is a point of extraordinary, principal importance — Dasein bears within itself an echo of *Sein*, Being, as the primary ontological reality. Thus, as we can see, the "initiation" from Yorck and Dilthey,

---

27 Heidegger, "Dilthey's Research,", 285; idem, *"Issledovatel'skaia rabota,"* 157. My italics.

28 Ibid.

29 We leave this central term of Heidegger's hermeneutic philosophy untranslated, since any translation is inadequate in one way or another. While with other terms of Heidegger's such inadequacies can be recompensed by the explanatory context, in the case of *Dasein*, which is the "pillar" of hermeneutics, any imprecision of understanding threatens to distort the whole picture of Heideggerian philosophizing.

to which Heidegger himself, in a rare instance, testified, was from the very beginning transformed by this philosopher's thinking to the point that it gained, alongside its starting intention, a completely new, original, Heideggerian meaning: alongside the historicality of concrete human life, there is the meaning of historicality itself, which is identified with the being of beings. Heidegger will subsequently never mention Yorck or Dilthey as theoretical sources for the category of Dasein or, in the very least, for the interpretation of this category, but this may be regarded as quite explainable and justified: the link between Yorck and Dilthey's "historicality" and Heidegger's "Dasein" is more inner and "spiritual" than logico-theoretical, and such vague references would have already been inappropriate in 1925-1926, when Heidegger decided to approach the complex problem of the grounding of metaphysics. To the extent that it could have been agreeable, Heidegger showed in the Kassel lectures where he drew from Dilthey and where he went further.

Thus, in speaking of Dilthey's influence on Heidegger's philosophy, we can say that this influence was expressed in: (1) recognizing the foundational role of the principle of historicality (of concrete human existence) and (2) in the hermeneutic method by which the problem of concrete human existence is studied and developed. On the other hand, introducing the term Dasein brought the possibility of an ontological interpretation to the problem of historicality, which we will soon discuss in connection with the ontologization of hermeneutics amidst the transition from the *Hermeneutics of Facticity to Being and Time*.

The second point from which Heidegger set off in developing his hermeneutics was *Nietzsche's nihilism*, as imprinted in the formulation that "God is dead." In the fifth book of *The Gay Science*, "We Fearless Ones," the 343rd aphorism entitled "How to understand our cheerfulness" says: "The greatest recent event — that 'God is dead'; that the belief in the Christian God has become unbelievable —

is already starting to cast its first shadow over Europe."[30] Nietzsche here is not putting forth another philosophical construct or another all-solving method; rather, he is bearing witness to an event that is really, objectively taking place, albeit on those planes of actuality that are more accessible to philosophers and poets than anyone else. This is the meaning that Heidegger imparts to Nietzsche's philosophizing in his interpreting. In accordance with one of the principles of Heidegger's hermeneutic method, namely, "thinking in the wake of and beyond the author's thought more consistently than the author himself," the event to which Nietzsche bore witness and in which he saw his mission — "God is dead," values have been devalued — is an event which Heidegger endows with completely different and more profound meaning than it had for its original author.

Just as in the case with Dilthey, Heidegger is strictly reflecting and sharing those points that he takes from his predecessors, interpreting them in his own way, as well as identifying the limitations of their approaches and pointing out the source of those limitations. Heidegger takes from Nietzsche only the starting point, namely, the indication of the event that is taking place in the fate of Western European mankind: "God is dead, values have been devalued." This is the challenge man faces in the midst of the loss of any meaningfulness in the world. Nietzsche did not discover this challenge, but he was the one who gave it the most succinct expression. As for everything else pertaining to the response to this challenge — the will to power, the transvaluation of values — Heidegger regards Nietzsche's position not only as limited, but as harboring a significant danger. Where Nietzsche is simply formulating a problem, a challenge, Heidegger follows him:

---

30   Friedrich Nietzsche, *The Gay Science*, trans. Josefine Nauckhoff and Adrian del Caro, ed. Bernard Williams (Cambridge: Cambridge University Press, 2001), 199.

> In a note from the year 1887, Nietzsche poses the question, "What does nihilism mean?" (*Will to Power*, Aph. 2). He answers: "*That the highest values are devaluing themselves.*" This answer is underlined and is furnished with the explanatory amplification: "The aim is lacking; 'Why?' finds no answer." According to this note Nietzsche understands nihilism as an ongoing historical event. He interprets that event as the devaluing of the highest values up to now... And yet the highest values are already devaluing themselves through the emerging of the insight that the ideal world is not and is never to be realized within the real world. The obligatory character of the highest values begins to totter. The question arises: Of what avail are these highest values if they do not simultaneously render secure the warrant and the ways and means for a realization of the goals posited in them?[31]

Here we can see that Heidegger's interpretation of Nietzsche, although quite independent, does not in essence go beyond the boundaries of what Nietzsche himself had in mind, namely, the devaluation of values. However, it is clarified over the course of his interpreting that Nietzsche was testifying to the devaluation of values and was proposing his own answers to this challenge to man without fully thinking through what exactly this event in the "fate of Western history" — which underlies the whole problem — truly is. From this point on begins the critique of Nietzsche — not a critique of rejection, but a creative critique that takes its point and impetus of departure from examining the limitation of the critiqued position and opens up the possibility of expanding, modifying, and refining it. The root of the devaluation of values that Nietzsche saw lies, according to Heidegger, in the following:

> That thinking is concerned unceasingly with one single happening: In the history of Western thinking, indeed continually from the beginning, what is, is thought in reference to Being; yet the truth of Being remains unthought, and not only is that truth denied to thinking as a possible experience, but Western thinking itself,

---

31 Heidegger, "The Word of Nietzsche," 66; idem, *Raboty i razmyshleniia raznykh let*, 179.

and indeed in the form of metaphysics, expressly, but nevertheless unknowingly, veils the happening of that denial.[32]

Heidegger takes from Nietzsche none other than the challenging indication of the oblivion of Being and the ensuing devaluation of values. We will be able to see the importance of this starting point for all of hermeneutics only later on, when we arrive at discussing the influence of Husserl's phenomenology on Heidegger's hermeneutics. As I hope to show, both phenomenology and hermeneutics can be fruitfully interpreted as two logically possible variations of human thinking's response to the challenge that the meaninglessness of the world poses to man. Although hermeneutics emerged much earlier and had already been developed more fully (in Dilthey), the historically first option of a response to this challenge came with Husserl's phenomenology, on the basis of which different hermeneutic resolutions of the problem began to appear.

The response to the devaluation of values that Nietzsche himself put forth could not satisfy Husserl or Heidegger. Heidegger wrote the following about this:

> The pronouncement "God is dead" means: The suprasensory world is without effective power. It bestows no life. Metaphysics, i.e., for Nietzsche Western philosophy understood as Platonism, is at an end. Nietzsche understands his own philosophy as the countermovement to metaphysics, and that means for him a movement in opposition to Platonism. *Nevertheless, as a mere countermovement it necessarily remains, as does everything "anti," held fast in the essence of that over against which it moves.*[33]

According to Heidegger, Nietzsche's philosophy, while claiming to overcome metaphysics as Platonism, ends up being merely an inversion of the latter:

---

32 Ibid., 56; idem, *Raboty i razmyshleniia raznykh let*, 170.

33 Ibid., 61; idem, *Raboty i razmyshleniia raznykh let*, 174. My italics. Following the "Turn," Heidegger will address the same reproach to himself for having attempted to "overcome metaphysics." In the end, he acknowledged that metaphysics needs to be left to itself.

The reversal of Platonism, according to which for Nietzsche the sensuous becomes the true world and the suprasensuous becomes the untrue world, is thoroughly caught in metaphysics... It looks as if the 'meta,' the transcendence to the suprasensuous, were replaced by the persistence in the elemental world of sensuousness, whereas actually *the oblivion of Being is only completed and the suprasensuous is let loose and furthered by the will to power*.[34]

The next source that influenced Heidegger's hermeneutics, and which deserves its own examination, is Edmund Husserl's phenomenology, to which we shall now turn.

§2. The Role of Husserl's Phenomenology in the Formation of Heidegger's Hermeneutics[35]

At the outset, let us note in general terms the main stages in the development of Heidegger's hermeneutics and its changing relationship to Husserl's phenomenology.

1. *The development of hermeneutics (1916-1923)*: In the first period, between 1916 and 1921, hermeneutics figures as the very same phenomenological method in its application to the "existential structures" of Dasein. In 1923, in the final section of the *Hermeneutics of Facticity* lectures, we see Heidegger's first attempt to pose the question of Being hermeneutically. At this stage, his hermeneutics only begins to recognize (or, in any case, to openly proclaim) its independence from the phenomenological method.

2. *Christmas 1923 to 1924 — the "discovery" of time*: the beginning of Heidegger's reflections on the role of time and temporality for interpreting the being of Dasein.

---

34 Heidegger, "Overcoming Metaphysics," 92; N.V. Motroshilov (ed.), *Filosofiia Martina Khaideggera i sovremennost'* (Moscow: Nauka, 1991), 217. My italics.

35 The main part of this section was first published as an article in the *Philosophy* series of *Vestnik MGU* (*Bulletin of Moscow State University*) 5 (2000).

3. *1924 to Summer 1925*: in this period, we see Heidegger developing and working out the question of the being of Dasein, which is to say that the very same material that appeared in 1923 under the rubric of the "existential analytic of Dasein" is now used for the "ontological analytic" (whose central terms, which we will soon analyze, include "significance," "encountering," "concern," "care"). Insofar as Heidegger was already planning his "ontological" project, he started avoiding the use of the term "hermeneutics", replacing it with "phenomenology" (as in the "phenomenological interpretation of Dasein"). The question of time only begins to be worked out in *History of the Concept of Time: Prolegomena* and in the Kassel lectures (1925).

4. *Late 1925 to early 1926*: reworking the developed form of the question of Being and the question of time for the project of *Being and Time*. The connection between hermeneutics and phenomenology is once again "bracketed."

The question of the interrelationship between Heidegger's hermeneutics and Husserl's phenomenology can be approached on the historical plane and in theoretical terms. First, we will examine the history of this interrelationship, then we will move on to a theoretical, comparative analysis of these thinkers' respective views.

Husserl and Heidegger's personal relationship was inseparable from their philosophical collaboration between 1919, when Heidegger began teaching under Husserl's guidance at the Faculty of Philosophy at the University of Freiburg, and 1929, when a long-brewing rift in their philosophical and personal relationship took place. Husserl's personal influence on Heidegger's formation as a philosopher cannot be underestimated. Heidegger himself described his mentor's teaching thusly: "Husserl's teaching took place in the form of a step-by-step training in phenomenological 'seeing' which at the same time demanded that one relinquish the untested use of philosophical knowledge. But it also demanded that one give up introducing the authority of the great thinkers into the conversation."[36] This training in the skill or art of the "presuppositionless insight into essences" provided what would subsequently constitute one of the main traits of Heidegger's independent philosophizing. At the same time, from the very outset, Heidegger was never a blind follower of his teacher. Until 1927, Husserl's thinking remained a monologue, and as a mentor he left his students (in phenomenology, of course) significant space for their own independent activity. Heidegger made full use of this freedom. As he recalled: "Husserl watched me in a generous fashion, but at the bottom in disagreement, as I worked on the *Logical Investigations* every week in special seminars with advanced students in addition to my lectures and regular seminars."[37] Husserl's *Logical Investigations* aroused in Heidegger what he himself called "perplexity" and "unrest," firstly because "Husserl's own programmatic explanations and methodological presentations rather strengthened the misunderstanding that through 'phenomenology' a beginning of philosophy was claimed which denied all previous thinking," and secondly because such "made one suspect that it came from the inability to attain the act of philosophical thinking called 'phenomenology' simply by reading the philosophical literature."[38] The independent development of Heidegger's philosophical thought, for the time being "within the scope of phenomenology," proceeded in both directions stemming from this misunderstanding, which then "dissipated," as it were, over the course of his personal contact with Husserl. Despite the phenomenological requirement of refraining from citing philosophical authorities, Heidegger was increasingly drawn to interpreting Aristotle as his "phenomenological seeing opened up." In fact, Heidegger's independent hermeneutic method

---

36 Martin Heidegger, "My Way to Phenomenology" in idem, *On Time and Being*, trans. Joan Stambaugh (New York: Harper Torchbooks, 1972,) 78; idem, "Moi put' v fenomenologiiu," 305.

37 Ibid., 79; "Moi put' v fenomenologiiu," 307.

38 Ibid., 78; "Moi put' v fenomenologiiu," 306.

in its historico-philosophical application developed precisely under the rubric of a "phenomenological interpretation of Aristotle." Moreover, Heidegger discovered in Greek thinking the foundations that were then being rediscovered by phenomenology. This allowed Heidegger, increasingly drawn to the philosophy of the Greeks, to reformulate the main phenomenological principles and conquer yet another dimension of freedom in relation to phenomenology. In Aristotle, for example, Heidegger discovered a "phenomenological" treatment of phenomena as self-manifesting:

> What occurs for the phenomenology of the acts of consciousness as the self-manifestation of phenomena is thought more originally by Aristotle and in all Greek thinking and existence as *aletheia*, as the unconcealedness of what-is present, its being revealed, its showing itself. That which phenomenological investigations rediscovered as the supporting attitude of thought proves to be the fundamental trait of Greek thinking, if not indeed of philosophy as such.[39]

No matter how nearsighted Husserl might have been, physically as well as in the realm of human relations, Heidegger's independence gradually became clearer to him. In 1923, when Heidegger already presented a generally negative assessment of phenomenology in his *Hermeneutics of Facticity* lectures, Husserl began to experience negative feelings, albeit without talking (perhaps not even to himself) about the causes. "It is difficult to write, much weighs heavily on the soul, although *privatim* I cannot complain," Husserl wrote in a letter to Ingarden on 31 August 1923.[40] In 1925, Husserl's only hopes for the further development of phenomenology remained with Ingarden alone: "No one is more capable of benefiting from my results than you are, no one is more selfless [*Ichloser*]. Only in phenomenologists who are genuinely pure and *not burdened by self* do I place my serious hopes."[41] It is obvious

---

39 Ibid., 79; "*Moi put' v fenomenologiiu*," 307.
40 Quoted in Heidegger, "*Moi put' v fenomenologiiu*," 243.
41 Ibid., 294. My italics.

that Husserl counted Heidegger, in the depths of his soul, among those "burdened by self," and experienced Heidegger's departure from the initial principles of phenomenology as philosophical betrayal. Nevertheless, in 1926, he still helped Heidegger proofread *Being and Time*. Due to his nearsightedness, reading caused Husserl great agony, especially when it came to others' texts; perhaps this is why only in 1927, and fully only later, in 1929, did Husserl recognize how far *Being and Time* had departed from the principles of phenomenology: "What have deeper 'Heidegger studies' yielded? I've come to the conclusion that I cannot regard his work as belonging to my phenomenology, and, unfortunately, I am compelled to decisively reject not only the method in it but also, foremost, the content."[42] In the philosophical systems of his iconic students — Scheler, Heidegger, etc. — Husserl saw only "rolling into old philosophical naiveties, albeit high in spirit."[43]

Heidegger's assessment of Husserl's phenomenology is a separate question. We already noted Heidegger's impression of the *Logical Investigations* from the beginning of his philosophical cooperation with Husserl. Subsequently, his evaluation of phenomenology became even more critical. According to Mikhailov, the content of the 1923 *Hermeneutics of Facticity* lectures testifies that Heidegger "(a) considered the tradition of Dilthey to be more significant than phenomenology; (b) had subjected the tradition of phenomenology represented by Husserl to rather harsh critique and declared it to lack prospects and have reached a dead-end; (c) proposes what is in essence a completely new, more radical concept of phenomenology."[44] We have also already spoken of Heidegger's approach to Dilthey. Thus, Heidegger's emerging evaluation of the state of the phenomenological tradition was presented in section 14 of the second part of *Hermeneutics of Facticity*:

---

42 Ibid., 298.
43 Ibid.
44 Ibid., 291.

1. Thus transcendental idealism entered into phenomenology. And the countermovement to this also arose in phenomenology by taking up traditional realism. These opposites became the guiding foci for academic discussions within the different directions phenomenology took. No one raised the radical question of whether epistemological questions might not in fact be meaningless in phenomenology. Everyone went to work within a bad tradition.

2. The investigations carried out in the field of logic were also applied to other traditional domains of inquiry. In line with the approach and the kind of person doing the work, a specific model of inquiry was in each case picked up from the tradition. One set to work with a limited fund of phenomenological distinctions.

3. The drive for a system is noticeable everywhere...

4. What has resulted from the escalation of these three moments and from the infiltration of traditional terminology into phenomenology is a general watering down... Phenomenological research, which was supposed to provide a basis for scientific work, has sunk to the level of wishy-washiness, thoughtlessness, and summariness, to the level of the philosophical noise of the day... The business is hopeless! All such tendencies are a betrayal of phenomenology and its possibilities. The ruin can no longer be halted![45]

It bears noting that the critique expressed in these assessments is not accompanied by any conscious reflection on how Heidegger's own position had departed from phenomenology and in what ways he remained connected to it. This pertains to the "dilemma" of Heidegger's situation: he had not yet established a sufficiently stable basis for his own philosophizing from which he might announce his own approach independent of phenomenology. This approach already existed in the form of a hermeneutic method that was fully independent of phenomenology and was being tried and tested in his interpreting of the existential structures

---

45 Martin Heidegger, *Ontology — The Hermeneutics of Facticity*, trans. John van Buren (Bloomington: Indiana University Press, 2008), 57-58; idem, *Gesamtausgabe* [GA] 63, Abt. 2, *Vorlesungen, 1923-1944: Ontologie (Hermeneutik der Faktizität)* (Frankfurt am Main: Vittorio Klostermann, 1988), 73-74.

of human Dasein (the *Hermeneutics of Facticity* lectures). However, a pure form of hermeneutics, one that had not gone far enough beyond Dilthey, seemed to Heidegger to be an insufficiently reliable foundation for departing from phenomenology. In order to do so, Heidegger would need to *ontologize* hermeneutics in *Being and Time*. Establishing his own ontology would make Heidegger a genuinely significant figure beyond the phenomenological tradition. Until then, he was compelled to work as a "phenomenologist" within the scope of "phenomenology." And to this end, he firstly had to define what phenomenology is in his own way (the "distinctive *how of research*"[46]) and secondly, to postulate the necessity of "setting off from" phenomenology itself through its own "demonstration": "Phenomenology can only be appropriated phenomenologically, i.e., only through *demonstration* and not in such a way that one repeats propositions, takes over fundamental principles, or subscribes to academic dogmas."[47]

Finally, upon attentive examination, the "more radical concept of phenomenology" approached in the *Hermeneutics of Facticity* lectures would discover the principles which, here seen hermeneutically, will be reinterpreted ontologically to become the basis of *Being and Time*: "Objects are to be taken just as they show themselves in themselves..."[48] — this is essentially one of the main methodological premises of phenomenology, but taking it further entails changing its meaning in a cardinal way: "just as they are encountered by a *definite manner of looking toward them and seeing them* [*wie sie für ein bestimmtes Hinsehen begegnen*]. This seeing arises out of and on the basis of a being-oriented regarding the objects, and already-being-familiar with these beings."[49] Heidegger is indicating the fundamental condition, or presupposition, of our seeing the world, and thus one of the main requirements

---

46 Ibid., 58; GA 63, 74.
47 Ibid., 37; GA 63, 74.
48 Ibid., 58; GA 63, 74-75.
49 Ibid., 58-59; GA 63, 75.

of phenomenology — presuppositionlessness — is rejected. The ensuing development of Heidegger's thought in the *Hermeneutics of Facticity* lectures follows this alternative path of hermeneutically interpreting the phenomenological tradition's own presuppositions concerning the human seeing of the world, that is the *existentials*, or "Dasein's ways of being in a world."

In essence, if Heidegger had been a "phenomenologist," then already in 1923 he was such only nominally. In the Kassel lectures in 1925, Heidegger developed in conversation with Dilthey his own understanding of "phenomenology" and pointed out its fundamental limitation, which suggests that Heidegger already had his own position, but was only presenting it in individual strokes rather than in direct opposition to phenomenology. Heidegger reproached Husserl for psychologizing phenomenology:

> Phenomenology to a large extent still worked within the confines of early psychology when the discovery of intentionality was made, a discovery that moves its research onto another level.[50] Husserl himself misunderstood his own work when he wrote the preface[51] to his ground book, where he advanced the thoroughly perverse interpretation of phenomenology as an improvement upon psychology.[52]

Further on, Heidegger discusses the problem that phenomenology should have placed before itself: "What is the character of being of the whole being? Phenomenology defines the human being as a context of life experiences that is held together by the unity of the ego as a center of acts. But no one asked about the character of being of this center."[53] It is this question of the "character of being" of the center of all acts and experiences that, according to Heidegger, neither Dilthey nor Husserl raised. Naturally, this question could

---

50 By "another level," Heidegger obviously has in mind the ontological plane.

51 Heidegger has in mind the preface to the second volume of *Logical Investigations*.

52 Heidegger, "Dilthey's Research," 258; idem, "*Issledovatel'skaia rabota*," 160.

53 Ibid.; idem, "*Issledovatel'skaia rabota*," 161.

not have been posed by them because, for various reasons, neither Dilthey nor Husserl were endeavoring to construct an ontology. The possibility of an ontological interpretation appeared only in Heidegger's work as a result of synthesizing Dilthey's hermeneutics and Husserl's phenomenology, along with the unique peculiarities of the German word *Dasein* which allowed Heidegger to bring together therein Being (*Sein*), historicality, and the temporality of human existence (Dasein).[54]

The turning point in Heidegger's relation to phenomenology, the maturation of which has been discussed in the preceding, came after 1925: in *Kant and the Problem of Metaphysics* and in *Being and Time*, Heidegger announced himself as an independent thinker engaged in working out the ontology of human Dasein. In this respect, references to any connection to phenomenology practically disappear, save for the dedication of the first edition of *Being and Time* to Husserl. Subsequently, Heidegger would return to the question of his relation to phenomenology only in the works of his late period.[55] It is obvious that Heidegger had no interest in thoroughly developing this theme, as all of his attention turned to developing his own question.

Such is the "exterior" history of the relationship between Heidegger and phenomenology. We shall now endeavor to present a critical, comparative analysis of Heidegger's position vis-à-vis phenomenology, in which the similarities and differences that have hitherto remained hidden might be disclosed.

It would be appropriate and expedient to examine the "internal" connection between phenomenology and Heidegger's

---

54 The emphasis on the *Da*, that is, on the "hereness" of being, is already derivative of temporality and the temporal character of Dasein, and not vice versa. Therefore, it is preferable to not separate *Da* and *Sein*, as has been the case in some Russian translations (such as *zdes' bytie*). This is another reason why we leave Dasein untranslated.

55 See, for example, his short article cited above, "My Way to Phenomenology," in *On Time and Being*.

hermeneutics in the broader context of the turn from phenomenology to hermeneutics that took place in 20th-century European philosophy. It is of great interest and importance to highlight the essential reasons for this turn and to trace what results it led to, that is, to the variations of hermeneutics it entailed.

Phenomenology was conceived by Husserl in accordance with the model of a "hard" or "precise" science (although the realization of this project deviated from this model to a significant extent). Unlike hermeneutics, phenomenology only dispassionately states facts — it does not *interpret* them. (The principle of *epokhe*, or refraining from judgment, belongs to the forefather of ancient Greek skepticism, Pyrrho). This means discarding all the preconditions that stipulate the human being and human perception, such as authorities, customary stereotypes, and self-evident dogmas on the "natural state of affairs," in order to get to *the things themselves* (*zu den Sachen Selbst*). The Russian word for "thing," *veshch'*, corresponds to the German *Ding*. Only a *Ding* is really "thingly," "substantial" [*veshchestvenno*].

> "*Zur Sache*" means both "to the essence of the matter" and to that "something" with which a certain scientific discipline is engaged, but first and foremost it does not mean to the "thingliness" [*veshchestvennost'*] with which it is engaged, for only then (in secondary order) can "thing" [*veshch'*] and "thingness" [*veshchnost'*] name the "tangible," "graspable" aspect of that with which the discipline is engaged.[56]

In other words, it could be said that both phenomenology and hermeneutics are oriented to things themselves, but phenomenology predominantly to the *Sache* and hermeneutics to the *Ding*. We could say that hermeneutics preserves, or more accurately, creatively appropriates the very principle of presuppositionlessness by setting off from its phenomenological understanding. For Husserl, presuppositionlessness means that phenomenology does not incorporate any premises that

---
56 Shpet and Heidegger, *Dva teksta*, 196.

are not phenomenologically determinable. As already noted, Heidegger does not believe in the possibility of achieving any presuppositionless "insight into essence": the human seeing of things is always conditioned by the human's position in the world, by the human's "specific looking," and the human and the world constitute a single interconnection. But Heidegger's hermeneutics appropriates the demand for presuppositionlessness as a general methodological principle: hermeneutics should not incorporate any premises that are not definable hermeneutically. Interpretation begins *as if* in an empty space, from nothing, with questions alone. Only over the course of interpretation — each time anew — does hermeneutics re-discover and re-develop its founding principles. "Presuppositionlessness" should obviously always remain relative, for one or another specific answer is already inlaid in the very formulation of a question, in the very research attitude.

It is also obvious that in his interpretation of the principle of presuppositionlessness and the demand to go "to the things themselves," Heidegger is proceed from Husserl's interpretation, but he takes from it only what aligns with his own task of, firstly, developing hermeneutics, and then, on that basis, ontology. The main discoveries of phenomenology that served as the impetus for the independent development of Heidegger's thinking were "categorial intuition" and "intentionality." In the Kassel lectures, Heidegger deemed such to be "decisive discoveries."[57] The categorial intuition was then treated in the sixth section of his *History of the Concept of Time: Prolegomena* (1925), where we read:

> Intuition means: simple apprehension of what is itself bodily found just as it shows itself [*schlichtes Erfassen von leibhaftig Gegebenem, wie es sich zeigt*]... The discovery of categorial intuition is the demonstration, first, that there is a simple apprehension of the categorial, such constituents in entities which in traditional fashion are designated as categories... Second it is above all the

---
57 Heidegger, "*Issledovatel'skaia rabota*," 157.

demonstration that this apprehension is invested in the most everyday of perceptions and in every experience.⁵⁸

In the Kassel lectures, Heidegger spoke of the categorial intuition altogether briefly: "We have already distinguished being from beings by noting that being, unlike beings, is not accessible through sense intuition. Nevertheless, the *sense* of being which is meant when I say 'is' must somehow be demonstrable. The act which opens the way to this demonstration is categorial intuition."⁵⁹ The interpretations in the *Prolegomena* and in the Kassel lectures differ noticeably, and at first glance they do not even offer any idea as to how the categorial intuition can be deemed one of the "decisive discoveries" of phenomenology. In order to unpack this question, it is necessary to turn to Husserl's and Heidegger's texts' discussions of the fundamental points of phenomenology and hermeneutics. One such fundamental point is the question of the relation between perceiving consciousness and thing, of which Husserl asserted in his *Ideas pertaining to a Pure Phenomenology*: "As a consequence, one must not let oneself be deceived by speaking of the physical thing as transcending consciousness or as 'existing in itself.'"⁶⁰ Husserl does not recognize the existence of Kantian "things in themselves," as they do not correspond to the methodological principle of presuppositionlessness and cannot be established phenomenologically. What follows is fundamental to both phenomenology and hermeneutics: *there is nothing in things besides the meaning that is imparted to them by perceiving consciousness in the course of its experience of them.* This formulation holds for both Husserl and Heidegger, but both

---

58 Martin Heidegger, *History of the Concept of Time: Prolegomena*, trans. Theodore Kisiel (Bloomington: Indiana University Press, 1985), 47-48; idem, *Gesamtausgabe* [GA] 20, Abt. 2: *Vorlesungen, 1923-1944: Prolegomena zur Geschichte des Zeitbegriffs* (Frankfurt a.M.: Vittorio Klostermann, 1979), 64.

59 Heidegger, "Dilthey's Research," 258; idem, "*Issledovatel'skaia rabota*," 160.

60 Edmund Husserl, *Ideas pertaining to a Pure Phenomenology and to a Phenomenological Philosophy, Book 1: General Introduction to a Pure Phenomenology*, trans. F. Kersten (The Hague: Martinus Nijhoff Publishers, 1983), 106.

of them interpret it in different ways and draw their own conclusion. Husserl's is: "In so far as their respective senses are concerned, a veritable abyss yawns between consciousness and reality"; "whatever physical things are... they are as experienceable physical things. It is experience alone that prescribes their sense."[61] On the other hand, a thing is always a thing "belonging to my surrounding world."[62] Thus, for Husserl, a thing in itself (outside of consciousness) has no meaning.

Three aspects can be distinguished in Husserl's premise and interpretation. Firstly, *a thing has meaning only in the <u>context</u> of other things of the "surrounding world."* Like a sign in a written text (which is also important for the hermeneutic interpretation of this thesis), a thing attains its meaning only from the context in which it is incorporated; the broader the context we take, the greater and deeper the meaning. Hence, Husserl introduced (not without Heidegger's influence) the notion of the "lifeworld," or the "horizon of all horizons," that is, a "whole in which we live as historical beings" (as per Gadamer's formulation).

Secondly, *all things of the "surrounding world" are united by the fact that they are objects of the perception and experience of "a certain <u>subject</u>."* For Husserl, the primordial and unifying center of experience is transcendental subjectivity, which is rigorously distinguished from the empirical and psychological ego. This subjectivity is taken in one aspect alone: the *structures of perception* immanently inlaid in it. As Piama Gaidenko writes, "the object of direct perception that remains after 'bracketing' the empirical world as transcending consciousness is the *pure structure of consciousness itself*, which is given to us immanently."[63] Let us add that this structure is that of the *perceiving* consciousness.

---

61 Husserl, *Ideas pertaining to a Pure Phenomenology*, 111, 106.

62 Ibid., 99.

63 P.P. Gaidenko, "Nauchnaia ratsional'nost i filosofskii razum v interpretatsii Edmunda Gusserlia," *Voprosy filosofii* 7 (1992), 120. My italics.

Thirdly, all the objects of experience, taken as a whole and separately, *obtain meaning from no other source than the perceiving consciousness of the subject* that is carrying out "categorial intuition." In my opinion, Heidegger regards the categorial intuition as one of phenomenology's "decisive discoveries" not as much because it, unlike sense intuition, somehow sees categories rather than the exterior form of "apprehended corporeality," but because "categorial intuition" pertains in general to any act of *generating* meaning by consciousness and the *imparting* of this meaning to the objects given in experience: "to be consciousness," according to Husserl, means "to give meaning." Of no less importance is the converse: there is no meaning that does not have its source in the meaning-positing activity of consciousness. Thus, categorial intuition turns out to be inextricably bound to the intentionality of consciousness, as though these were two aspects of the same meaning-positing act of consciousness: the fundamental directedness of consciousness towards something beyond it (intentionality) explains the very possibility of positing meaning, while categorial intuition is the form in which this possibility is actualized.

Heidegger did not merely assess the categorial intuition to be a decisive discovery of phenomenology; he also placed it, upon rethinking it in his own way, at the core of his own hermeneutic method. Of analogous significance is the other phenomenological discovery that Heidegger mentioned in the Kassel lectures: intentionality. Intentionality, according to Husserl, is the essence of transcendental subjectivity: "By intentionality we understand the characteristic quality of experiences of 'being conscious of something.'"[64] Gaidenko further expounds the Husserlian understanding of intentionality in the following way: intentionality makes consciousness *teleological*, and the unity of consciousness is ensured by what it is directed towards, that is, its "end," its

---

64 Gaidenko, "*Nauchnaia ratsional'nost*," 120.

telos.⁶⁵ The objective (ideal) signification of the intentional act is the *noema*, and the actual way in which an object is given in the act of consciousness is *noesis*. The core of *noema* is the entelechy that ensures the fundamental unity of the transcendental Ego as the purposive, meaning-giving principle. An object always figures as a certain actualized horizon, but it is also *always* within the backdrop of a potential horizon. The *active* character of intentionality lies in the actualization of potential possibilities. Hence arises the question: how active is consciousness in the act of perception, or how (in whatever respect) passive is it? Or, in other words, is the perception of an object the constitution of this object? Yes and no. That which is described both does and does not exist before its description. "Such describing, which presumes the existence of what is described before the description and at the same time first creates it, is what Husserl calls 'constituting.'"⁶⁶

We always (potentially) have within consciousness the horizon of a thing, which presupposes the existence of a thing. But, in discovering this horizon (actualizing it), we learn what we did not know before, and we have therefore created a new object. *Intentionality, thus, is at once both active and passive*. In *Kant and the Problem of Metaphysics*, Heidegger shows that Kant in this very same sense and with almost the very same expressions speaks of the dual character, both creative and perceptive, of the productive power of the imagination.

Having characterized, albeit not to any exhaustive extent, the two "discoveries" of phenomenology — categorial intuition and intentionality — we can now turn to examine how these discoveries made their way into and were transformed within the fabric of Heidegger's hermeneutics. The categorial intuition ends up refracted in Heidegger's philosophizing

---

65 Ibid.
66 Ibid.

in accordance with his unique (distinct from Husserl's) orientation towards things in the sense of *Ding*, not *Sache*:

> It is now a matter of regarding the basic structures in which this being-in-the-world takes place and plays itself out. How is the world given? Originally not as an object of theoretical knowledge, but as an environing world in which I look and move around, do something and take care of it. These objects are primarily not objects of theoretical knowledge, but are matters I have to deal with, which carry within themselves references to what they are used for and how they are employed, their usefulness... The immediate world is a world of practical concern.[67]

Heidegger here is speaking out against the Cartesian and generally rationalistic approach to the world, whereas Husserl, as is well known, developed Descartes' standpoint (cf. Husserl's *Cartesian Meditations*). Heidegger says: "But his [Descartes'] conception of the human being, in which only the ego is first given, is itself uncritical. It is based on the presupposition that consciousness is something like a box, where the ego is inside and reality is outside the box. Yet *natural consciousness* knows nothing at all of this."[68] Following Dilthey, Heidegger also opposes transplanting the methods and apodictic claims of mathematical natural science into the domain of the "sciences of the spirit." Descartes, according to Heidegger, "wanted an axiom for deduction *rather than a presentation of the full being of the human being*."[69] In line with the task of "presenting the full being of the human being" in its living, practical existence, Heidegger rethinks the premises that we highlighted in the Husserlian categorial intuition:[70] instead of *transcendental subjectivity* in the role of

---

67 Heidegger, "Dilthey's Research," 259; idem, "*Issledovatel'skaia rabota*," 162-163.

68 Ibid. My italics.

69 Ibid. My italics. Giordano Bruno addressed an analogous reproach to Aristotle.

70 Gaidenko believes that the possibility of ontological interpretation was already inlaid in phenomenology: "The core of intentionality is temporality, which means historicity. Time constitutes the deepest layer of the ultimate reality, the transcendental Ego. Husserl sees every individual phenomenon within the horizon of time, which is the universal horizon of the life of the transcendental

the unifying center of experience and the singular source of all accessible meanings, Heidegger puts forth the category of *Dasein*. Dasein is not "beyond" the "natural attitude" of the world, but is initially given and structured as "being in the world," and Heidegger designates Dasein's ways of "entry" or "being-in" the world with the term "existentials." In this new terminology, the essence of categorial intuition, i.e., that only consciousness is the source of all meanings, is expressed by Heidegger in *Being and Time* in the following formulation: "*Meaning is an existential of Dasein*, not a property that is attached to beings, which lies 'behind' them or floats somewhere as a 'realm between.'"[71] In *Hermeneutics of Facticity*, Heidegger designates the contextual interconnection between things in the totality of human experience with the complex notion of *Verweisungszusammenhang*, "context of references."

In *Being and Time*, intentionality, as the fundamental directedness of consciousness beyond itself, corresponds to the notion of (*Entwurf*), that is "project," "projection," or "projecting." Heidegger writes: "Why does understanding always penetrate into possibilities from among all the essential dimensions of what can be disclosed to it? Because understanding in itself has the existential structure which we call *project* [*Entwurf*]."[72] And further: "The project character of understanding constitutes being-in-the-world with regard to the disclosedness of its there as the there

---

I and, as such, takes on the characteristic of being... Being is transcendental subjectivity in its meaning-constituting activity. It is absolute in the sense that it is the only temporal, 'absolute' source of meaning and significance. Insofar as phenomenology is the science of the subjectivity constituting meaning, it is at the same time actual ontology." Gaidenko, "*Nauchnaia ratsional'nost'*," 125, 127. Nevertheless, if phenomenology did harbor the possibility of ontological interpretation, then Heidegger needed to carry out the essential transformations under discussion here in order for these potentialities to be realized. In the meanwhile, any connection to phenomenology remains behind the veil of silence.

71 Martin Heidegger, *Being and Time*, trans. Joan Stambaugh, rev. Dennis J. Schmidt (Albany: State University of New York Press, 2010), 147; idem, *Raboty i razmyshleniia raznykh let*, 14. My italics.

72 Ibid., 140; idem, *Raboty i razmyshleniia raznykh let*, 5-6.

of a potentiality of being."⁷³ In this passage, "understanding" is contextually interchangeable with Dasein (cf. *Being and Time* §31, "Dasein as understanding"), which is to say that "project" is the "existential structure" of Dasein, the structure of Dasein's "entry" in the world in which it initially already dwells (being-in-the-world).

For Husserl, the primary law of consciousness is its outward directedness towards something that it itself is not. But Heidegger believes that consciousness (by its very nature) *posits the being* of its object: the object is not consciousness, and consequently the object is something other than consciousness. The object "is," of course, not "in itself," but rather "for consciousness," yet it is nevertheless the first and only *being*. From this can follow the conclusion that Husserl's demand to refrain in *epokhe* from any "postulating of being" directly contradicts the nature of consciousness, its main law and concrete being, turning it into Berkeley's "immeasurable abstraction" and dividing what is in actuality indivisible. But Husserl is relying on yet another "law of consciousness": "I am I, therefore I am." In this case, the postulating of being follows *after* the self-positing of the pure subject. Insofar as Heidegger, like Hegel and Nietzsche before him, dethroned the "pure subject" as a self-delusion, the "postulating of being" is for Heidegger the very law of consciousness.

Husserl's and Heidegger's positions on this question serve as archetypal examples of two fundamentally different approaches to consciousness:

1. Consciousness is the light that illuminates (knows) everything, including — and first and foremost — itself, but consciousness can never become an object for itself.

2. Consciousness is a *ray of attention* emanating from the subject, and this ray of attention can make itself an object, but only indirectly, in its reflection or refraction in the mirror of other-being. This approach can be called "hermeneutic" in a broad

---

73 Ibid., 140-141; idem, *Raboty i razmyshleniia raznykh let*, 6.

sense: in its self-knowing, consciousness moves in a circle that is analogous to the hermeneutic circle proper, extracting itself as meaning out of other-being in the form of signs.

Both of these approaches can be traced throughout all the eras of the history of philosophy and in diverse countries. For example, it is also one of the main points of dispute between the different schools of India. For instance, Prabhākara and Śālikanātha, followers of the *Pūrva Mīmāmsā*, treat consciousness in the first sense and believe that consciousness can never become an object for itself, but it has no need to do so, for it is already incorporated into every act of cognizing external objects. To the contrary, Kumārila adhered to the point of view that we have called "hermeneutic" by maintaining that consciousness can and should make itself into its own object in the act of *reflecting* on object consciousness. The same dispute was carried on by representatives of Vedānta. Śankara believed that "[Ultimate consciousness] is the absolute vision that is its own visibility,"[74] which is to say that consciousness, in the very least in its own deep essence, is always *self-consciousness*. To the contrary, Rāmānuja adhered to the second approach and believed that "The self is not self-luminous knowledge, but only the subject of it,"[75] and hence consciousness can become an object, for instance, in the case of communication between two subjects. A similar view of consciousness was maintained by the Sāṃkhya and Yoga schools: "We cognise the conscious occurrence even as we see the face reflected in a mirror. Only in this way can consciousness have a vision of itself."[76]

What did Heidegger achieve by way of introducing new terminology to designate his reinterpretation of Husserl's categories of "transcendental subjectivity" and "intentionality" — respectively, "Dasein" and "project"?

---

74 Radhakrishnan, *Indian Philosophy*, vol. II (New York: Macmillan Company, 1958), 485.

75 Ibid., 681.

76 Ibid., 296.

In sections 31 and 32 of *Being and Time*, Heidegger speaks of Dasein as understanding and as "project" (*Entwurf*) that has understanding. "Project" can be correlated with "intentionality" as Husserl understood it only if we introduce a number of fundamental corrections. Instead of consciousness, whose essence in phenomenology consists in "giving meaning," we put forth Dasein, the essence of which lies in "understanding." It would not be a mistake to say that "understanding" is "giving meaning," so what, then, is achieved by this replacement? The point is that Husserl's intentionality is rather methodological abstract in character and pertains to transcendental subjectivity, and therefore it cannot be positioned at the foundation of ontology. Setting before himself the task of creating a fundamental ontology, Heidegger replaces the category of "consciousness" (and "transcendental subjectivity") with Dasein as "understanding." On the one hand, Dasein bears a shade of concreteness, of vitality ("life," "existence"); on the other hand, it is close to Being, *das Sein* — this is the category on which ontology can be built. At the same time, the meaning-positing function of "abstract consciousness" in phenomenology is fully transferred to Dasein: "Only Dasein 'has' meaning in that the disclosedness of being-in-the-world can be 'fulfilled' through the beings discoverable in it."[77] In speaking of the meaning-positing function of understanding, Heidegger, unlike Husserl, emphasizes above all the generation of one concrete, most fundamental meaning: the meaning that we always presuppose when we believe that a thing is, that is, *the meaning of Being*. Thus, whenever *Being and Time* discusses the meaning-positing activity of Dasein, Heidegger speaks of *Being* (or of *possibility*). In phenomenology, a thing acquires meaning by virtue of the directedness of consciousness towards the world and the act of categorial intuition. In *Being and Time*, "possibilities" are constituted as a result of Dasein's "projecting" itself out into and upon the world in

---

77   Heidegger, *Being and Time*, 147; idem, *Raboty i razmyshelniia razynkh let*, 14.

the act of understanding. As in the case of meaning, which is meaning for consciousness and therefore not something abstract, possibility is not modality in general; rather, it is the possibility for Dasein to be in a certain way or to do something: "Dasein is in the way that in each case it understands (or, alternatively, has not understood) to be in this or that way."[78] It is thanks to this reinterpretation of phenomenological intentionality that Heidegger gained the possibility of building fundamental ontology on the basis of a phenomenology aligned with hermeneutics, the brilliant embodiment of which is presented in *Being and Time*.

Within the scope of the question of the influence of phenomenology on Heidegger, we are left with examining the question of the "inner spring" whose "springing" was expressed in the transition from phenomenology to hermeneutics. To get a fuller picture, we can also consider the hermeneutics of Gustav Shpet, which became one of the variations of the "hermeneutic turn in philosophy" alongside Heidegger's. The common point of departure for Husserl, Shpet, and Heidegger is the phenomenological thesis that "to be consciousness is to give meaning," or the converse: meaning does not exist apart from consciousness. But in the interpretation of the enigma of consciousness, Husserl, Shpet, and Heidegger represent three different approaches. For Husserl, this is transcendental subjectivity, pure consciousness, and the category corresponding to the phenomenological attitude of presuppositionlessness; moreover, if we follow Husserl, then we adopt the Cartesian thesis of the absolute self-evidence of consciousness for itself (*ego cogito*). For Shpet, as well as for Heidegger, the fundamental question is the "owner" of consciousness, whereas the "transcendental purity" of consciousness does not interest them. In this pivot of interest for these thinkers lies, in my opinion, the driving force of the passage from phenomenology to hermeneutics. The point is that, for these thinkers, the challenge that Nietzsche posed to man remains in force:

---

78 Ibid., 140; idem, *Raboty i razmyshelniia razynkh let*, 4-5.

God is dead, the world has lost meaning, there are no objective values, all meanings are derivative of consciousness. "To be consciousness is to give meaning" is merely a more productive expression of the event "God is dead." Husserl, Shpet, and Heidegger offer three variations of a response to this discovery. Husserl, in accordance with the ideal of scientific knowledge, proposes to abstract ourselves from the world of the "natural attitude" in the very least until the structure of the meaning-positing activity of consciousness, from which the world gains meaning, is sufficiently studied. Shpet and Heidegger, like the masses of ordinary people, do not believe that abandoning the "natural attitude" of the world is appropriate, even if the world obtains the entirety of its meaning from consciousness. Instead, they seek a replacement for Husserl's "transcendental subjectivity" that would enable the establishment of the ontological foundation of the human being's lifeworld. Shpet put forth in this role the "socially-determined *logos*," the lingual consciousness that is fixed in concepts. Heidegger at first put forth Dasein as existence rooted in its "being-in-the-world." But this gave rise to a second danger: if Husserl's "transcendental subjectivity" is too abstract and faceless, then Dasein, provided that it applies to every human being, is too many-faced to see in it any guarantee of the reality of the world, and it is, therefore, once again faceless. If everyone is responsible for something, then no one bears responsibility. Therefore, after the "Turn" in the 1930s, Heidegger (after Shpet, but independently of him and in a completely different sense) will put forth that the guarantee of the reality and meaningfulness of the world is language, and he will see the concrete subject and creator of language in the poet.

§3. The Interpretation of Actuality in Heidegger's Early Hermeneutics[79]

Historically, hermeneutics is a very heterogeneous phenomenon. Over the course of its history, its object and methods of interpretation have changed, as has its understanding of the very process of interpretation and the role of human intellect therein. Here we will attempt to examine some aspects of Heidegger's early hermeneutics primarily from the point of view of the particularity of its object.

In examining the evolution of hermeneutics in Western culture since its very beginning, we find the preconditions for understanding actuality as a sign that bears definite meaning. For example, in Plato's *Cratylus*, "body," *soma*, is pseudo-etymologically correlated with *sema*, "sign." Besides Plato, we might also mention the *logoi spermatikoi* of the Stoics and the doctrine of "two books," the Book of Revelation and the Book of Nature, that was popular in the late Middle Ages and the Renaissance. Yet, it is in Indian philosophy that this point of view has been most consistently developed: God is the only true reality, and man, insofar as he really exists, also carries God in the depth of his essence; however, for a number of reasons, this is hidden from man, who is constantly turned outwards (from Being to beings, in Heidegger's language). Insofar as God is concealed within the essence of every thing, man, in coming to know the world, thereby also comes to know himself as God. In other words, consciousness has lost itself among beings, and all things are, as it were, a hint or a sign calling upon and awakening man to penetrate behind the veil of all signs to their one source — God. As a sign or a set of signs (a "text"), actuality is subject to deep interpretation. It is in this very same sense that Western hermeneutics treated

---

[79] This section was first published as an article in *Vestnik MGU* (*Bulletin of Moscow State University*), *Filosofiia* 5 (1997).

the texts of Homer and Scripture. As the *Bhagavad Gita* (XVIII, 61) says:

> God abides in the heart of all beings
> Turning them as on a potter's wheel
> By the māyā of the three gunas.

Having before us such an exemplification of the possibility of understanding actuality as a sign, we will try to see what meaning the interpretation of actuality takes on in Heidegger's early hermeneutics as it grew out of the Western tradition of textual interpretation. We will take as our basis Heidegger's early lectures entitled *Ontology — The Hermeneutics of Facticity*, which he delivered in Freiburg in the summer semester of 1923 (his last lectures there before he moved to Marburg).

Following Nietzsche and his formulation that "God is dead," the meaninglessness, dubiousness, and precariousness of the world became a fact that human thought needed to withstand. As I hope to show, phenomenology and hermeneutics became two ways by which thought responded to the challenge that the meaninglessness of the world posed to man. Although hermeneutics as a method had been developed much earlier and to a fuller extent by Dilthey, Husserl's phenomenology became the first variation of a response to this challenge, and it is on the basis of phenomenology that different versions of hermeneutic solutions to the problem arose.

On the basis of the preceding, we can affirm that both phenomenology and hermeneutics have not only many points of contiguity, but are also based on a series of common premises, even though hermeneutics does not necessarily emphasize this commonality. For Husserl and Heidegger (as well as for Shpet), the premise that "to be consciousness is to give meaning" remains in force, as does its converse: "there is no meaning apart from consciousness." But the method of the phenomenological reduction and the abstraction from the "natural attitude" find no close analogy in hermeneutics. As a response to the meaninglessness of the world, the meaning of the phenomenological reduction can, to the maximally possible extent of simplification, be presented in the following terms: insofar as the world has no inherent meaning outside of consciousness, which means that it has no independent reality, we must abstract ourselves from the world in its "natural attitude" in order to get to the depths of the source of all meanings, including the meaning of reality, and this depth is absolute consciousness. As Husserl said: "consciousness considered in its '*purity*' must be held to be a *self-contained complex of being*, a complex of *absolute being* into which nothing can penetrate and out of which nothing can slip."[80] Proceeding from the discovery that man ordinarily invests meaning and existence in the objects of his experience *unconsciously*, Husserl draws one possible conclusion: it is necessary to refrain from attributing meaning, at least until the nature of meaning-postulating consciousness is thoroughly studied. Thus, phenomenology is based primarily on the second of the three premises which hermeneutics holds in common: (1) meaning exists only in the context of experience; (2) meaning is generated by consciousness; (3) consciousness is intentionally directed outwards, beyond itself, and the proposed response to the meaninglessness of the world is a scientific, or scientifically structured, analysis of meaning-postulating activity and its subject, that is, absolute consciousness.

This response was one possible answer to the problem, but by the time of the mature Husserl, this answer was far from satisfying for everyone. It was unsatisfying in that it not only left the "natural attitude" of the world meaningless and unreal, but also because it theoretically substantiated this unreality in conjunction with emphasizing the necessity of rejecting any presumption of the existence of things as naive. Heidegger's hermeneutics reflects an altogether different tendency that took shape in the early 1920s: it

---

80 Husserl, *Ideas pertaining to a Pure Phenomenology*, 112.

does not follow from the meaninglessness of the world that it is necessary to abandon the world; to the contrary, it is necessary to turn back around to this world in its "natural attitude" and *creatively fill it with the reality of living, genuine meaning*; and, as it turns out, it is the metaphysical practice of fleeing from the world that has ultimately led to the loss of meaning and to falling into a sphere of beings torn away from its roots in Being. From this recognition comes the turn from phenomenology to hermeneutics that was characteristic of 20th-century philosophy. In order to draw on the world of concrete experience (not in the methodological sense of the empiricists, but in the meaning attributed to it in its "natural attitude"), hermeneutics had to sacrifice the classical ideal of scienticity and take upon itself the difficult labor of defining its relationship to science. Hermeneutics' aspiration to introduce its own terminology, even where it is drawing upon positions held in common with phenomenology, is perhaps connected to this fundamental reorientation. In the case of the third common ground between phenomenology and hermeneutics, namely, the principle of the outward directedness of consciousness, we can see substantive results yielded by hermeneutics' introduction of its own, new terminology.

On the one hand, Dasein bears a tint of concreteness, particularity, and vitality ("life," "existence"); on the other hand, it is close to Being, *das Sein*, the category on which ontology can be built. Therefore, in speaking of "project" as the founding structure of Dasein's being, Heidegger is speaking not about the generation of new meaning through "projecting" in general, but rather is emphasizing the generation of one concrete meaning — reality, being. Instead of imparting meaning to something in an intentional act, we are dealing with the constituting of possibilities in the acts of Dasein's "projecting" from within itself out upon the world. Just as meaning is not something abstract, but meaning for consciousness, so is possibility not simply modality, but possibility for Dasein to *be* something or to do something.

Thanks to this rethinking of phenomenological intentionality, Dasein, as the source of any meaning and reality in the world, is also "embedded" in the world — not an abstract, philosophical world, but the living, concrete world. Thus, as it were, the world obtains proof of its own non-illusory character, the "natural attitude" is implicitly rehabilitated, and vast expanses open up for filling the world with meaning and reality through hermeneutic interpreting. At the same time, however, Heidegger's relationship to the "natural attitude" is more complex: if the latter is understood to be the "unconscious postulating of the being of a being outside of us," then Heidegger "removes" this "natural attitude," but in a different way than Husserl — being is to be postulated, but *consciously*, and is not to be substituted at the outset by a being.

"Project," thus, does not have a merely abstract-methodological meaning, but allows for describing and interpreting the manners of human "being in the world." Dasein carries out understanding as a "project," which means that it cannot understand the world or itself without going beyond its boundaries into ex-isting, standing-out, "projecting" itself. In *Being and Time*, the emphasis is on Dasein's ex-isting, on its "going beyond itself" in "projecting." This is a continuation of the phenomenological line of interpreting intentionality, but here we can already trace Heidegger's tendency to see Dasein in a more immanent dimension: even in going out of itself, in ex-isting, in projecting, Dasein still remains itself.

> Because of the kind of being which is constituted by the existential of projecting, Dasein is constantly "more" than it actually is… But it is never more than it factically is because its potentiality of being belongs essentially to its facticity. But, as being-possible, Dasein is also never less. It is existentially that which it is *not yet* in its potentiality of being.[81]

Everything that Dasein understands, and thereby constitutes, in its going out and beyond itself towards the world, turns

---

81 Heidegger, *Being and Time*, 141; idem, *Raboty i razmyshleniia raznykh let*, 6.

out to belong to Dasein itself, i.e., Dasein can never really leave itself or escape itself. Everything that it "projects" is its own self-projection. What compels Dasein to constantly "project" the world from itself? Such is its "existential," that is, its way of being. The desire for happiness, satisfaction, confidence, and identifying with something better or bigger than you are, the desire to possess many things and beings for satisfaction — these are some of the reasons that lead Dasein to "live in projection." Is this bad or good? Heidegger is not engaging in any evaluation, but rather sets the task of acknowledging what there is in full *transparency* (in "seeing," *Sehen*), acknowledging that Dasein nevertheless remains itself, within itself, in and as existing. With this acknowledgment, if it is full and clear, Dasein's predatory impulses towards beings should fade away, for such impulses have but one aim: fleeing from oneself, getting out of oneself, becoming something other than what we essentially are.

Thus, we can see that substituting "Dasein" as understanding and as "project" for "consciousness" and "intentionality" not only enabled Heidegger to develop ontology on a hermeneutic basis, but also contains a certain possibility for ethical interpretation. "The interpretation [the development of understanding projecting itself] can draw the conceptuality belonging to the beings to be interpreted from these themselves, or else the interpretation can force those beings into concepts to which they are opposed in accordance with their kind of being."[82] After *Being and Time*, Heidegger will be increasingly inclined to treat any "project" whatsoever as violent, while Dasein's task is proclaimed, such as in *On the Way to Language*, to be "returning to where we are always already abiding." In this critique of metaphysical, conceptual language as killing life, Heidegger has authoritative forerunners: for instance, in the preface to his *Phenomenology of Spirit*, Hegel spoke in the same sense against "rationalizing" and called for creating a "dialectical"

---

82 Heidegger, *Being and Time*, 145-146; idem, *Raboty i razmyshleniia raznykh let*, 12.

language in which the inner development of concepts would not be shackled by immobile forms of preconceptions: "only a philosophical exposition that rigidly excludes the usual way of relating the parts of a proposition could achieve the goal of plasticity."[83] Nietzsche also wrote of philosophers in *Twilight of the Idols*:

> They think they are doing a thing an *honour* when they dehistoricize it, *sub specie aeterni* — when they make a mummy out of it. All that philosophers have been handling for thousands of years is conceptual mummies; nothing real has ever left their hands alive. They kill things and stuff them, these servants of conceptual idols, when they worship — they become a mortal danger to everything when they worship.[84]

Whereas in Hegel's case we can hardly speak of any direct influence on Heidegger, Nietzsche exerted a powerful impact on all aspects of Heidegger's philosophy.

Thus, it becomes more or less clear why and in what sense actuality ("facticity") is in need of interpretation and thus becomes an object of hermeneutics. In the wake of Nietzsche's words that "God is dead," Heidegger rethought Dilthey's hermeneutics in such a way that the intentional character of meaning-postulating consciousness in Husserl's phenomenology could be creatively used to fill the world with actual meaning and reality.

Let us move on to a direct examination of Heidegger's *Hermeneutics of Facticity* lectures. In particular, let us examine the terminology of these lectures: firstly, this terminology will remain in many respects definitive of what will appear in *Being and Time* and remain up until the "Turn" in the 1930s (only after which will Heidegger's terminology and style change cardinally); secondly, in the creation of such special terminology lies a significant aspect of hermeneutics

---

83 G.W.F. Hegel, *Phenomenology of Spirit*, trans. A.V. Miller (Oxford: Oxford University Press, 1977), 39.

84 Friedrich Nietzsche, *Twilight of the Idols or How to Philosophize with a Hammer*, trans. Duncan Large (Oxford: Oxford University Press, 1998), 16.

in general. Insofar as hermeneutic interpretation cannot represent a theoretical structure, it develops as a constant explication of certain key terms and the unfolding of the possibilities of interpretation consciously inlaid in them by the author.

The most important and, at the same time, the most ambiguous term in the *Hermeneutics of Facticity* lectures, as well as in all of Heidegger's works up to the "Turn," is Dasein. In my view, to reiterate, this term is most appropriately and expediently left untranslated. For example, translating Dasein as "here-being" (such as in the Russian *zdes'-bytie*) accentuates the ontological aspect of Dasein, whereas in Heidegger this term always retains the resonance of "life" and "existing." There is no unambiguous, once-and-for-all established definition of Dasein to be found in Heidegger's works; rather, it is always defined contextually, colored and coloring in corresponding tones. For instance, when Heidegger speaks of "curiosity" (*Neugier*), Dasein is defined in terms of curiosity; when Heidegger discusses "being moved," "agitation," "being concerned," and "care" (*Bewegtheit, Sorge*), Dasein emerges in each of these respective terms. In Heidegger's texts, "Dasein" can be likened to a "floating marker" which indicates that a given phenomenon or problem is related to the very essence of hermeneutics (and subsequently ontology). In tracing Dasein's "entry" and "being-in" in various contexts, both within one work and in multiple works from different years, one can highlight the dynamism of the philosopher's movement of thought from problem to problem, from one object of interpretation to another. In the *Hermeneutics of Facticity* lectures, two problems of completely different dimensions are consistently examined under the rubric of "Dasein," and the passage from one to the other is very telling for the philosophical situation of the time.

The first circle of questions associated with Dasein pertains to the concepts associated with *"das Man"* — the "everyone" or "anybody," the "average," "talk," "hearsay," the "exposure" of "publicness," and "interpretedness" (or "having-been-interpreted"):

> the following can be defined for the time being: The being-there of Dasein has its *open space of publicness* and its ways of seeing [*Sicht*] there. It moves (a basic phenomenon) around in a definite mode of discourse [*des Redens*] about itself: talk (technical term) [*das Gerede*]. This discourse "about" itself is the public and average manner in which Dasein take itself in hand, holds onto itself, and preserves itself... This talk is thus the how [*das Wie*] in which a definite manner of Dasein's *having-been-interpreted* stands at its disposal. This being-interpreted is not something which would have been added to Dasein, externally applied to it, affixed to it, but rather something into which it has come of itself, from out of which it lives, on the basis of which it is *lived* (a how of its being).[85]

This "having-been-interpreted" of Dasein is, as it were, what the hermeneutics of Dasein as facticity strives to interpret: "The theme of this investigation is facticity, i.e., our own Dasein insofar as it is interrogated with respect to, on the basis of, and with a view to the character of its being."[86] After all, the task of hermeneutics is interpretation. But, insofar as Dasein is understanding, the very meaning-generating activity that interpretedness is must in some way be intrinsic to Dasein in its concreteness. Heidegger sees this interpretedness at first in the "talk" or "discourse" that dominates "public opinion." He uncompromisingly exposes the structures of the everyday, average "spirit": "an example of an exponent of being-interpreted in the today is... the talk heard in the public realm from the average educated mind — today: the modern 'mind.'"[87]

Each factical life needs recognition by others, for it is only on this recognition that it builds its own notion of

---

85 Heidegger, *Hermeneutics of Facticity*, 25-26; GA 61, 31.
86 Ibid., 24; GA 61, 29.
87 Ibid., 27; GA 61, 32.

itself, and this opinion then conditions others.[88] It is not the ontological sense of Dasein that is emphasized here, but rather the aspect of life and concrete human relations. In generating all meanings, Dasein subordinates itself to one of the laws of meaning: meaning is always in a concrete context. Human relations, ties, and acquaintances are the "context" in which a concrete Dasein acquires meaning (i.e., existence, i.e., itself). Dasein is always conditioned and limited by this context, but it is not burdened by this unfreedom, for it therein finds protection from an even deeper vision of itself:

> being-interpreted... is what gives to the "there" [Da] of the factical being-there of Dasein [Da-sein] its characteristic of being-oriented in a definite manner, of a definite circumscription of the kind of sight possible for it and of its scope. Dasein speaks about itself and sees itself in such and such a manner, and yet this is only a *mask* which it holds up before itself in order not to be frightened by itself. The warding off 'of' anxiety.[89]

Being-interpreted, by definition, belongs to the essence of Dasein itself; it is interior, not exterior, and hence it could even be said that Dasein is a certain kind of interpretedness; consequently, *Dasein is doomed to always acquire itself "secondhand,"* as it were, that is, to depend upon others, to create by talk and hearsay, to be a mask hiding itself from itself and a "warding off 'of' anxiety."

Through talk and hearsay, it would seem that Dasein's interpretedness does not belong to the essence of Dasein itself, but only "sticks" to it as if it were a "nagging." But man does not give birth to himself, grow up, or live in solitude. Even before a person is born, as soon as their mother feels their presence, she begins to talk about them and with them — about what she expects, what she wishes, or what she fears. What is thus said, even if only in the mind, is the first manifestation of the actuality with which a person has to encounter from birth to death, the very form (*soma—sema*

---

88   Ibid., 77; GA 61, 99.

89   Ibid., 26; GA 61, 32.

in the *Cratylus*) into which a soul-sense is supposed to be embodied, the context in which this meaning will live and be perceived by others. Dasein is a being among other beings, a sign among signs, a word in the self-writing and self-developing Book of Life (cf. Revelation 5:1: "I saw in the right hand of him who sat on the throne a scroll with writing on both sides"). This whole book is a coherent narrative, and the word (Dasein) cannot be taken out of a sentence. Even if it is the best word in the Book, it is the Book that makes it such. Moreover, Dasein is not only a sign — it is also *being* (*Sein*), that is, meaning, and it therefore belongs to its own embodiment (being-in-the-world) as well as to the whole Book, like meaning to a sign. Of course, talk and hearsay are the most exterior, alienated, and burdensome level of the Language of Life, but man must *act* in society, which means being judged and "treated" ("interpreted about"). It is another matter that "hearsay" cannot be taken too close to heart, for these "traces" of existence, this infinite game of reflections, is always already behind oneself and can never capture the essence of existence that is Being.

Bringing readers to this thesis, Heidegger compels us to think with him and to seek the way to something more authentic and profound in Dasein than everyday interpretedness. The task is to "see it [Dasein] in its peculiar character there where everyone least suspects [*Wo man es nicht vermutet*]."[90] Dasein does not "consist of experiences, and still less is it a subject (an ego) standing over against objects (which aren't the ego)"; rather, Dasein "is a distinctive being [*Seiendes*] which precisely insofar as it 'is there' for itself in an authentic manner is not an object — in formal terms: the toward-which of a being-directed toward it [*das Worauf eines meinenden gerichtetseins*]."[91]

This new definition of Dasein marks the passage into a new, problematic domain of the hermeneutics of facticity.

---

90 Ibid., 38; GA 61, 48.
91 Ibid., 37; GA 61, 47.

If Dasein is only the directedness of consciousness (towards the greatest self-interpretedness), then, without contradicting Dasein's nature, we can move forward in hermeneutic interpretation and break the structures of everydayness so as to bring Dasein to that which resounds in the second meaning inlaid in it (alongside "life" and "existence"): "being" (*das Sein*). In so doing, we do not deny that Dasein can exist only in context, but instead of ordinary human relations there arises the context of the categories of Being. Nor is "interpretedness" discarded, but now Dasein receives it from something other than "talk."

A separate section of the lectures in question is devoted to how Dasein acquires its interpretedness firstly by means of history and secondly by means of philosophy. Dasein's task in both of these directions of interpretation is to objectively demonstrate itself, to bring itself into the here. History confirms Dasein as a structure that develops in time, in historical fulfillment, while philosophy considers Dasein from the point of view of eternity, that is absolutely. Insofar as history and philosophy are modes of interpreting Dasein, and since Dasein itself is a certain interpretedness, Heidegger even says that "history and philosophy are...something which Dasein itself is," or "modes of its having itself in a definite manner."[92]

Upon concluding a brief exposition of the historical and philosophical self-interpretation of Dasein, Heidegger moves to the rung of interpreting that would subsequently become the basis of "fundamental ontology" or the "Dasein analytic" in *Being and Time*. All of the levels of Dasein's self-interpretedness — whether through talk, public opinion, or historical and philosophical self-consciousness — turn out to be superficial, limited, and limiting; Dasein nowhere ever appears in the full depths of its living reality, its being. Here, once again, the indeterminacy, ambiguity, and "floating character" of the term Dasein is redeployed: through setting

---

92 Ibid., 39; GA 61, 48-49.

up a new context of existential characteristics, or existentials, the very meaning of Dasein changes, increasingly dissipating into the "*da*" that emphasizes its concreteness, its "hereness," its "embeddedness" in the world, as well as alongside "*Sein*," the being in every being that fills the "natural attitude" of the world with ontological weight and significance.

Heidegger writes in italics: "*Dasein (factical life) is being in a world*"[93] — this will later be "being-in-the-world" (*In-der-Welt-Sein*). This is a highly significant definition: now Dasein is not so much "a being," even a "special kind," but is "being" (*Sein*). Intrinsic to this being are certain main characteristics or ways in which Dasein "enters" or "is being-in" the world and responds to its challenges. The further interpretation of Dasein lies in examining these main characteristics, or "existentials."

At this point, let us recall that we are examining the terminology of the *Hermeneutics of Facticity* lectures and tracing how the contextually defined understanding of the term Dasein develops within them. The first question that stood before us was: How (in what sense) can actuality be an object of interpretation? We now have some grounds to advance a hypothesis: Dasein in its concrete particularity is facticity.[94] Actuality has (acquires) meaning only insofar as it is interpreted and understood by Dasein. Therefore, the interpretation of actuality, that is, the disclosure of the meanings imparted to it, leads Heidegger to Dasein as being rooted and "embedded" in the world. The hermeneutics of actuality is thus replaced by a hermeneutics of Dasein (i.e., hermeneutics has the tendency of passing into ontology). The ways in which Dasein "enters" or is "being-in-" the world (likewise, how the world "enters" or is "in" Dasein) are the "existentials," and these "existentials" constitute an especially important article in the terminology of the *Hermeneutics of Facticity* lectures.

---

93   Ibid., 62; GA 61, 80.

94   Such is indicated in the title of Part One, Chapter Two, §6 of the lectures.

Just as the contextual understanding of Dasein laid out by Heidegger consists of two complementary and intersecting meanings ("life" and "being here"), so can we confidently highlight two semantic layers in the interpretation of Dasein's existentials: the first pertains to "everyday interpretedness," to the plane of the "life manifestations" of existence, and the second to the plane of "existential determinations."

Dasein's existentials can be arranged into a single sequence that reflects the course of the hermeneutic clarification of Dasein's "existential situation" and "position" (*Lage*) in the world:

- "Curiosity" (*Neugier*)
- "Movement" or "agitation" (*Bewegtheit*)
- "Care" or "concern" (*Sorge*)
- "Encountering" (*Begegnende*)
- "Familiarity" (*Vertrautheit*)
- "Availability" ("being-present-at-hand", *Vorhandenheit*) and "being-ready-to-hand" (*Zuhandensein*)
- "Significance" (*Bedeutsamkeit*)
- "Context of references" (*Verweisungszusammenhang*)

It is impossible to examine these existentials in separation from each other, as each of them represents a certain stage in bringing into relief Dasein's authentic position in the world.

Heidegger turns to the phenomenon of curiosity directly in the wake of examining the historical and philosophical modes of Dasein's "making itself certain about itself." Curiosity connects Dasein to interpretedness through talk and hearsay. It is typical of the human being to search for proof of the credibility of their own ideas of themselves in other people, in history, in philosophy, and in science. On the one hand, the aspiration to find such proof leads a person into an infinite multiplication of knowledge, from street gossip to scientific theories; on the other hand, this aspiration shows that Dasein is not in the world in a state of bliss: being in the world "hits a nerve" and agitates it (*Bewegtheit*). The reality of the world and, first and foremost, the reality of Dasein itself turn out to be a challenge to which one must constantly seek a response. "The basic phenomenon of *curiosity*... shows Dasein in its peculiar kind of *movement* [*Bewegtheit*]."[95] "Curiosity [is] a movement in such a manner that the Dasein which 'is' this movement 'has' itself there in it," and therefore "what needs to be explained, brought into relief... is in what sense Dasein is movement."[96]

In German, *Bewegtheit*, in the sense of "agitation" or "being moved," comes close to "concerned" or "care" (*Sorge*), which will be one of the main categories on the stage of *Being and Time*. In the *Hermeneutics of Facticity* lectures, "care" is already defined as the "fundamental phenomenon of the being-there of Dasein."[97] Like Dasein itself, the category of "care" bears a dual meaning: with respect to Dasein as life, care means the main tune and "attunement," that is, the psychological state of seriousness and responsibility. But, above all else, care is the characteristic of the being of Dasein; if we recall that the main aspiration of hermeneutics is to confirm the world in its natural attitude, then it becomes clear that care (and not even "love") shows the fullest engagement of Dasein in the world — love might go beyond the world, but care presupposes an actual object. "Care" arises out of "curiosity": Dasein's first concern in the world is confirming itself by means of the world. Insofar as this "certification" is mediated by something, Dasein in caring becomes capable of forgetting about itself and going towards the world beyond its own limitations.

The very phenomenon of "going out," of "projecting" (*Entwurf*) will be examined in more detail in other works. Here, Heidegger passes from care to the notion of "encountering" (*Begegnende*). This is a very profound characteristic of

---
95 Heidegger, *Hermeneutics of Facticity*, 51; GA 61, 64-65.
96 Ibid.
97 Ibid., 80; GA 61, 103.

being that is of key significance in the chain of existentials. Everything that constitutes Dasein's "lifeworld," everything that is accessible to its understanding and has value for it, is "encountered" by man when he is "actively concerned" or "taking care."

Three existentials immediately and organically arise out of "encountering": "significance" (*Bedeutsamkeit*), "being-present-at-hand" (*Vorhandenheit*), and the "context of references" (*Verweisungszusammenhang*). "The *as-what* and how of their ["things'"] being-encountered can be designated as *significance*."[98] The world has significance namely because it has the character of being-encountered. "Significance" can be directly associated with care: the state of being concerned is characterized by the fact that the human being is inclined to give more meaning to something (out of the things that are encountered) that has a relation to an object of care. Further, Heidegger writes: "what is being encountered in a 'worldly' manner shows itself as being a means to..., used to..., no longer really suitable for..., no longer used to...: its being-there [*Da-seiende*] is a being-*there-for-this*. 'Therein-in-order-to-do-this' [*Vorhandenheit*] means: ready-to-hand [*Zuhandensein*] for *being-occupied-with* [*Verfugbarsein*]..."[99] In *Being and Time*, this "being-present-at-hand" [*Vorhandenheit*] will be contrasted to "being-ready-to-hand" as an object of scientific representation. These existentials significantly clarify the picture of Dasein's position in the world. Dasein, defined as "actively concernful" or "taking care," enters a particular world and imparts various objects with significance insofar as they help or hinder Dasein's task of affirming itself in the world. From unreliable self-assertion by means of talk, and then by means of history and philosophy, we arrive here at a more sturdy grounding of the objects of everyday use in the world. Dasein enters along with the world into a very tight familiarity and proximity (*Vertrautheit*). It cannot be said whether this closeness pertains, and whether to an equal or

---

98 Ibid., 71; GA 61, 93.

99 Ibid.

different degree, to people and objects. What is important for Heidegger is the positionedness of the being of Dasein in the world, and this "intimate closeness" is a rather full characterization of such.

At this stage of interpretation, Dasein's rootedness in the world of the "natural attitude" turns out to be altogether full and deep. Now, having firmly put Dasein as the source of all meaning in the center of the life world, this world can be filled with the meaning and significance which it needs. Dasein's lifeworld, a world of significances which are unified, like their source, by care, and yet are manifold in their relations between one another, is now imagined like an extensively branching network of meaningful relations between objects as they are given in everyday being. A hammer refers to an anvil, and the anvil to the hammer. The whole totality of references is designated by Heidegger with a single construct, *Verweisungszusammenhang*, "context of references": "The phenomenal whole of disclosedness, from out of which and on the basis of which something being encountered in a factical manner signifies and points itself into its there, is itself a peculiar context of references."[100]

On this point we can conclude our survey of the existentials that characterize Dasein's position in the world and its relationship to the world as they are presented in the *Hermeneutics of Facticity* lectures of Heidegger's hermeneutic period. Overall, this relationship can be characterized as *hermeneutic in the strictest sense of the* world. This means that the interpretation that constitutes the essence of hermeneutics is, so to speak, the mode of Dasein's being and self-realization in the world. Dasein is simultaneously that which understands (life), that which is understood (facticity), and that which is understanding (interpreting). Dasein is at once both "subject" (life) and "object" (facticity), but these aspects are "pulled off" in the *act of interpreting*. Interpretation is primary in relation to life as well as in

---

100 Ibid., 76; GA 61, 99.

relation to facticity. It is primary in relation to life because life first "comes to know" of itself and becomes certain about itself out of facticity, and it is primary to facticity because facticity is only the projection of Dasein as "an interpreting life."

Thus, Dasein cannot be "verified" or "understood" outside of this very hermeneutic relationship. Hermeneutics, therefore, obtains Dasein, "being here," the only verifiable being, in its full disposition, and this hermeneutics will soon naturally grow into the fundamental ontology of *Being and Time*.[101]

The picture of the world and existence that Heidegger draws with the existentials develops the ideas that were inlaid in phenomenology, but also goes far beyond them. Just as in phenomenology, much depends on the point of view from which we observe an object. Point of view constitutes horizons and determines *what* we see. But Husserl's understanding of "point of view" is rather "speculative" in the theoretico-optical sense. In Heidegger, this point of view is not firstly in the theoretical-optical, "speculative" space, but in the world of things among which we find ourselves in a pre-given hermeneutic situation. In other words, Heidegger illuminates the *role of practice in cognition*. Contemporary studies in the field of the physiology of sense perception confirm that we perceive (even feel) any "encountered" thing not as a ready given, but as a field and material for possible *activity*. A blacksmith looking at a hammer is sizing up how he might smith with it. According to Heidegger, *there is nothing else to a thing for the human being*, that is, everything that we see and call a "thing" is a sum of "estimations," possible "hows," "I could...," etc.

In the preceding, we defined meaning as the possibility for Dasein to become something else, to be otherwise. Now it becomes clear that at least one way for being "other" is the possibility for action, for play. Here we can see an analogy

---

[101] In *Hermeneutics of Facticity*, the mode of temporality is derived from care, but is not yet attributed decisive significance.

that anticipates Postmodernity: a thing (a sign) in a playing field has only the meaning that the game gives it. Outside of the game, there is *nothing*, no meaning, for us. More precisely, the contrast between practice and theory, between action and speculation, is removed by hermeneutics: both are unified within the notion of *interpretation*. Any action is Dasein's "project" and "othering," a creative act that *"creates-with"* or *"creates-upon"* a new meaning and links or "invests" it into what is being done. Interpretation does not reveal a ready meaning, but creates it, inserts it: interpreting is also an action. No matter what a person does, the object of their action will, for themselves and for all others, bear the imprint of their spirit, their uniqueness, and be reminiscent of them. The human, being a "sign" in the Book of Life, a living sign that develops through its interpretation of itself, incorporates the object of its action into the context of its life and thereby gives it and "imbues" it with new meaning. The tighter a person weaves something into the fabric of their life, the greater the meaning with which it is endowed. Therefore, *any action is interpretation*, and Dasein — the human engaged in "becoming other" — is, according to Heidegger, the product of all of its (and others') actions, i.e., Dasein is "interpretedness."

Now, having examined some aspects of Heidegger's hermeneutics, can we answer the question: how, and in what sense, according to Heidegger, can actuality be an object of interpretation? Actuality is none other than Dasein itself in the mode of "projection," Dasein in its concrete particularity. Actuality is no more than the meaning and significance that "care-taking" Dasein imparts to the known and familiar objects surrounding it. Therefore, actuality can be interpreted by bringing into relief, firstly, the inner, meaningful connection of actuality (e.g., hammer — anvil) and, secondly, the finite, single source of all significances and meanings, that is Dasein in the "attunement of care." At this stage, like phenomenology, hermeneutics is not a system, but a method — a method for imparting meaning to actuality. Just like phenomenology, hermeneutics proceeds from the premise, already discovered in phenomenology, that man *unconsciously* assigns the meaning of existence and all other significances to the world of the "natural attitude." Unlike phenomenology, however, hermeneutics sets the task of doing the same thing (investing meaning) *consciously*. For Husserl, "between consciousness and actuality lies an abyss of meaning," just as for Kant the "thing in itself" is hidden behind the veil of phenomena weaved by the "productive power of the imagination," and for the Vedantists the unconditioned reality of *Brahman-Ātman* is hidden behind the veil of *māyā*. Just as Buddhism tore down the veil of *māyā* and showed that there is Nothing behind it, and just as Schelling, Fichte, and Hegel showed that there is no "thing in itself," so does Heidegger, in turn, abolish the *noema*, the ideal content of acts of consciousness, and leaves man as a creator alone with his creation — alone with the world and his own life within it.

§4. Heidegger's "Discovery" of the Principle of "Temporality" (Historicity)

In the *Hermeneutics of Facticity* lectures, "temporality" is derived alongside other existentials from the mode of "being concerned" that is intrinsic to Dasein's being in the world. Part II, §26 (*Der Begegnischarakter der Welt*) says:

> The being-there which is being encountered has its own *temporality*, and this is something we are concerned about and attend to in a broader sense. What we are concerned about and attend to is there as not yet, as to be... for the first time, as already, as approaching, as until now, as for the time being, as finally... It is only on the basis of this temporality that all the basic moments of time can be understood.[102]

The principle of temporality is devoted very little attention in these lectures, and it would indeed have been difficult to

---
102 Heidegger, *Hermeneutics of Facticity*, 78; GA 61, 101.

presuppose that just two and a half years later Heidegger's fundamental work would be completed, in which "time" is put on par with the fundamental category of ontology, "Being." In our striving to reconstruct the whole context and line of development of Heidegger's thought, we would seek in vain to find in the *Hermeneutics of Facticity* lectures the prerequisites for the shift in relation to the principle of time besides the above-cited mention in passing, which we have reproduced almost in full. It is obvious that following the Hermeneutics of Facticity lectures in Autumn 1923, Heidegger went on to accomplish a very important, fundamental, unexpected discovery that prompted him to put the principle of temporality at the center of the ontological problematic.

In *Prolegomena to the History of the Concept of Time* (summer semester lecture, 1925), Heidegger issues a highly significant caveat: "On the basis of the foregoing, I could now leap ahead and relate all sorts of things to you about time."[103] If this were true, then this means that Heidegger had been thinking about time (which he already thought about in 1916) *in addition to* his "phenomenological studies," but that he did not yet have sufficient grounds to incorporate time into the circle of his Dasein analytic. The formal reason for this was the Kantian definition of time as a "form of inner sense" and Kant's use of time in the doctrine of the pure schematism of rational concepts, as Heidegger wrote in *Being and Time*: "Kant is the first and only one who traversed a stretch of the path toward investigating the dimension of temporality — or allowed himself to be driven there by the compelling force of the phenomena themselves."[104]

However, there is every reason to presume that the real motive that prompted Heidegger to "discover the principle

---

103 Heidegger, *History of the Concept of Time*, 307; idem, *Prolegomeny k istorii poniatiia vremeni*, 323.

104 Heidegger, *Being and Time*, 22; idem, *Bytie i vremia*, trans. V.V. Bibikhin (Moscow: Ad Marginem, 1997), 23.

of temporality" was Dilthey's correspondence with Count Yorck von Wartenburg, which had just been published by Rothacker and sent to Heidegger ahead of Christmas 1923-24. It was uncharacteristic of Heidegger to ever cite sources and leave them without interpretation. One unique case, however, was his quoting of Count Yorck towards the end of the Kassel lectures:

> Yorck von Wartenburg had perhaps an even better sense than Dilthey of this need for historical meditation-on-meaning [*Besinnung*]. On August 21, 1889, he wrote: "It seems to me that the oscillations brought about by the principle of eccentricity, which led to a new era more than four hundred years ago, have now become extremely broad and flat. Knowledge has progressed to the point where it annuls itself and human beings are so removed from themselves that they can no longer see themselves. 'Modern man,' i.e., man since the Renaissance, is ready for burial." And then on February 11, 1884: "Since to philosophize is to live, there is in my opinion — Do not be alarmed! — a philosophy of history. But who could write it?... That is also why there can be no real philosophizing that is not historical. The distinction between systematic philosophy and historical presentation is in its essence incorrect... I am dismayed by the monastic cell of modern man in these times when life's waves surge so high and when, if any time, knowledge should be power. But if science has a native ground, it is to be found in the world of the past, in *antiquity*."[105]

Following Heidegger, we have reproduced these quotes in full because, in our opinion, they became Heidegger's real program for developing his philosophy. The whole development of Heidegger's philosophy can be interpreted as an evolution of understanding the principle of "historicality" and "temporality." The Kassel lectures repeated, with only small modifications, the bringing into relief of "temporality" out of "care" that had been given in *Hermeneutics of Facticity*, where time did not yet occupy an important place:

---

[105] Heidegger, "Dilthey's Research," 273; idem, "*Issledovatel'skaia rabota*," 182-183; Dilthey, *Briefwechsel*, 83.

> Concern fulfills its meaning by managing to make available what is not yet available; it has the sense of bringing what has been placed under its care into the present. There is in care a certain expectation or waiting, that is, a definite relation to the future. I expect something from the future which concerns me; it is not something that I am, but rather something I have to do. To concern oneself in this way with the future is at once to forget.[106]

"Care," of course, is one of the main existential characteristics of Dasein, but in *Hermeneutics of Facticity* time is derived from care in the same way as space, significance, etc. In the very same way, time could be derived from encountering, curiosity, or any other existential (e.g., the "encountering now," the "no longer encountered," the "already being encountered"). A turn was needed in the very trajectory of Heidegger's thought in order to arrive at the understanding of the role of time presented in some of the expressions of the Kassel lectures and in the ensuing lectures *The Concept of Time* (25 July 1924) and *Prolegomena to the History of the Concept of Time* (summer semester 1925). In the Kassel lectures, Dasein itself, the "floating marker" of the *Hermeneutics of Facticity*, is already defined as "time": "We will now venture a preliminary definition of the being of human being that will serve as a basis for the proper definition, wherein the sense of the being of human being will turn out to be time."[107] Further:

> *Dasein* is nothing but *being time* itself. Time is not something that occurs out there in the world, it is rather what I myself am.... Time defines the wholeness of Dasein. Dasein is in each instance [*jeweilig*] not only in the moment, but rather is itself in the full stretch of its possibilities and of its past.[108]

That is, "time" is the answer to the question of the being of beings, the center that connects all experiences and acts of consciousness, to which neither Dilthey nor Husserl could furnish an answer. In accordance with the general tendency

---

106 Heidegger, "Dilthey's Research," 266; idem, "*Issledovatel'skaia rabota*," 172.
107 Ibid., 258; idem, "*Issledovatel'skaia rabota*," 161.
108 Ibid., 265; idem, "*Issledovatel'skaia rabota*," 171.

of the era to impart abstract categories with the ethical meaning of concrete human relations, Heidegger correlates the "future" with "resoluteness" ("decision") to commit any kind of action, the present with acting as such, and the past with consciousness of responsibility. "Every action is at once guilt," or as Goethe put it, "He who acts is always without conscience."[109]

If we were to assess the actual role of the concept of "temporality" in the works of 1924-1925, then the conclusion may be drawn that there is a certain rift between an awareness of the first-rate importance of the principle of time in ontology (and philosophy in general) and the actual place of this principle in the interpretation of the characteristics of the being of Dasein. The "discovery" of the principle of temporality under the influence of the Yorck-Dilthey correspondence was not absolutely unexpected. Heidegger's first work devoted to the concept of time dates back to 1916 (!),[110] but there was still a long way to go before time would be posed at the center of the ontological problematic. When Heidegger identified Dasein with time in the Kassel lectures, this could only mean one thing: the next object to which the hermeneutic method is to be applied would be time. But we know that hermeneutics draws positive results of any kind not from out of itself, but always from the interpretation of philosophical sources or categories; therefore, it is only natural that Heidegger had to go through a certain period (namely, just over two years) of working out the connection: between early 1924, when Heidegger evidently "discovered" the principle of temporality, and Spring 1926, when he finished *Being and Time*. During this period, Heidegger busied himself with the intensive engagement of "hermeneutically working out" the concept of time and endowing it with the profound substance that would become part of *Being and Time*.

---

109 Ibid.

110 See Martin Heidegger, "Der Zeitbegriff in der Geschichtswissenschaft," *Zeitschrift für Philosophie und philosophische Kritik* 16:1 (1916), 355-375.

II
HERMENEUTICS IN THE PERIOD OF *BEING AND TIME* (1925-1929)

§1. *Prolegomena to the History of the Concept of Time* (1925): Posing the Question of Being

Heidegger's posing of the problem of Being at the center of his philosophizing was anticipated by a number of factors in the "spiritual situation of the time" (in Jasper's terminology).

1. *The crisis of worldview.* Many thinking people in Europe during the interwar period felt something akin to an "inflation of reality": things were becoming empty, meaningless, and evasive in their ephemerality. Accordingly, Dasein, which derives the ground for its existence from things, loses its existential foundation. Things are no longer what they once were — no longer goods, substantial, or true things — but mere signs, increasingly reduced to bare functions. When things lose their meaning, life itself becomes empty. In addition, the First World War showed how quickly human life could be devalued to the status of "expendable material" needed for the functioning of the military-industrial machine. All of this generated, or aggravated, a deep spiritual and moral crisis that touched the very foundations of human existence in the world. As a result, the question of the deep grounds of this existence — of Being — became acutely actual and relevant.

One example of how a moral or spiritual crisis always raises the question of Being can be found in Hamlet's famous dialogue: it is not "to live or not to live," but "to be or not to be, that is the question." One can live, i.e., "exist," but still *not be* anyone or anything in the face of the reality of death.

2. The crisis of science. Heidegger stated in *Prolegomena to the History of the Concept of Time*:

> the real crisis is internal to the sciences themselves, wherein their basic relationship to the subject matter which each of them investigates has become questionable. The basic relationship to the subject matters is becoming insecure, which activates the tendency to carry out a propaedeutic reflection on their basic structure. Such a reflection seeks to dispel the insecurity over the fundamental concepts of the science in question or to secure those concepts in a more original understanding of its subject matter.[111]

In mathematics, this manifested as the crisis of foundations and the problem of psychologism, which was the subject of the fundamental dispute between formalism and intuitionism: formalists believed that the foundation of mathematics is simply the best currently known system of axioms satisfying a number of formal signs (fullness, non-contradiction, etc.); intuitionists believed that the foundational mathematical exams are expressions of some kind of initial intuitions. Moreover, not all physicists were ready to embrace the theses of Einstein's general theory of relativity, whose conclusions did not align with the world view of ordinary experience and Newtonian physics.

The sciences in crisis looked to philosophy for substantiation, demanding that philosophy, in Heidegger's words, bring "the subject matters under investigation to an original experience, before their concealment by a particular scientific inquiry."[112] Husserl had already put forth the call to go "back to the things themselves!," but for him "thing" was the German *Sache*, which meant "object," the object of research, rather than a "thing" as such. This object is itself constituted within a given science and therefore cannot serve

---

[111] Heidegger, *History of the Concept of Time*, 3; idem, *Prolegomeny k istorii poniatiia vremeni*, 9.

[112] Ibid., 5; idem, *Prolegomeny k istorii poniatiia vremeni*, 11.

as a sufficiently durable foundation. For Heidegger, "thing" is *Ding*, the pre-scientific thing of everyday experience. Irreducible to scientific concepts and underivable from them, it is the thing itself (*Ding*) that should, according to Heidegger, become the sturdy foundation for the teetering edifice of science. As in other cases, Heidegger followed Husserl, but went further than him.

3. The crisis of phenomenology. In Heidegger's view, the main reason for what he saw as the obvious crisis of phenomenology was its neglect of the question of Being. Although phenomenology is first and foremost a method, not an ontology, Heidegger did not believe it to be free from the unfolding resolution of its own founding question: out of all the multiplicity of beings, why is it intentionality that is phenomenology's topic? The answer to this question should have been, according to Heidegger, to take phenomenology towards the problematic of the being of human Dasein.

Posing the Question of Being by Hermeneutic Means

From the very outset, Heidegger posited the possibility of a dual interpretation of Dasein: on the one hand as "life" and "existence," and on the other as "being" ("-here"). In the face of the challenge that the meaninglessness of the world poses to man, the main undertaking of hermeneutics is to find a way to creatively impart meaning through "interpreting," that is, through establishing a contextual link to the source of all meanings that is Dasein (Husserl's "absolute consciousness" fulfilled this function as part of a different task). The first stage of interpretation, where Dasein is understood in terms of life and human relations, inextricably links Dasein to the context of the "natural attitude." As soon as ontological meaning begins to be disclosed in Dasein, Being is found "embedded" in this given being as such, not outside of or beyond it. In other words, Being is not transcendent, but rather is "transcending" in the sense of constantly compelling this being to go beyond its own limits (to ex-ist), all the while remaining itself. In essence, what *Being and Time* called "fundamental ontology" is merely a development of one of the degrees of Dasein's interpretation in the "hermeneutics of facticity." It is ontology in terms of its task, but in terms of its essence, method, and principles, it is a hermeneutics of Dasein and its existentials.

The question of Being gradually ripened in Heidegger's consciousness alongside his dissatisfaction with the phenomenological approach to consciousness, where the latter is taken in "pure" form. Husserl turned to Descartes and Kant as though Hegel, Nietzsche, Freud, or Marx had never happened. Husserl's attempt to revive transcendentalism was interesting, but the era had changed, and few believed in the possibility of "pure consciousness." Hermeneutics, therefore, raised the question of *the being of the intentional*, that is, the being of consciousness. However, substantiating the posing of this question in view of the centuries-long tradition of metaphysical ontologies was no simple task and required serious preparation. Heidegger began such preparations in 1923, he was in the middle of it in 1924-1925, and he was at the end of it in 1926-1927.

1. *The question of Being, posed hermeneutically, is the question of the meaning of Being.* In the final analysis, this question's resolution does not lie in what "Being" is or how it pertains to beings. There is no "objective" or purely "subjective" Being. "Being" is only one meaning that we (as Dasein) invest in our "projecting" of reality. Therefore, it would be more accurate to say that the question is not about the "meaning of Being" as one thing that "has meaning," but about "the meaning: being." To answer this question, Heidegger suggests that we must first understand the meaning of the word "is" in everyday language.

2. *The question of the meaning of "Being" is addressed to (that is, it "turns towards") beings.* In German, the words "Being" (*Sein*) and "being(s)" (*Seiende*) have the same root, hence Heidegger has no difficulty in guiding the reader to think of the question of Being as directed towards the "basic character of the entity": "the sense of being of an entity implies the entity itself."[113] That is, the question of the meaning of "is" should not be posed without examining *what* is (and what this *what* is).

Heidegger consciously allows that which would be considered a circularity from a logical standpoint: a being ("what") should be taken not simply as a being, but as something "be-*ing*," "existing," that is, in the aspect of its Being. For this, there should always be some kind of vague pre-understanding of what "to be" is. This is not a *petitio principii*[114], nor is it a *circulus vitiosus*[115] — it is the hermeneutic circle. Heidegger uses a different term, "circle of searching,"[116] but with the same meaning. This does not correspond to the ideal of scientific substantiation, but the choice is simple: either we move around the circle of the grounding of Being, or the entirety of science and worldview remain groundless due to the fact that the question of Being has not been clarified.

3. *The question of Being is addressed to ("turns towards") a special being.* "The questioning is itself an entity."[117] Being lies at the core of any being, but in an ordinary being the relation between such a being and Being is hidden, unmanifest. The being that asks about Being, *Dasein*, is the only being

---

113 Heidegger, *History of the Concept of Time*, 144; idem, *Prolegomeny k istorii poniatiia vremeni*, 151.

114 In Latin, "the pretense to become a basis for proof," a logical error that lies in allowing for the basis of a proof to be a premise which itself is still in need of proof.

115 In Latin, "vicious circle," a logical error that lies in allowing for the basis of a proof to be a premise that is itself derived from such a proof.

116 Heidegger, *History of the Concept of Time*, 147.

117 Ibid.; idem, *Prolegomeny k istorii poniatiia vremeni*, 151.

whose relationship to Being constitutes its essence. This relation becomes more manifest as Dasein questions something that transcends the realm of beings in general, and thereby *goes beyond it*. The question of Being is therefore turned towards not just any being, but to Dasein: "being demands the exhibition of the entity *Dasein*."[118] Thus, Dasein itself demands attentive examination. In the *Prolegomena to the History of the Concept of Time* lectures, Heidegger still calls this research "phenomenology," but it is in essence *hermeneutic* research, *interpretation* in the strict sense of the word.

4. *This being is the closest to us, but in the sense of its givenness (its certainty) it is the furthest away.* On this point, Heidegger challenges Descartes and Husserl's certainty as to the "subject's self-evidence to itself." For the latter, the pure consciousness of the subject understands itself directly in the act of *ego cogito*, in intellectual intuition. Heidegger returns to the ancient Greek words of Heraclitus: "What the gods have given us first becomes known last" and "However far you go, you will not find the boundaries of the soul, for so deep is its *logos*." Heidegger does not simply discount the concept of the "subject" out of some "willful decision," but rather calls it into doubt as a very artificial and derivative concept in need of substantiation. Husserl "critiqued" (in the philosophical sense) the natural attitude and reduced the "natural person" to "transcendental subjectivity." For Heidegger, on the contrary, *the "natural person" is more certain*, albeit with two qualifications: (1) this is only an initial certainty — the certainty of a being — from which it is necessary to depart in order to ascend to Being. It is also necessary to demonstrate how the "natural person" can ever "be certain of itself" (through a being); (2) this is not the natural person of Husserl and the sciences (the *animal rationale*), because the sciences and phenomenology cannot grasp the notion of the "natural person" as it is given to oneself *before* and *beyond* scientific concepts themselves (and yet, scientists themselves

---

118 Ibid., 149; idem, *Prolegomeny k istorii poniatiia vremeni*, 154.

are persons!). Later, and in many respects continuing the work begun here by Heidegger, Foucault would engage in the study of "technologies of the self," i.e., the means by which a person acquires a notion of himself, or becomes aware and thinks of himself as a subject.

Why is Dasein the "furthest away?" In Heidegger's words, "the phenomenal context to be laid open in this entity is the mistaking and misinterpreting indigenous to our intimate familiarity with the entity."[119] The "misinterpreting" here does not mean, as per the classical understanding of truth, a "lack of correspondence between thought and actuality," for there can be no *a priori* criteria of truth and falsehood concerning Dasein's pre-scientific experience. The "mistaking" is a distortion by a scientific and even philosophical conceptual apparatus. But, as Heidegger himself argues, there can be no "presuppositionless" seeing, hence all that we have left to do is to move from more distorted seeing to less distorted seeing, though we can never reach the "boundaries of the soul" (Heraclitus). But where are the criteria which would indicate that we are at the very least moving in the right direction towards a deeper, more authentic self-interpretation? The problem of criteria will always remain an acute one for Heidegger: how do the active and passive sides in the Kantian "productive power of the imagination," the Husserlian "constituting," and the Heideggerian "projecting" correlate? What plays the role of the "object" that constrains the subject's arbitrariness? If we can speak of any criteria of correspondence at all when it comes to hermeneutic discourse, then it is the facelessness, the absence of any personal interestedness apart from striving towards the truth of Being, and, as Heidegger will write later, "rigor of meditation, carefulness in saying, frugality with words."[120]

---

119 Ibid., 152; idem, *Prolegomeny k istorii poniatiia vremeni*, 159.

120 Martin Heidegger, "Letter on 'Humanism,'" trans. Frank A. Capuzzi, in idem, *Pathmarks*, ed. William McNeill (Cambridge: Cambridge University Press, 1998), 276. idem,"*Pis'mo o gumanizme*" in idem, *Vremia i bytie. Stat'i i vystupleniia*, trans./ed. Vladimir V. Bibikhin (Moscow: Respublika, 1993), 220.

5. *Dasein, as a being, should be examined not from the point of view of its "beingness," but from the point of view of its Being.* This means that there is no need to examine its composition, its structure, or its functioning; rather, what needs to be attended to is only *how* this being *is* (the "way of being" of this being). One of the important consequences of this posing of the question of Being is that Heidegger breaks with the entirety of religious, mystical, and spiritual tradition. The latter proceeds from the duality of matter and spirit in man, where everything is one in the spirit, the spirit itself being bottomless and ultimately rooted in God. Heidegger tries to show that "wakefulness" (*Wachsein*) is not a religious "vigilance over oneself," for the body, the soul, and the spirit all pertain to *a being*, whereas what interests Heidegger is *Being itself*. In this sense, Heidegger contrasts Christian theology as a positive (ontic) science of beings with philosophy as a more primordial, ontological science.[121]

Heidegger will later acknowledge that his employment of European metaphysics' traditional notion of "Being" (*Sein*) led to an enormous confusion that conflated, on the one hand, Being as the being of a being, and on the other, Being as the "clearing" (*Lichtung*). In his early works, Heidegger not only allows for such confusion, but also fails to avoid it himself. In the first sense, he speaks of Being as the word "is" in the conventional form for naming a noun. Thus, Dasein's questioning of its own Being is a questioning of how it is, how it can be itself. But as soon as it is said of Dasein that it stands in one or another relation to Being, "Being" is implicitly substantialized and intuitively perceived as a kind of substance to which a being (Dasein) stands in relation.

In this seemingly inconspicuous step, Heidegger moves directly from positions related to Mahāyāna Buddhism to something more like Vedānta. For Buddhism, *nirvāna* ("Being") is, like for Heidegger here, merely a manner of

---

121 See Martin Heidegger, "Phenomenology and Theology," trans. James G. Hart and John C. Maraldo, in idem, *Pathmarks*, 39-62.

the Being of that being which is; there is no *nirvāna* apart from this being, and the attainment of *nirvāna* is only the attainment of full wakefulness (*Wachsein*), awareness, and paying heed to the *manner of one's being*. As soon as this "truth" in a being is separated from the being itself, the Vedāntist concept of *Ātman-Brahman* arises — the absolute reality that one reaches through *transcensus*, by going beyond any conditioned existence.

6. *Dasein should be examined in the mode of its everydayness (Jeweiligkeit).* In other words, in order to answer the question of the Being of Dasein, we need to examine not some rare, exceptional, selected moments or instances in its existence, but take it in its routine current, in the proverbial "how it happens to be" or "the way it goes." This follows from hermeneutically rethinking the requirement of *presuppositionlessness*: any scientific (or any other) concept that is predicated on an object distorts the latter if this concept does not originate in the preliminary, non-conceptual experience of it. Therefore, Dasein needs to be taken *firstly* in its "pre-conceptual" form, in its "natural environment," that is, in its everyday being. But, once again, it should not be taken as one or another being in relation to its composition, but only in the aspect of its *Being*. In Russian, the word *byt*, "everyday life," is of the same root as *bytie*, "Being," and therefore best expresses Heidegger's thought on the "ontological" significance of everydayness. Insofar as "to be" and "to impart meaning" are one and the same for Dasein, with the latter being even more primordial (since "Being" is only one meaning that Dasein imparts to the things of the surrounding world), Heidegger's analytic of "Being—occurring—everyday life" [*bytie—byvanie—byt*] boils down to examining how Dasein imparts meaning and "projects" itself in the world.

7. *The "fundamental constitution" of "being-in" that is primordially intrinsic to Dasein is radically different from the "being-in" of things that are present-at-hand.* Here Heidegger first introduces the distinction between man and things (the natural world): present-at-hand things are only spatially present within something, whereas Dasein, by virtue of its nature of going beyond its own boundaries (intentionality), "enters into reaction" with its surroundings. At this point, an old problem of philosophy rears its head to face Heidegger: do animals possess consciousness, i.e., intentionality, and do they have existence? According to Heidegger, they do not. There would be no meaning in the world without man.

8. *Hence the critique of the gnoseological "pure subject": cognition, as a way of Dasein's Being, is ontically grounded as being-in-the-world.* The cognizing subject is a being among other beings, but of a special kind. This special character does not confine its "place" among beings in the sense that it could "autocratically rule" on its own. The subject is entirely permeated by the whole world's currents, smells, and pains, and the special character that distinguishes it from present-at-hand beings lies in its capacity to ask about the meaning of its own Being as well as that of others. While remaining a being, Dasein asks about itself: the question itself is also "a being." Descartes' subject is based on the intuition of an "inner," autonomous world of consciousness that is different from the "external" world of things and independent of it. But, according to Heidegger, spatial relations are first established by Dasein itself, and therefore it is not subject to the unconditional authority of spatial limitations, particularly the categories of "inside" and "outside."

According to Heidegger, traditional gnoseology's question of "knowing the truth" is a pseudo-problem, because scientific cognition is by default taken to be the *main way* of Dasein's being in the world, but this is not the case at all. The real question that should replace the problem of pure gnoseology is: "How does the Dasein, which at any given time is in a particular but primarily non-cognitive and not merely cognitive mode of being, *disclose* its world in which it already is?"[122]

---

[122] Heidegger, *History of the Concept of Time*, 162; idem, *Prolegomeny k istorii poniatiia vremeni*, 172.

The stages along which Dasein is led to knowledge should be seen hermeneutically as phases of its meaning-positing activity. According to Heidegger, these stages can be outlined as follows:

1. Self-directedness-towards: the act of directing-oneself-towards, projecting — this is analogous to Husserlian intentionality;
2. Abiding-by: while maintaining the object of directedness in the circle of the "project," in the sphere of the concerned-acting attention, even while being "by" or "under" the object of cognition, Dasein remains "within" itself;
3. *Vernehmen* ("apprehending," "perceiving"[123]), clarifying, and interpreting: imparting meaning by way of establishing a tight connection between Dasein in its being and an object;
4. Preserving that which is apprehended, possessing it: not in the final analysis, but by way of conceptually capturing something in scientific and metaphysical notions.

Heidegger traces his gnoseological concept back to Augustine and Pascal, for whom knowledge through love and hatred is the highest and primary way of knowing, while cold, rational knowledge is secondary and derivative: "Knowing is rather more likely to cover up something which was originally uncovered in non-cognitive comportment."[124] Here we can recall Empedocles' words: "Thought is blood washing the heart."

9. The disclosing of the world. According to Heidegger, the world which Dasein inhabits has its own intrinsic, special way of being which, by virtue of its uniqueness, the philosopher calls "worlding" (*Welten*). "The world worlds" (*das Welt weltet*), i.e., the world has the character of "worldliness" — all of these definitions are meant to indicate the special way of the

---

123 While *Vernehmen* is translated as "apprehending," "perceiving," and "coming to awareness" in the English edition of the *History of the Concept of Time* lectures, we will have more to discuss around the rendering and meaning of this term in Chapter III, §5 and §6 below.

124 Heidegger, *History of the Concept of Time*, 165; idem, *Prolegomeny k istorii poniatiia vremeni*, 172.

world's being and are employed to analyze the "characteristics of encounter of the world."[125]

Thus, in the *History of the Concept of Time* lectures, Heidegger introduces a number of new points which were absent in the earlier variations of the Dasein analytic. Firstly, the emphasis falls on the primacy of the "context of references" (*Verweisungszusammenhang*), the "world" as a sphere of "being appropriated" in relation to a specific "reference," i.e., a thing. A thing "catches the eye" and can claim distinct significance in Dasein's life when it falls out of the context, "breaks," or rises up against the whole, against the world: "surroundings, especially the most familiar ones, become a compelling presence when something is *missing* in them. Because the specific presence of the environing world lies precisely in the familiar totality of references, missing something can allow us to encounter the inconspicuous extant thing."[126] Secondly, the world is no one in particular's: the world is the world of *das Man*. Thirdly, the "world of concern" is reinterpreted as the "work-world."

Although Heidegger here appears to be discussing Dasein's "ways of being" in the world, he is in essence — insofar as hermeneutics lies at the core of the determination of all these questions of Being — analyzing the *connections of meaning* in the world as a self-developing text. The "author" of this text, Dasein, is incorporated in the text itself as one of its signs, albeit of a special type. The "references" (*Verweisungen*) are the meaningful connections in the context itself, the "context of references." The authentic task of hermeneutics — to interpret the world as a text — develops along the model of the hermeneutic circle: the whole can be understood only by proceeding from understanding its parts (and itself as one of its parts), and vice versa. However, before we know something about the parts, we have a pre-understanding of the whole, the "haziness" of which needs to be clarified.

---

125 Ibid., 186; idem, *Prolegomeny k istorii poniatiia vremeni*, 194.

126 Ibid., 189; idem, *Prolegomeny k istorii poniatiia vremeni*, 197.

Insofar as we ourselves are incorporated in this whole, our pre-understanding of the world will be a hazy feeling of the world as a "world" that is "at peace," i.e., a world that is harmonious, that fits together, that is measured in its flow, which carries us *without requiring* our conscious participation, but which leaves open this possibility. Hermeneutics, as the inter-interpreting of the world through oneself and oneself through the world, makes Dasein a *conscious participant in the projection of "world,"* of which it is the co-author anew in every moment. We can thus interpret the ultimate aim of hermeneutics to be bringing Dasein into a state of "wakefulness" (*Wachsein*) in relation to itself in its own "is."

§2. Working out the Question of Being by Hermeneutic Means

The question of Being is the question of what it means for Dasein *to be*. The first answer is that it means to be "its own" (*eigentlich*) and "not its own" (*uneigentlich*), i.e., "authentic" or "inauthentic." Therefore, working out the question of Being by hermeneutic means unfolds into and brings into relief Dasein's "own" ("authentic") and "not its own" ("inauthentic") modes of being:

1. Dasein's being-in-the-world (*In-der-Welt-Sein*)
2. Being-with-others (*Miteinandersein*)
3. Being-towards-death (*Sein-zum-Tode*)
4. Being time (which Heidegger does not fully work through).

Being-in-the-World

1. *The reality of the world does not need proof.* The meaninglessness of doubting the being of the world is demonstrated in the following manner in the *Prolegomena*:

"It is absurd to wish to subject to a proof of existence that which founds in their very being all questioning of a world and all attempts to prove and demonstrate that the world exists."[127]

2. *Reality is irreducible to objectivity and intelligibility.* The world is not an "object" for a certain consciousness or subject. It is irreducible to phenomena, whether in Kant's or Husserl's sense. On the other hand, however:

3. *Reality is not something "in itself";*

4. *Corporeality does not yield a primary understanding of reality.* Corporeality is given in "pure perception," but this is a mode of "defective significance," whereas full significance is the whole "system of references" of living Dasein. "Pure perception" is only a truncated form.

5. *The spatiality of the world is not its primordial quality.* If it is treated as such (as Descartes did), it transforms the world into extreme alienation. The homogeneity of space-time can be seen as a direct prerequisite for the moral indifference of the sciences.

In and of itself, being-in-the-world (the analogue of Husserl's "natural attitude") cannot yet be called Dasein's "own" mode of being, but neither can it be called "not its own." Being-in-the-world is the structure of Dasein, its fundamental way of being within which both the "own" and "not own" modes are possible.

Being-in-the-world cannot simply dispense with the "inauthentic" mode — not because the world is always "mixed in" with Dasein, nor because Dasein as interpretedness is in need of material as a means to interpret itself, but rather because there is always (in every moment of time) the real danger of "getting carried away" by an interpretation and thereby forgetting that the interpretation is us ourselves; there is also the danger of "falling" into the text-of-beings and

---

[127] Heidegger, *History of the Concept of Time*, 215; idem, *Prolegomeny k istorii poniatiia vremeni*, 225.

living within it like an object, forgetting that we ourselves are the author of the text. Moreover, this forgetfulness itself is intrinsic to Dasein (in *Being and Time*, this is called Dasein's "thrownness"). The Being of Dasein (that is Dasein for itself) is itself a "setting off": it is what we would like to know in the last analysis, and it is that from which we always shield ourselves by covering ourselves with beings.[128]

Hermeneutics, the aim of which is to make Dasein "accessible" (*zugänglich*) to itself, is therefore always *violent* and contrasts how Dasein otherwise tends to dissolve itself amidst beings into oblivion, into *das Man*. In this regard, hermeneutics is analogous to the attitudes of Marx, Nietzsche, and Freud, which, although by all means different from one another, similarly draw the subject into discourse against its own will and tell it what it does not want to hear. If we translate this onto the plane of "truth" and "errancy," then error (concealment) turns out to be an inextricable quality of Dasein which must be overcome through constantly renewed effort.

Hence arises the question of *intelligible space*. Cassirer, in my view, was not quite right when, at the discussion in Davos, he reduced Heidegger's interpretation of space to the spatiality of the "ready-to-hand" (*Zuhandene*) and the everyday dealings associated with it. According to Heidegger, the "ready-to-hand" is the phenomenologically first mode of spatiality that presents itself to man before any critique, but it is not the only one. Intrinsic to the "present-at-hand" (*Vorhandene*) is the scientific-theoretical manner of constituting spatiality, which Heidegger critiques on the grounds that in the 17th-20th centuries it unjustifiably claimed to be the exclusive and primary mode. Heidegger demonstrates that the abstract space of modern geometry and physics is derivative of the space of "everyday concerns," but it does

---

128 Heidegger here does not clarify the reason for this "setting off," since this is not required for the task of interpreting "factical Dasein." Only many years later, after the Turn, will Heidegger find in Hölderlin's poetry a "poetic founding" of this trait of the being of Dasein.

not follow that Heidegger tries to deny this manner of constituting. For Heidegger, these two aspects of space rather precisely correspond to the first two "symbolic functions" of Cassirer's philosophy of symbolic forms — expression and representation. But the third function — meaning — corresponds in Heidegger to a certain mode of spatiality which, while not being clearly determinable, is nevertheless always present at all stages of the philosopher's thought. This semantic space is the space of meaning and points of view which take on some of the traits of the "intelligible space" (*noetos topos*) in Plato's *Phaedrus*.

For Heidegger, man is "universally meaningful" in essence; by the very fact of his existence, man testifies to a certain universality. Man is human in that he is understood, in that he understands, and in that he participates in the *event* of understanding. Understanding is nothing other than the establishing of com-munication ("making meaning common"), of a common "sphere of understanding" between two "points" in intelligible space, between "points of view." If consciousness is narrow, which is to say that its sphere of understanding has a small radius, then it is beyond its power to understand something far removed in intelligible space, i.e., "foreign" points of view. Even a broader consciousness would deflect something coming towards it. Enmity between people — whether religious, national, political, economic, etc. — will never cease as long as *ideational enmity* persists. This enmity can only be resolved in one way: by *expanding consciousness*. In order to expand consciousness, one needs awareness of a singular, whole intelligible space.

Being-with-Others, Dasein's Temporality, and Being-towards-Death

1. The Kassel lectures repeat the derivation of time from care that Heidegger first introduced in the *Hermeneutics of*

Facticity: care is aimed at what is not yet, i.e., the future, and from out of this future it consigns the past to oblivion.

2. Then the question is posed of the totality of Dasein and the totality of its understanding. This arises in connection with the problem of death, since Dasein (in its first signification as "life in time") attains totality only with its demise (its conclusion, completion), up to which Dasein is always open (incomplete, problematic).

It is evident that posing the question of the *integrality* of Dasein in no way flows from the preceding analysis of Dasein; rather, posing this question appears to be a device which Heidegger employs in order to introduce the dimension of time into the Dasein analytic, and he proceeds to do so by turning to interpret death. This "device" looks rather artificial. Nevertheless, the problem of time, of course, pertains to the essence of Dasein as life, as does the problem of death. But it would have been more logical and natural to derive time from the very *openness* of Dasein, from the fact that Dasein, in its essence, as a being, is "being-possibility," which either does or does not come to be in one manner or another. Dasein is "open" to the world, but this does not mean that Dasein is open to accepting the world as something external which is to be internalized, as though it were a matter of consciousness or perception. Dasein is open towards some kind of "space" consisting of all the events that are possible for this Dasein; every point of this continuum is a certain event in which Dasein *might come to be.* This is a peculiar "continuum of possibilities" constituting, as it were, the "ontological body" or "aura of being" of Dasein. Actual Dasein is only a small and derivative part of this sphere of possibilities, and the boundaries of this sphere are never *given* for it, although they constitute a "playing field" or "framework" for Dasein. If we adhere to the logic of the Dasein analytic rather than populist biography, the question of the "finitude" of Dasein should pertain to this projected sphere of possibilities, not to human life on earth that ends in death, and the finitude of this sphere will not at all be as obvious as the finitude of human life in time. But a "possible event," even the event of human life, is also an event, and any event is particular, concrete, and therefore finite. Dasein therefore has death as its limit not only in the temporal dimension, but also in the *ontological* dimension.

A "phenomenological judgment" on death at first seems to be impossible, since (a) one's own death cannot be an object of experience; and (b) someone else's death, although it might be an object of experience, cannot be one's own — death is always my own and no one else's. However, an examination of death in the Dasein analytic is not only possible, but necessary: "Death does not stand out in Dasein, but *stands before* Dasein in its being. In other words, death is always already *impending*. As such death belongs to Dasein itself even when it is not yet whole and not yet finished, even when it is not dying."[129] Thus, it turns out that Dasein not only attains totality in the moment of death, but *always* has this totality thanks to the presencing of death in every moment.

Unlike the Cartesian and Husserlian subject's self-comprehension as a "thinking thing" (*res cogitans*), Heidegger's Dasein comprehends itself in a more original way in its mortality as *sum moribundus* ("I am dying"): "For *I myself am this constant and utmost possibility of myself*, namely, to be no more."[130] Like any possibility, *the possibility of death is itself a being*: "Dasein can... be this its utmost possibility either in this or that way,"[131] i.e., we can distinguish the "own" or "authentic" and "not own" or "inauthentic" modes in Dasein's relation to death.

The *inauthentic approach* rests in merely stating the empirical law that "everyone dies." Death is seen as a moment in time when the life-activity of the biological organism of

---

129 Heidegger, *History of the Concept of Time*, 313; idem, *Prolegomeny k istorii poniatiia vremeni*, 329.

130 Ibid.; idem, *Prolegomeny k istorii poniatiia vremeni*, 330.

131 Ibid., 315; idem, *Prolegomeny k istorii poniatiia vremeni*, 330.

man ends. This ordinary representation of death contains a determinacy in regard to the very fact and an indeterminacy in regard to its moment. The certifiable inevitability of death in the future drives man into thrownness, compelling him to use all the opportunities offered by beings to forget about death. The indeterminacy of the time of death serves as grounds for self-consolation: "Yes, everyone dies, but at any rate I'm not dying now."

The *authentic approach*, expressed in the ancient maxim *memento mori*, "remember death," is the right way to pass from the forgetful averageness of *das Man* to wakefulness (*Wachsein*). First of all, death is always only my own alone, i.e., it reminds me of myself, of what is "my own" (*eigentlich*). Secondly, death reminds us that the world and other people will no longer be accessible to me in the moment of death, i.e., my connection with them is not eternal. This recognition *stirs one up* and thus *is an awakening*.

The inauthentic relation to death, unlike the inauthentic relation to beings, the world, and people, is counterintuitive at its root, because death (as well as birth) is what "throws Dasein back to itself," tears it out of average, half-asleep being. Therefore, in the case of death, it seems as though Heidegger's analysis anticipates a more decisive conclusion for the ethics of the necessity of being wakeful (*memento mori*). In relation to things, on the contrary, "falling" is the "main motion of Dasein," i.e., the inauthentic mode of being in some way belongs to Dasein itself and constitutes it as possibility. Dasein overcomes the alienation of the world through understanding and interpreting, but things always remain "unknown" by nature.

When it comes to *other people*, it turns out that any intersubjectivity, any *Mit-Sein* and *Miteinandersein*, takes on the form of *das Man*, that is, average, alienated being. Being-with-others is the only way of Dasein's being for which Heidegger finds no possible "authentic" mode. Heidegger tries to overcome the problem of intersubjectivity by saying that *Mit-Sein* is just as fundamental a structure of Dasein as is Dasein's being-in-the-world, *In-der-Welt-Sein*, which is to say that man is primordially correlated with others, is essentially "common," since he first gains a notion of himself — and therefore himself as interpretedness — "secondhand," but this dense involvement and embeddedness of Dasein in "being-with-others" turns out to be a primordially "inauthentic" mode of being. In this mode, the deep solitude of existence is hidden from Dasein and becomes an object of experience only in the experience of death as one's own mortality.[132]

Time also has authentic and inauthentic ways of being. Unlike many other philosophers, Heidegger places the "present," the "here and now," in the inauthentic mode, since it flees from the future, which in the final analysis means running away from death, as well as from the past, from its accountability and feeling of guilt. Like Augustine, Heidegger says that the future *already is* for Dasein, is already present in its "sphere of possibilities," and he calls being-towards-the-future "resoluteness," and being-towards-the-past "guilt." Heidegger quotes Goethe: "He who acts is always without conscience"[133] — because action is finite, while accountability is infinite. Insofar as the past does not disappear, but remains, every new present asks the past about itself, about its causes, and so does every new "now" until infinity.

Furthermore, Dasein's inauthentic mode of being is, of course, felt in the world and our representations of it. For Heidegger, every representation of the world in traditional philosophy (especially in modern philosophy) is a reflection of the "inauthentic" mode of being which distorts the primordial phenomena of "world" and "things."

---

132 We will further unravel Heidegger's analysis of "being-towards-death" in the next section.

133 Heidegger, *History of the Concept of Time*, 319; idem, *Prolegomeny k istorii poniatiia vremeni*, 336.

Although the task of hermeneutics (as we have already defined it) is to bring Dasein to the "authentic" mode of being in the world, this does not eliminate the "inauthentic" mode, nor does it even "cancel" it in a dialectical sense: Dasein always remains in the space between its "own" and "not own," between authentic and inauthentic, between "wakefulness" (*Wachsein*) and "everydayness" (*Jeweiligkeit*). Moreover, this space, this possibility of choice, this "being-possibility" to be or to not be oneself in the authentic sense, *is also a being*, for this possibility is not an abstract not-yet-realization, but a positive possibility-capacity.

Dasein can never cease to be a being, a being which stands before the choice of *one or another self*. All that hermeneutics can do is bring a clear awareness of this choice, because we usually choose the inauthentic way of being without even considering that something else is possible (inasmuch as Dasein is, for itself, a setting-off from itself).

The authentic and inauthentic modes are not some kind of fixed models, but rather infinite lines of coordinates for any of Dasein's actions, and they are established by Dasein itself. Dasein's flight from itself has no unconditional boundaries, and its return to itself cannot be absolute. Moreover, Dasein's actions are realized in the space established by these "poles," wherein they are possible thanks to this duality.

The fundamental duality disclosed in the analysis of Dasein's being in the world lies in that Dasein discovers itself *as part* of a world of which it itself is the "*author*" (albeit unconsciously, in the mode of *das Man*). It is not the case that first there was Dasein which "made up" the world as if an "addition" to its own existence, nor is it the case that first there was a world which one part of it, "Dasein" (or *das Man*), then joined and became its author. How can one be the author of a play without simultaneously being its actor — *always already* its actor? If the work-world — the main foundation of our present-at-hand world — is created by *das Man*, by the inauthentic way of Dasein's being, then does this mean that the world in general is not the truth, i.e., is an illusion? According to Heidegger, if we are talking about "the world in general," then this is indeed so, for "the world in general" does not exist; rather, the world is "my world," in which I am in intimate relationship, uncovering the truth of its conditional forms (conditioned by *das Man*).

§3. The Analytic of Dasein in its Temporality (Historicity)

The essence of the "discovery" of temporality as an object of hermeneutic interpretation lies in its providing an answer to the question of the ground of Dasein's totality. Already in phenomenology, upon eliminating the Cartesian "subject" as an arbitrary concept, there arose the old *problem of the unity of consciousness*, the unity of intentional acts. Husserl explained this unity as the unity of the transcendental subjectivity, but Heidegger critiqued this subjectivity as "unfounded." As a result, Heidegger is left with a multiplicity of intentional acts, "projects," which seemingly turn out to be disconnected, "dissipating" without a kernel linking them together.

Before the discovery of temporality, these acts were connected, first, by their belonging to Dasein (which imparted Dasein with traits of a Cartesian subject), and second, by links of meaning ("context of references"). However, this network itself, rather than grounding Dasein, was derived from the totality of Dasein as such. Heidegger thus found himself confronted with the possibility of life being "flattened," reduced to something like the "surface effects" of Postmodernism pursued by Foucault and Deleuze following the "death of the subject."

Heidegger endeavored to employ the discovery of time as the foundation for the totality of Dasein. As a present being, Dasein is, of course, historical, but it is completely submerged in the flow of becoming and does not yield any stable ground for a *synthesis of acts of consciousness*. Still, Dasein is limited in time by its birth and death, and is therefore *whole*. Heidegger grasps the phenomenon of death and translates it from the level of "present beings" onto the plane of ways of Being, where, it turns out, death is no mere indeterminate possibility in the future, but is an "*existential part of Dasein itself*," and in this sense is always already "here and now."

The temporality of Dasein is derived from its being-towards-death as anticipating (*Vorlaufen*, that is literally "running forward towards") and from resoluteness towards being-guilty, that is, conscience. Heidegger defines the inauthentic way of being-towards-death as anticipating. What is being-towards-death in the authentic sense? It is a state in which the very possibility of death is an object of care. However:

(1) Being-towards-death is not a possibility in the sense of doing something or becoming something; if death were such a possibility, then being-towards-death would be an orientation toward the fulfillment of death, that is, to die. Of course, death can be an object for "objective" concern in two cases, but these are examples of the "inauthentic" relation to death: (a) suicide, which makes one's death into an "act," bringing it down from the plane of Being to the plane of beings; (b) Eastern man believes in the infinitude of existence (Dasein) and is concerned not with accelerating death, but with a *correct* death, i.e., with being prepared so that his final thought before death is directed towards the supreme, for his posthumous existence depends on this to a large extent. The "art of dying" as developed in the Renaissance on the basis of Christian beliefs in the posthumous tribulations of the soul came close to this.

(2) Authentic being-towards-death does not mean constantly "thinking about death," which would be an "incorrect use" or even "abuse" of death, i.e., an attempt to turn death into something presently given, depriving it of the character of possibility, eliminating the "ontological gap" between actuality and possibility, and thus making death less horrifying. In Russian villages, elders used to dig their graves and sleep in them in order to get used to death, to no longer fear it, as if growing accustomed to death would mean something after death.

(3) Authentic being-towards-death is *anticipating possibility*. What does this mean? Firstly, it is *absolute possibility* that does not presume any "becoming given," any presence. More precisely, upon passing into the mode of being presently given, there arises the "absolute impossibility of existing," which is the "absolute [ontological] possibility of absolute [ontic] impossibility." Secondly, in anticipating this possibility, *death increases* to the point that it becomes *boundless*: after all, death has no "more" nor "less" (one cannot be "more dead"). Thirdly, anticipating the possibility of death is a way of being of Dasein itself *in the condition of its disclosedness*, i.e., in its ex-isting (going beyond its boundaries).

Evidently, anticipating therefore means entering into a *correct* relation with death as the ultimate possibility, which means:

(a). Death as the "ownmost possibility" is not relative; it does not depend on another being or on other people; it is the ultimate possibility that first constitutes the being of Dasein as its own, that is, as its authentic being.

(b). Death as such a possibility is *necessary*. Anticipating death "liberates one from one's lostness in chance possibilities urging themselves upon us"[134] (cf. *Dhammapada* 10.135: "As a herdsman drives cows out to pasture with a stick, so do old age and death drive the life out of living beings").

---

134 Heidegger, *Being and Time*, 253; idem, *Bytie i vremia*, 264.

Hence, "Anticipation reveals to Dasein its lostness in [*das Man*], and brings it face to face with the possibility to be itself, primarily unsupported by concern that takes care, but to be itself in... freedom toward death."[135]

(c). This possibility is *certain* — and this certainty is higher than any perception or judgment.

(d). However, in all its certainty, this possibility always remains undetermined from the point of view of the moment it happens in time.

One of the results of Heidegger's analysis of death is that death, as an "ontological phenomenon", is factically separated from death as an ontic event that has a time and place, medical symptoms, and can be studied by an ontic (positive) science like thanatology. Even if we could imagine a person living on earth for an indeterminately long or even infinite time, this person, being "extantly" immortal, would still not be free from the necessity of choosing himself out of given possibilities, and this means that he is existentially mortal. Conversely, the greater the sphere of possibilities open in existence, the more painful it is to reject all other possibilities in favor of one that is chosen to be fulfilled.

The death of which Heidegger speaks is one with life; it is the space in which life can live, and yet this space is not homogenous like the space of geometry, but rather is akin to a forcefield that organizes the phenomena of life and keeps them in manifestation. Paradoxically, "death" in Heidegger can be correlated with the "prime matter" of Aristotle, which is also "pure possibility," although, of course, Heidegger's interpretation of the category of possibility essentially differs from Aristotle's. For Heidegger, "possibility" is substantial only in the positive sense as "ability," not as that which is "absent" or "lacking."

Has the analysis of death yielded an answer to the question of the totality of Dasein? No, because "existential

---
135 Ibid., 255; idem, *Bytie i vremia*, 266.

death" itself is omnipresent, fluid, and mobile; it does not set any exterior boundaries for Dasein, nor is it the inner center of the synthesis of acts of consciousness. Although death is *one* and although all "projects" are aimed towards it alone, it is still *indeterminate*.

Thus, temporality could already be derived from the "ontological phenomenon" of death: time is the dimension of Dasein's passage into "its own other," into possibility, and in the final analysis, into the "utmost possibility" that is death. We could even propose one possible definition: "time is unfolding death." However, Heidegger defines "being-towards-death" and "anticipating death" only as an *existential possibility*, and he raises the question of the ontic confirmation of this possibility "from Dasein itself" (from life), unlike Kant, who left aside the question of the factual realization of the act of the categorical imperative in the ethical behavior of one rational being.

In hermeneutics, however, a question never arises without being called to be by an emerging answer: just as "words accrue to significations,"[136] so do *answers accrue to questions*. The answer to the question of the ontic confirmation of the possibility of being-towards-death is already in waiting: it is conscience as resoluteness (the analysis of which is to be found in the second chapter of the second section of *Prolegomena to the History of the Concept of Time*).

1. Conscience is the call (the summons) of Dasein "to its ownmost potentiality-of-being-a-self," that is, in the mode of "summoning it to its ownmost being-guilty."[137] Choosing to be oneself is *resoluteness*. That is, conscience *summons* Dasein out of *das Man* towards itself, which, of course, remains *being-in-the-world* (albeit, at this point, without "others"). Heidegger breaks the question of conscience as "call" down

---

136 Heidegger, *Being and Time*, 156; idem, *Raboty i razmyshleniia raznykh let*, 24.
137 Ibid.,, 259; idem, *Raboty i razmyshleniia raznykh let*, 269.

into three questions: *Towards what* does conscience call? *Whom* does it call? *Who* (or *what*) calls in this call?

2. *Towards what* does conscience call? Conscience summons towards silence and summons in silence. Dasein, as interpretation and as interpretedness, is inclined to acquire its having-been-interpreted, that is, itself, from second and third hands, from *das Man*, through talk and hearsay. According to Heidegger, almost any discourse between two or more people is idle chatter, whereas true speech is to oneself and to no one. Dasein is always listening to Others (*das Man*). We can hardly bear silence, yet silence is when we ourselves speak, voicelessly, in thinking, reading, or writing.

The call of conscience calls Dasein away from *das Man* and *towards itself*. But, after all, Dasein by its very nature is an interpreting strung out between that which is interpreting and that which is interpreted, it is "projected" and thrown into the world, "thrown upside-down" into its possibilities. To what self does conscience call? Towards one's "ownmost possibilities to be," of course. That is, in the final analysis, conscience is the call to open up towards one's ultimate possibility, death, which removes all masks. Dasein is interpreting, that is, speaking; hence, falling silent and ceasing to listen (ceasing any participating in discourse) is for Dasein tantamount to death. But then what we said earlier about the "omnipresence" of death, its "spilling over" into and throughout all of life, is comparable to the *pauses* between words, amidst the very backdrop against which words can "*figure*" or "*perform*" at all. This backdrop allows for the feeling of one's "disposition-of-being" to appear to pure understanding as something incalculable and pre-conceptual (cf. the lyrics of Sergei Nikitin's song: "Let us pause in words"). The call of conscience "forces the Dasein thus summoned and called upon into the reticence of itself."[138]

---

138 Ibid., 263; idem, *Bytie i vremia*, 273.

3. *The call of conscience is ontically indifferent, but ontologically particular.* The call of conscience cannot be understood as the voice of some Other, and it is not "compromised" by the various understandings and verbal expressions that we give to it. Conscience cannot be *explained* psychologically, biologically, religiously, or even philosophically. It can only be felt, but it can only be fully felt in particularity — as the call of one being to Being, from the "what" and "how" of something extant to its Being, from meanings to the understanding that grounds them, from words to silence.

4. *Who is calling* in the call of conscience? It is the ultimate, most proper, ownmost possibilities that call — Dasein is calling upon itself as something greater that incorporates the "projection" of its possibilities. Indeed, feelings of regret or shame in one's conscience are associated with abandoned possibilities, with missed opportunities. If something was not possible for us, then conscience as a call would not have the space in which it might unfold and resound. "The call calls from afar to afar."[139] What is important here is that it is not just any possibilities that call, but only one's *own* possibilities — the possibilities for one to be, or become, *oneself* in one way or another. The possibilities of stealing, killing, and cheating are not one's own possibilities, for they are caused by circumstances, values, and meanings which are exterior to Dasein, imposed upon it from without, obscuring and perverting Dasein's own Being.

Dasein is called by its "project," by what we could become if we seized upon *all of our possibilities.* Is this possible in principle? It should be *ontologically* possible (cf. the Kantian "ought implies can"): the possibilities that particular Dasein has are also concrete, which means that they are exhaustible, although they exceed any ordinary representation by "people" (*das Man*). It is not our *"concept"* or *"representation"* of what

---

139 Heidegger, *Being and Time*, 261; idem, *Bytie i vremia*, 271.

we could be that calls (such can yield only frustration, disappointment, stubbornness, but not conscience and not shame), but rather what we could indeed be. The stubbornness and insubordination of conscience against a particular Dasein's will and representation confirm that "possible Dasein" is *real* in the sense of a *positive possibility*, and from its own sphere, really affects "factical" Dasein, "pulling" it towards itself. It must be remembered, however, that we are always this greater Dasein to the same extent that we are this lesser, factical Dasein.

The one calling in conscience is Dasein "in the ground of its uncanniness."[140] This "uncanniness" unfolds as the angst of the regrets of conscience. This angst is rooted in Dasein itself, in the "greater Dasein," the Dasein that is possible. It is angst in view of the fact that *all* possibilities cannot *factically* be fulfilled. It is, therefore, the angst of possibilities themselves before their own annihilation. Seen as an event, not seizing the possibility to build a house is the same as destroying a house. Not giving birth to a child is the same as killing a person. In choosing itself in each and every moment, Dasein is both killing and killed, and thus is pure angst for itself. Hence, wherever this angst is rooted in Dasein, in its Being, the voice of conscience reaches factical Dasein (its consciousness, or at least its feelings). This consciousness gives rise to a special attunement in Dasein: being-guilty.

5. In *being-guilty*, Dasein "is guilty in the ground of its being," and this guilt is defined by Heidegger as "being the (null) ground of a nullity,"[141] that is, a refusal of something in Being, a rejection of something coming to be. In its essence, in projecting and choosing itself, Dasein destroys the self that it does not choose, which means that it is the cause for its "own nullity" (its own not-being-something or being-nothing).

---

140 Heidegger, *Being and Time*, 255; idem, *Bytie i vremia*, 276.

141 Heidegger, *Being and Time*, 263-264.

Factical Dasein in its concrete particularity is not the possibilities that it has chosen and realized, but rather is those which it has refused and has thereby cast into nothing. *Dasein is the totality of its abandoned opportunities.* Or, in other words, Dasein is nothing (a mode of "nihilating" more so than a mode of being). This nothingness is the guilt and the angst of itself from which Dasein flees out of panic into beings and into *das Man*; it is the void that it strives to fill with feelings of satisfaction and suffering, emotions of joy and bitterness, and concepts of truth (being) and nothing.

The influence of the Christian worldview's inextricable feeling of innate guilt is obvious here, but it is traceable back to even deeper historical roots in the philosophical form in which Heidegger expresses this feeling. An indication of this guilt can be seen in the only certifiable fragment of Anaximander that has come down to us: "...and they repay each other for harm (untruth)." This is "harm" done to Being, harm that is inflicted by each and every thing insofar as it is already something determined, and every determination, as is well known, is a *negation*. The determinateness of the essence of each and every thing consists completely in the negations to which it has subjected being-possibility. The positive essence of a thing is the only Being in which a thing is one with all others. For its determinedness, every being pays the price of negation, or in a determinate sense, "ontological sacrifice." In bringing Dasein back to the "wakefulness" over itself, Heidegger brings it back to consciousness of its pure negativity. Therefore, Heidegger's being-guilty has only a very conditional relation to the feeling of innate pain which Nietzsche, one of Heidegger's main authorities, disclosed with scientific rigor as *ressentiment*.

Nevertheless, why is it the case that Dasein is not its realized possibilities? In its very manner of being, Dasein is a project, a projection of itself. *As soon as a possibility* is realized, it is turned into a present being and "falls out" of existing *Dasein*, literally "falling out" like precipitate from a solution.

Just as in logic, the greater the content of a concept, the greater its volume, and the more significances are excluded from it, so it is with Dasein: the fuller and more substantial its life, the more it acts, the more possibilities it rejects and drops — that is, the more it "an-nihilates" itself. But factical Dasein, consisting of rejected possibilities and having negated past ones, is each time projecting from itself new possibilities that open up before it.

Heidegger is often reproached (as he was by Cassirer) for lacking an "ethical dimension" in his philosophy, and sometimes even more specifically for never writing an *Ethics*, or for never devoting even a single chapter of one of his works to morality. But if by "ethics" one means the substantiation of "eternal values," then we will not find any such "ethics" in Buddha, Confucius, or Laozi, yet no one would accuse them of lacking an "ethical dimension." After Nietzsche, it became clear in Europe that the values of morals are nothing other than modes of establishing and upholding their will. Therefore, the necessary, "*a priori*" condition for the existence of values would be active, conscious, "noble" will. For Heidegger, therefore, the task is not to indicate exterior orientations for will which can never be finally grounded and must therefore be imposed, but to bring will to such a sharp and transparent self-consciousness (*Durch-sehen*) so that within it there might be awakened the insurmountable impulse to reject false, empty, imposed values, an impulse that strives to "live in truth." To what extent Heidegger succeeded in doing so is a different question.

§4. "Projecting" as the Basic Structure of the Being of Dasein

1. In "projecting" (*Entwurf*), Dasein constitutes *possibilities* — possibilities for itself *to be* something or to do something. This is analogous to the various relations of Epicurus' *epibole* and Nicholas Cusanus' *possest*. In phenomenology, the intentional act, the archetype of "projecting," constituted *meaning*, whereas "project" seen as understanding constitutes meaning and establishes *possibilities*. It turns out that meaning, for Dasein, *is the possibility of being something* — obviously something other than what it is, since otherwise it would be an actuality, not a possibility. Meaning is the possibility of *becoming other*. The possibility *to do* something is already derivative of this becoming-other, because any act changes Dasein itself: Dasein *is* the doing or the having-done something. Thus, in the world of beings, what is meaningful for Dasein is that which, by impacting Dasein and "hitting a nerve," *changes* it, in the very least by *giving the chance* for it to change itself. Thus, we acquire a new formulation for defining meaning: *for Dasein, meaning is the possibility to become other*.

2. In "projecting," Dasein is simultaneously greater and lesser than itself: "thrown" Dasein is *Möglich-sein*, "being-possibility," which is Being in the broad sense of the word, provided that we understand "possibility" in the positive sense as a power, a capacity, and not in the narrow sense of the word as something which *is not yet* (i.e., possibility understood as "not-yet-actuality").

For Heidegger, Dasein *is* the sphere of its own possibilities. This sphere is not an "alienated form" or "alienated sphere" of Dasein, as is nature for Hegel's spirit, but, conversely, is Dasein's "ownmost," for Dasein itself is *understanding* (and not merely "that which understands," i.e, not simply a subject across from something which is understood, an object). Therefore, for Dasein, "being itself" means being open for possibilities, which is to be "resolute." In German, "resoluteness" and "openness" are words with the same root: *sich entschliessen* and *erschliessen*. As we have already clarified above, insofar as any possibility is essentially a possibility for Dasein to *become other*, "being oneself" for Dasein means resolving to change, for any change is, in a certain sense, the "death" of the old, which is to say that "to be oneself" is tantamount to "being resolute towards death."

Resoluteness to die is not heroism, but the norm of life; everything that is not *resolute* towards death will — in short time — be annihilated by death, whereas whatever is resolute towards death is reborn out of the destruction of the old, like a seed that dies in the moment of sprouting.

As with Hegel, in Heidegger *"experience"* is not a mechanical assemblage of ever new, colorful, and memorable impressions. The latter is a perverted or "inauthentic" existence. Authentic experience changes a person forever. Even when I forget about an experience, I can never again be who I was before it. In the same sense as Heidegger would later, Hegel wrote of experience: "Spirit becomes object because it is just this movement of becoming an other to itself, i.e. becoming an object to itself, and of suspending this otherness. And experience is the name we give to just this movement..."[142]

3. *The conceptuality drawn out of "projecting" can be "violent" towards beings, but it can also be drawn from beings themselves.* The condition of the "authentic" character of conceptuality is the presence of a "preliminary (pre-ontological) grasp of a being's disposition-of-being." What is this "preliminary grasp" and how can it be achieved? What does it precede? Obviously, it precedes any conceptuality. Before any conceptual grasp, the world is given to Dasein as a vague pre-understanding. Things are "concretized" in "falling out" of this pre-understanding when they fall out

---

142 Hegel, *Phenomenology of Spirit*, 21.

of the coherent, accustomed course of things in Dasein's world. Evidently, it is only when "a nerve is hit" in Dasein by a thing falling out of its "world order" that Dasein attains this pre-conceptual grasp of the disposition-of-being of such a being. For example, the chauffeur of a car might, without any accurate knowledge of the car's mechanics, construct any number of hypotheses about the car's structure, movement, the laws of its motion, etc. However, when something breaks and announces itself through sounds, smoke, or a deviation in motion (or complete cessation of movement), the broken detail is "pre-conceptually grasped." When we open the hood and try to figure out why the car broke down, we understand what detail is broken, and then it is grasped conceptually, i.e., we create the "concept" of a carburetor, its functions, construction, etc. Trying to squeeze a being into the concept of a carburetor before the breakdown would have been violent for Dasein and would be perceived only as *"information."* Of course, this information would turn out to be useful during a real breakdown thanks to the fact that it was the fruit of a past being-experience had by "people" (*das Man*). In the sciences, fundamental concepts like space, time, number, line, force, and life are often not grounded (and Heidegger will later argue that they are never grounded) in an onto-experience of absence, lack, or disharmony. However, this does not address whether such an experience is possible or impossible. At this point, whether a grasp on the being of the basic concepts of science is possible remains an open question for Heidegger. Later, his answer will be unambiguous: such a grasp is impossible when it comes to the concepts of traditional Western science.

4. *In "projecting," Dasein "sees"; it is able to understand what it itself is within the world.* That is, it "sees" or "understands" itself — which is dying (as being-possibility). For man, the only thing that "is" in the world is whatever gives him the possibility to do something (or not to do something), to become something (or not to become something), which, once

again, means the possibility *to be dying*. *The world manifests itself to man through death* — much like how a developer sees what appears on photographic film. Just as photographic film already contains information about light and dark, so has Dasein, in its pre-understanding of the world, already correlated itself with the world and discerned those objects which "death shines through" — that is, those objects that hold the greatest possibilities for transforming Dasein. Death merely manifests this preordained structure.

The question might be asked: Why is any genuine change tantamount to death? Change is ordinarily understood to mean taking a predicate away from a certain subject and endowing it with a different predicate. But with the destruction of the concept of the subject in the Cartesian sense, there is no return to the old Scholastic understanding of the subject: any change, if it is authentic and not merely apparent, affects the whole being, whose whole "disposition-of-being" is changed; just as nothing is left of the old that would remain unchanged in the new, we can speak of the "death" of the old in the new.

5. Dasein "buys" its world at the cost of itself (with its death, even if only in terms of potentiality). For Dasein, the world is the totality of "doorways into other-being." Anything that is not such a door is simply not perceived, not present, and, strictly speaking, does not exist.

One could argue that this interpretation of death unnecessarily dramatizes Heidegger's notion of "projecting," but for the philosopher himself, in principle, this is no cause for fear. Death is not the most terrifying thing, especially for a philosopher. In Heidegger, angst plays a very important role as the only "ontic" feeling that allows Dasein, albeit indirectly, to *experience its being*. This angst comes when Dasein is "thrown out" of its world, for example, by the death of a loved one or the prospect of its own death, when it is "thrown" unto itself alone. The most terrifying thing for

Dasein, even for philosophizing Dasein, is it itself (as being-in-the-world). What is so horrifying in this? Dasein is deprived of the possibility of interpreting itself in terms of the world and covering itself with the world. Instead, Dasein stands at a point of absolute freedom and absolute responsibility. As before, it is still concrete, particular being-in-the-world, disclosed as being-possibility, and in a particular sphere of its possibilities, but in employing these possibilities it now bears an *infinite responsibility*. The world "subsides," and we feel that the network of meanings of our pre-understanding of the world is shaken, shattering under the impact of the transcendent Nothing.

Fear is fear of beings posing a challenge to Dasein, a summons to change, a summons towards death. The whole of actuality is illuminated to Dasein by this fear. Angst is the horror of Being, the angst of being at all, of being-in-the-world. It is incomparable to mere fear, since one can run away from a particular being, but one cannot run away from the inevitability of Being and the need to be.

6. *The authentic manner of Dasein's being is "projecting."* As understanding that has the structure of "projecting," Dasein is "seeing" (*Sehen*). Just as "Being" in Heidegger is like an activity *without* a subject and object, so is understanding a "seeing" before and, in a certain sense, without a subject, like a "grin without a cat." Seeing is manifest in the world as an illuminating "clearing" (Heidegger will later speak of the "clearing of Being"), as if a circle of light emerged in the middle of a dark room and things and observers appeared within the circle. We can try to approximately outline the boundaries of this circle of light and call it a "subject" and the illuminated things "objects," but the *illuminating* is primary, and any seeing is illuminating by the ray of attention. The most authentic way of Dasein's being as such understanding-seeing (*Sehen*) is "looking into," "viewing," "seeing through the transparency" (*Durchsehen*), a way of seeing in which there are no longer any "opaque" realms — in fact, such a realm would be what is usually the subject, the "I." In this transparency, Dasein sees itself as *consisting* of numerous *references* to the world and *possibilities* which have been realized or which are still open. Secondly, all objects are looked-into and viewed in their essence as signs which are established by Dasein — there is *nothing in Dasein that does not concern Dasein itself*, that does not bear the possibility of its "death" and new life.[143]

The question may be asked: Is this a return to subjectivism? Does only that which pertains to the subject, to myself, exist? Why couldn't something exist that might not concern Dasein, either due to its excessive greatness or insignificance? Heidegger might respond that absolutely everything that is known to science today, from quarks to metagalaxies, "affects" man in the mode of *das Man*, and his curiosity always seeks to look on even beyond these boundaries. But, perhaps conversely, hasn't the curiosity of *das Man* already gone too far into what really does not touch us, such as genetic engineering, cloning, etc.? The "transparency" should show man what it is that really, actually concerns himself.

All forms of "contemplative viewing," even speculative thinking, as well as pure cognition, are merely individual derivatives of understanding as seeing. Concepts like "subject," "object," "pure consciousness," "phenomenon," and so on can fully well fit among these derivatives, but in the existential analytic these concepts are unacceptable in the same way that the laws and constants of Newtonian mechanics are inoperative in the micro-world and in relative physics.

7. *Understanding and interpretation*: Interpretation is the form in which understanding comes to be. Understanding is primary, as it establishes the sphere of meaning, while interpreting "appropriates" this sphere anew by means of significance.

---

143 Here we can also see an anticipatory parallel with Postmodernism: looking without a subject, the grin without a cat, an effect without depth. "Viewing" is rather close to the "surface effect."

8. *The circle of interpretating is the hermeneutic circle.* Here, Heidegger already goes on the offensive, not only justifying the hermeneutic circle as the rightful "circle of searching," but also demonstrating the superiority of knowledge obtained through this circle compared to the "linear," demonstrative knowledge of, for instance, mathematics. It turns out that *any grounding of knowledge can come to be only by means of the circle*: subjectivism, realism, idealism, and materialism cannot provide a foundation for knowledge.

It would be fully logical to see Dasein itself as "circular": after all, Dasein is understanding coming to be through interpretation that always originates in some kind of pre-understanding — this is the vague (unthematized) image of the world as a "horizon" of Dasein's being-possibility. Understanding something out of its pre-understanding, Dasein chooses itself as one or another possibility and therefore passes into a different sphere of possibilities, a different pre-understanding of the world. This does not mean that Dasein, like a squirrel on a hamster wheel, is infinitely rotating between understanding and pre-understanding; rather, Dasein itself is this circling. However, Heidegger attributes this structure of the circle only to the domain of beings, not to Dasein: "However, if we note that the 'circle' belongs ontologically to a kind of being of objective presence (subsistence), we shall in general have to avoid characterizing something like Dasein ontologically in terms of this phenomenon."[144]

After describing Dasein as understanding and interpreting through projecting, Heidegger passes to "statement," "discourse," and "language." Statement turns out to be a derivative of understanding, whereas discourse is — unexpectedly — equiprimordial! Language is understood as discourse that is "thrown" into the world. The problem of discourse and the essence of language is still only being placed here, although it had already reared its head in the *Prolegomena.* However, in his

---

144 Heidegger, *Being and Time,* 149; idem, *Raboty i razmyshleniia raznykh let,* 15.

preparatory period for writing *Being and Time,* Heidegger concentrated all of his attention on the problem of time, not language. Although discourse is deemed "equiprimordial" with understanding, over the course of the analysis it turns out to be rather derivative of understanding:

(1). Understanding constitutes *meaning;* meaning that is distinctly expressed ("articulated") is *"significance."* Although Heidegger says that "intelligibility is also always already articulated before its appropriative interpretation,"[145] it is logical to suppose that in "pre-understanding," where there is already understanding, albeit vague and not "interpreted," there is meaning, but not significance, and thus words are only possible, not given. This is conformed by the fact that:

(2). "Words accrue to significations."[146] Words emerge *along with* their significations *inasmuch* as meaning is articulated internally. This clarifies why meaning is articulated for expression.

(3). Discourse grows out of a lack of understanding: wherever everything is clear between two speakers, no words are needed (the language of semi-gestures and semi-breaths created by lovers has almost no need for words). Whenever there is a gap, a shortcoming, in the totality of understanding, the contours of this gap are filled with meaning and shaped into *significance* that is ready to be expressed: the word is not given to significance like any ordinary means of expression, but is itself the main participant in outlining the contours of the gap in understanding — "the word accrues to significations." This is confirmed by an even more particular phenomenon:

(4). In discourse, we are above all hearing unknown words; whatever is clear and understood returns to the undivided totality of pre-understanding, modifying it. But whatever is not understood shapes new gaps in understanding which are to be filled with new "word-significations."

---

[145] Ibid., 155; idem, *Raboty i razmyshleniia raznykh let,* 24.
[146] Ibid., 156; idem, *Raboty i razmyshleniia raznykh let,* 24.

Somewhat running ahead of ourselves, here we can point to one of the main premises of hermeneutics after the Turn that is already inlaid here: "There is no thing where there is no word." Although understanding is more primordial than the word, there are not yet any "things" in understanding, only a vague feeling of a world that is full of meaning but is "inarticulate," "indistinct," not yet differentiated into significances. Thus, it is not only words that "accrue to significations": *things themselves accrue along with them*. After all, there are no "things" for Dasein apart from meanings or, more accurately, significances. After the Turn, language will be more primordial in relation to discourse, to beings, and to Dasein, that is, to man himself.

Several very important hermeneutic conclusions follow from this understanding of meaning. If no "objective" meaning exists (neither in actuality nor in a text), then what should interpretation strive for? Only for the sake of being satisfied with the meaning that a text has "for me" whenever I inscribe such a thing (a text) into the context of my care? In any case, this is how the partisans of "objective meaning" try to frame Heidegger's position.

Another question arises to face this hermeneutic philosophy: What is *outside* of the circle of Dasein's project? Is there, in any sense, something that is "disproportionately beyond" Dasein, that doesn't concern it, or are we once again returning to Berkeley's *esse est percipi*, "being is perceiving"? Heidegger's position on this question has already been expressed, but perhaps not clearly enough. Questioning itself, namely Dasein as questioning, is a being, and as such it outlines the circle of beings that are delineated by questioning. The question "What is outside of the circle?" is counter-intuitive and can only arise out of *curiosity*, because *beyond* this circle nothing *really* touches Dasein. We can recall Zeno of Elea's old proof against the finitude of the world: What would there be if we reached the end of the world and pierced it with a spear? Heidegger's response would be that Dasein's world expands to the depth of the spear, but it nevertheless remains thereby limited. Dasein's world will expand with each new attempt to go beyond only until the point that human curiosity — which is, after all, not limitless, like everything human — tires out. Devoting attention to "borders" and curiosity as to what is "behind" them is a sign of *das Man*, of Dasein fleeing from itself into beings, fleeing to the furthest removed "projection." Of course, it could also be said that the Unknown touches some of us, but this would no longer be curiosity; rather, it would be Dasein's own intrepid breakthrough into a sphere of new possibilities, not an attempt at overcoming its own complex of incompleteness by breaking out of its own boundaries and conquering new spheres of being, each of which would in turn become Dasein's "inner" and "own." The very question "What is beyond the circle of Dasein?" is a ray of light going beyond the boundaries of this circle, expanding it while remaining within it. The world is always the world for man, and even the unknown world is only such in relation to man, not "in general." Heidegger comes close to the "anthropic principle" of modern physics: we observe certain processes in nature because all other processes occur without observers. The question of the finitude or infinitude ("open-endedness") of the world does not arise for Heidegger. Instead, the world of the authentic existence of Dasein is finite in all relations except one, which is the most important: there is only one boundless dimension in the world, namely, the limitlessness of Dasein's changing, the movement of human life.

Indeed, an essential correction needs to be introduced into the image of Dasein as a circle of light in the darkness: Dasein is not a free-floating self-projecting, and the clearing of Being is not a circle or patch of light that freely runs through things. Rather, it is the *exuding of things themselves* as manifested by the death of Dasein. The illumination is the "surface effect" of exuding things. The question of the source of the light of Being has not yet been posed.

§5. "Hermeneutic Ontology" or "Phenomenological Hermeneutics of Dasein" in *Being and Time*

The main historico-philosophical problem confronting the present study of Heidegger's hermeneutics in connection with *Being and Time* is, in my view, the problem of the correlation between system and method in the process of constructing "fundamental ontology." This problem is closely bound up with the problem of correlating, on the one hand, the inner logic of the system of ontology which Heidegger is developing and maintaining, and on the other hand, the logic of the development of his ideas from work to work in the run up to *Being and Time*. The philosopher himself does not touch on the latter, but for the history of philosophy it is perhaps of even greater interest than the internal logic of *Being and Time* itself. This problem lies in the rift between logic and history which the scholar encounters. As I hope to show, *Being and Time* is, in essence, an integral, systematized exposition of the results which the application of the hermeneutic method to Dasein in the "mode of facticity" and to the principle of temporality yielded over the four to five years preceding the release of *Being and Time*. *Being and Time* itself contains such a direct indication: "Phenomenology of Dasein is *hermeneutics* in the original signification of that word, which designates the work of interpretation."[147] The status of "ontology" as a *system* of the "fundamental analysis of Dasein" is to a certain extent exterior to the *content* of *Being and Time*. The internal logic and structure of the work's development — from posing the question and explicating the main categories to unraveling the system of the existential analytic — does not organically emerge from the material itself. Although they might be sufficient within the framework of *Being and Time*, the grounds which Heidegger cites in favor of the interconnection of the categories do

---

147 Heidegger, *Being and Time*, 35; idem, *Bytie i vremia*, 37.

not reflect the motifs which *historically*, over the course of the development of Heidegger's philosophy, conditioned the involvement of these principles in precisely such a context; accordingly, the work does not reflect the *internal logic* of the development of hermeneutic philosophy.

Heidegger confronts the problem of introducing additional considerations for creating a certain continuity in the internal logic of the system of ontology at the very beginning of the work, in the very posing of the question. The point is that the hermeneutics with which Heidegger will now seek to establish the status of ontology was originally concerned not with "Being" as such, but with "Dasein," that is, life and existence. Heidegger is faced with finding an answer to a complex, difficult question: Why does Dasein, which overall pertains to the "ontic" sphere, become the main object of interpretation in fundamental *ontology*? Or, to be more succinct: Why Dasein? Heidegger tries to offer an answer to this question in the very beginning: he says that insofar as being is always the being of a being, the question of Being is also a question about a being. Which being can we prioritize to examine as a case study of the being of a being? Given that this question is very important, I will reproduce the whole passage in which Heidegger argues for "choosing" Dasein:

> If the question of being is to be explicitly formulated and brought to complete clarity concerning itself, then the elaboration of this question requires, in accord with what has been elucidated up to now, explication of the ways of regarding [*Hinsehen*] being, of understanding and conceptually grasping its meaning, preparation of the possibility of the right choice of the exemplary [*exemplarischen*] being, and elaboration of the genuine mode of access of this being. Regarding, understanding, and grasping, choosing, and gaining access to, are constitutive attitudes of inquiry and are thus themselves modes of being of a particular being, of *the* being we inquirers ourselves in each case are. Thus to work out the question of being means to make a being — one who questions — transparent [*Durchsichtigmachen*] in its

being... This being, which we ourselves in each case are and which includes inquiry among the possibilities of its being, we formulate terminologically as *Dasein*.[148]

In response to the question "Why do we choose Dasein, among all other beings, as an 'exemplary' case to use in working out the question of the meaning of Being?," the substantiation cited here might be satisfactory, but it is not exhaustive, and I would even say that it does not even touch the motifs that really guided Heidegger to choose Dasein as the main object of interpretation. Even from the point of view of the internal logic of *Being and Time*, all of this is far from obvious. Firstly, translating the question of Being onto the plane of the relation between Being and beings is in and of itself ambiguous. It is practically not substantiated here, but for Heidegger's philosophizing it is of decisive significance and should, therefore, be examined from the point of view of, if not its grounds, then in the very least its driving causes.

At this point, we are returning to the thesis that the fundamental ontology of *Being and Time* was not originally constructed as an integral metaphysical system, like the systems of German transcendental idealism, but rather was the result of the "ontologization" of hermeneutics, or more precisely, the ontological consequences derived from the materials of the "phenomenological interpretation of Dasein" (*Hermeneutics of Facticity*) as well as the phenomenological studies of Kant, Aristotle, Descartes, Hegel, and other representatives of the metaphysical tradition. The term Dasein was the central subject of interpretation and, perhaps from the very beginning, was chosen for the sake of the possibility of ontological interpretation (Da-sein, "here-being") as noted in the *Hermeneutics of Facticity*, which did not yet claim the role of a systematic ontology. Thus, Dasein in *Being and Time* is the legacy or, so to speak, the "birthmark" indicating the hermeneutic origin of "fundamental ontology." Insofar

---

148 Heidegger, *Being and Time*, 7; idem, *Bytie i vremia*, 7.

as Heidegger in *Being and Time* claims to be constructing a system of ontology, it is not in his interests to point to the hermeneutic sources of the founding category of Dasein (the same goes for the phenomenological, existentialist, and other sources). Heidegger is trying to create the "inner logic" of a system and to "re-ground" the choice of Dasein as the main subject of examination. This internal logic, however, has at least two weak points: firstly, passing from the question of Being to the question of beings; secondly, choosing Dasein as a being which is "exemplary" (*exemplarische*) from the point of view of the relation between beings and Being. In the history of the development of Heidegger's thought, the first passage (from the ontological to the ontic plane of examination) was conditioned by the fact that hermeneutics was initially engaged in interpreting the problem of beings, not Being, in accordance with the theoretical sources of Dilthey's hermeneutics, which engaged in interpreting the "life manifestations" of others. The second passage was conditioned by the fact that one being among all others is of predominant interest to hermeneutics, namely, the human being, which is the source of all the meanings imparted to actuality (phenomenology). The terms that Heidegger refers to as a "bridge" for passing on to Dasein — "looking upon," "understanding," "intelligible grasping" — are hermeneutic, *not ontological* relations.

Subsequently, over the course of substantiating the "ontic and ontological primacy of the question of Being," Heidegger readily replaces the aforementioned question with the problem of the "ontic and ontological primacy of Dasein." In other words, Dasein is not merely the center of the ontological problematic but fully encompasses it: the question of Being cannot be posed outside of the relationship between Being and Dasein. This once again underscores that Heidegger's "fundamental ontology" does not have a single element that would not be a result of the hermeneutic interpretation of Dasein in the works of the preceding period, works which did not claim the status of being an "ontology." It is for this reason that the terms "fundamental ontology" and "existential (fundamental, ontological) analytic of Dasein" are interchangeable, whereas outside of the context of Heidegger's philosophy this interchangeability is not at all obvious.

Heidegger returned to the question of "Why Dasein?" several times, evidently feeling that this is a really important problem of the whole work. In §8 he writes:

> The "special character" of the investigation does not belie the universality of the concept of being. For we may advance to being by way of a special interpretation of a particular being, Dasein, in which the horizon for an understanding and a possible interpretation of being is to be won. But this being is in itself "historical," so that its most proper ontological illumination necessarily becomes a "historical" interpretation.[149]

Here, however, the way in which the interpretation of Dasein as a "special kind of being" provides a horizon for understanding and interpreting Being is not fully substantiated. The link between Dasein and *Sein* remains mainly etymological, which is significant in hermeneutics, but insufficient for ontology. The other main categories of *Being and Time*, such as the category of temporality (*Zeitlichkeit*), face a similar situation to that of "grounding the choice of Dasein."

It is quite characteristic that, in grounding the task of the first part of the work as a whole (of which only two-thirds would be published), in the Introduction (§5), the task is formulated without using the terms "temporality" and "time." The section title reads "The Ontological Analysis of Dasein as Exposing the Horizon for an Interpretation of the Meaning of Being in General," while the first part is titled in a similar manner, but with the inclusion of the category of time: "The Interpretation of Dasein in Terms of Temporality and the Explication of Time as the Transcendental Horizon of the Question of Being." This duality in relation to the

---

149 Heidegger, *Being and Time*, 37; idem, *Sein und Zeit*, 39.

principle of temporality is explainable from the standpoint of the system of *Being and Time*, wherein the category of time is not yet brought into the discourse at this stage. But from the point of view of the integral context of Heidegger's thought, this testifies, in my opinion, to the later incorporation of time among the foundational categories of the Dasein analytic. We have seen that Heidegger "discovered" the principle of temporality in the correspondences of Dilthey and Count Yorck only in 1924, when the hermeneutics of Dasein in the mode of facticity had already been worked out to a significant extent. The discovery of the principle of temporality and its hermeneutic integration became the last component for Heidegger to complete the overall circle of the problem subsequently incorporated into *Being and Time* under the rubric of "fundamental ontology."

From a historico-philosophical point of view, in the structure of *Being and Time* we can easily see two sequential divisions. The first, "The Preparatory Fundamental Analysis of Dasein," corresponds to the period of the development of hermeneutics up to 1924, up to the discovery of temporality, and contains the results of the interpretation achieved at this stage. The second division, the section "Dasein and Temporality," has a mixed character and incorporates a "reinterpretation" of the main categories of the Dasein analytic from the preceding period. More precisely, it involves a reduction of these categories to the principle of temporality, of which they all become derivative. In substantiating the internal logic of the work, Heidegger tries, as in the case with the "choice" of Dasein, to construct a consistent chain of inferences. The entire Dasein analytic, corresponding to the hermeneutics of factical Dasein in the *Hermeneutics of Facticity* lectures, is referred to as the "preparatory analysis of Dasein" in the posing of the task of *Being and Time*.

> The analytic of Dasein thus understood is wholly oriented toward the guiding task of working out the question of being. Its limits are thereby determined... However, the analysis of Dasein is not

> only incomplete but at first also *preliminary*. It only brings out [*hebt heraus*] the being of this being without interpreting its meaning. Its aim is rather to expose the horizon for the most primordial interpretation of being. Once we have reached that horizon the preparatory analytic of Dasein requires repetition on a higher, genuinely ontological basis.[150]

From asserting the limited character of the preliminary analysis, Heidegger passes to the principle of temporality as a means of overcoming this limitation: "The meaning of being of that being we call Dasein will prove to be *temporality*. In order to demonstrate this we must repeat our interpretation of those structures of Dasein that shall have been indicated in a preliminary way — this time as modes of temporality."[151] Here, with the introduction of the principle of temporality, the internal logic of the system becomes less convincing than in the case of the "choice" of Dasein. The whole Dasein analytic from the period of the *Hermeneutics of Facticity* is declared to be "preliminary" and as "not grasping the meaning of Being." Even when viewed from the standpoint of the history of Heidegger's thought, this assertion means that, during the hermeneutic period of the *Hermeneutics of Facticity*, the focus is primarily on concrete, particular Dasein as human existence in the vein of Dilthey's philosophy, rather than on "Being" as the category of traditional metaphysics. At first, temporality is simply posited as a means of going beyond the limited scope of the preliminary analysis of Dasein which will in turn "justify itself" over the course of interpretation. Only then does the principle of temporality find a worthy place in the structure of Dasein's relation to Being:

> We intimated that a pre-ontological being belongs to Dasein as its ontic constitution. Dasein is in such a way that, by being, it understands something like being. Remembering this connection, we must show that *time* is that from which Dasein tacitly

---

150 *Being and Time*, 17; idem, *Sein und Zeit*, 17.
151 Ibid.

understands and interprets something like being at all... *in terms of temporality as the being of Dasein which understands being...* In the exposition of the problem of temporality the concrete answer to the question of the meaning of being is first given.[152]

The chapters of the second division of the first part of *Being and Time*, "Dasein and temporality," are a fusion of various influences, unified by the common hermeneutic method and language, which together create a single "artistic field" as depicted by Heidegger. The first chapter, "The Possible Being-a-Whole of Dasein and Being-towards-death," contains obvious traces of the influence of Kierkegaard. Although the category of "existentials," foundational for the whole of Heidegger's hermeneutics, can be attributed to this influence, this chapter is permeated by an "existential spirit" more so than the others. The third chapter, which interprets "Temporality as the Ontological Meaning of Care," and the fourth, "Temporality and Everydayness," are a direct continuation of the ideas of the *Hermeneutics of Facticity*, now reinterpreted with the employment of the concept of temporality. The fifth chapter, "Temporality and Historicity," contains elements of a philosophy of history that develops the ideas of Dilthey and, even more so, Count Yorck. Only the second and sixth chapters are of mixed origin, partially dealing with the hermeneutics of existentials, partially with interpreting Kant (the "internal sense of time," *Innerzeitlichkeit*) and Hegel (the "connection between time and spirit").

Emphasizing the "internal logic of the system" imparted by Heidegger so as to exclude the context of hermeneutic philosophy does not mean that the hermeneutic connections between the categories are completely eliminated. For example, as soon as Dasein is put at the center of ontology, which corresponds to the starting position of historical hermeneutics, the introduction of beings into the context of the ontological problematic becomes obvious — not on account of a retrospectively imposed "internal logic," but from

---
152 *Being and Time*, 17-18; idem, *Sein und Zeit*, 17-18.

the very logic of the development of the entire hermeneutic interpretation of Dasein: "in accordance with the kind of being belonging to it, Dasein tends to understand its own being [*Sein*] in terms of *the* being [*Seienden*] to which it is essentially, continually, and most closely related — the 'world.'"[153] Dasein is capable of knowing itself as none other than a means of knowing the world, which is a result of Dasein "self-projecting." Dasein's self-knowing by way of interpreting the world (as Dasein in the "mode of facticity") is the genuinely essential principle of hermeneutics: Dasein can clarify the structures of its own meaning-positing, the nature of the act of understanding that pertains to the essence of Dasein, only on the basis of the "material" of concrete, meaning-giving acts, which are disclosed as the ground and source of the everyday meanings that constitute our "world of everydayness." Bringing into relief and grounding Dasein as the genuine source of the meaningfulness of the world is, in my view, the essential intention of Heidegger's hermeneutics. It is no coincidence that, in "grounding" the introduction of the problem of beings in the context of ontology and the "choice" of Dasein as the most "exemplary" being, Heidegger is once again returning to the question of beings in ontology so as to bring into the context of the system of *Being and Time* a living, hermeneutic problem, one which, although not necessary from the point of view of the system itself, represents what is, in my opinion, the most valuable in "fundamental ontology."

The sense in which we can speak of a "hermeneutic ontology" in *Being and Time* has already been addressed above: hermeneutics is the primary method that emerged from Heidegger's engagement with phenomenology. This method generated a certain theoretical content only upon being applied to interpreting various sources, such as Aristotle, Dilthey (especially his correspondence with Yorck), and Kant's *Critique of Pure Reason*. Through the creative interpretation

---

153 *Being and Time*, 15-16; idem, *Sein und Zeit*, 15.

and synthesis and the results obtained therefrom, Heidegger acquired the possibility of developing an ontology on the basis of this hermeneutic method. Heidegger gives the name "fundamental ontology" to his project on the grounds that it poses and resolves the question of "Being," the main question of traditional metaphysical ontology. However, *Being and Time* cannot simply be seen as an "ontology," and I would even say that this is a dangerous move. Heidegger will later (in *On the Way to Language*) explain his choice of the term "Being" as having been compelled by his inability to find an adequate form of expression for what he was then seeking. Yet, in choosing this term with such a significant history of metaphysical understanding and employment, Heidegger was compelled to distance himself from the traditional understanding of "Being" and to introduce a new notion of his own. We know that Heidegger expressed this distance in the formulation of a "destruction of the history of ontology." But then the legitimate question arises: how much of the content of *Being and Time* can truly be considered an "ontology," and would it not be justified, albeit post factum, to give it a more adequate definition? In my view, it is possible to define *Being and Time* as "fundamental ontology," but this requires a preliminary, deep contextualization of the meaning that "Being" takes on in Heidegger's philosophizing. In other words, the philosophizing of *Being and Time* can be called "fundamental ontology" only *"from within"* the course of development of Heidegger's thought, but this is not simply a name: it is an *assertion* that can be understood only in its context. It is justifiable, but can also be critiqued. If we examine *Being and Time* in the broader context of the development of Heidegger's philosophizing as a whole, then a more adequate denomination for this work would, in my view, not be "ontology" (whether fundamental or hermeneutic), but rather *"phenomenological hermeneutics of Dasein."* This name contains an indication of the phenomenological basis of Heidegger's philosophizing, the guiding method of hermeneutics at work here, and the main object of the hermeneutic interpretation: Dasein. The whole problematic of *Being and Time*, with all its ambiguity, corresponds to the ambiguity and problematic of the very term "Dasein." Another variation for defining the content of *Being and Time* would be "Dasein analytic," and this is something which Heidegger would also later be compelled to additionally clarify.[154] Heidegger, in his words, "set off from" the Kantian understanding of "analytic" given in the *Critique of Pure Reason* (the section "Analytic of the Concepts"), which in Kant means "[tracing] the conditions for the possibility of scientific experience back to a unified whole, that is, the faculty of understanding," but Heidegger, as usual, redefines this in his own way as a "tracing back to a unity (synthesis) of the ontological possibility of the being of beings."[155] In working through the problem of the Kantian "grounding of metaphysics" in *Being and Time*, Heidegger borrows the concept of "analytic" from Kant. However, a more adequate denomination for the content of *Being and Time* should come not from the history of traditional metaphysics or from Kant's *Critique of Pure Reason*, but from the concepts of Heidegger's own philosophizing, hence it should be called the "phenomenological hermeneutics of Dasein." The hermeneutics of *Being and Time* is phenomenology inasmuch as it derives its main concepts from rethinking the corresponding concepts from Husserl's phenomenology, as we have already discussed above.

In what follows, we will examine only two main concepts from the plethora in *Being and Time*, insofar as they point to the genetic kinship between "fundamental ontology" and the "hermeneutics of human Dasein" preceding Heidegger's work, namely: "projecting" and the "hermeneutic circle." Although attestation of this kinship can be found in practically all the

---

154 Martin Heidegger, *Zollikoner seminare* (Frankfurt am Main: Vittorio Klostermann, 1987), 83.

155 Martin Heidegger, *Zollikon Seminars: Protocols — Conversations — Letters*, ed. Medard Boss, trans. Franz Mayr and Richard Askay (Evanston: Northwestern University Press, 2001), 114-115.

sections of *Being and Time*, this would, first, require a special, broader study that exceeds our present scope, and, second, some of the most important problems of *Being and Time* have already been examined above, as they were worked out in the *Prolegomena to the History of the Concept of Time*.

In *Being and Time*, Heidegger says of projecting:

> Because of the kind of being which is constituted by the existential of projecting, Dasein is constantly "more" than it actually is, assuming that one wanted to, and if one could, give an inventory of it as something objectively present in its content of being. But it is never more than it factically is because its potentiality of being belongs essentially to its facticity. But, as being-possible, Dasein is also never less. It is existentially that which it is *not yet* in its potentiality of being. And only because the being of the there gets its constitution through understanding and its character of project, only because it *is* what it becomes or does not become, can it say understandingly to itself: "become what you are!"[156]

The character of projecting is intrinsic to understanding; hence, just like Husserl's intentionality, projecting means Dasein's fundamental directedness towards something beyond itself. This is not the abstract-methodological directedness of consciousness towards an object, but the concrete possibility for the finite human being to do something or to be something. Dasein brings understanding into being as projecting, which means that it cannot understand the world, or itself within it, without going beyond itself in existing, in standing out, in "projecting" itself. Here, in *Being and Time*, the emphasis is evidently still on Dasein's existing, on its going out of itself in "projecting," whereas somewhat later this arrangement will shift words "holding oneself out into the Nothing." But even here we can already trace the more immanent interpretation of Dasein that will be characteristic of the later Heidegger: in going out of itself, in "projecting," in ex-isting, Dasein nevertheless remains itself. What it *is* not "in possibility," it *is* "existentially." Everything that Dasein

---

[156] Heidegger, *Being and Time*, 141; idem, *Raboty i razmyshleniia raznykh let*, 6.

understands in "getting ahead of itself" and encountering the world turns out to belong to Dasein itself, and it never actually manages to "get out of itself," to flee from itself, just as an unhappy person can never flee from the pain they carry in their heart.

Everything that Dasein "projects" is a self-projection of Dasein itself; in other words, man always sees, i.e., is capable of understanding in the world surrounding him, only that which is within himself, albeit hidden. It is in "projecting" the world from itself that Dasein first acquires the possibility to deal with all the "characteristics of being" that are inlaid in itself, such as "care," "curiosity," etc. The world as the self-projection of Dasein becomes the latter's possibility of knowing itself.

In *Being and Time*, projecting still bears traces of the phenomenological categorial intuition: "interpretation can draw the conceptuality belonging to the beings to be interpreted from these themselves, or else the interpretation can force those beings into concepts to which they are opposed in accordance with their kind of being."[157] This "drawing the conceptuality belonging to beings themselves" is essentially the categorial intuition, but here the condition of such a "drawing" is presumed to be the presence of a preliminary "grasp of a being's disposition-of-being." If there is no such preliminary grasp, then concepts inevitably become "violently imposed." The later Heidegger will be inclined to see projecting as *always* violent: a being is given to man only in his own projecting; it would be foolish to think that a human or humanized being is the only one possible. Instead, in order to "live in projecting," man should always try to orient himself to the essence of Being that resounds in the depths of his essence.

The method of the hermeneutic circle, one of the main methodological principles of hermeneutics, is in *Being and Time* developed out of projecting as an existential

---

[157] Heidegger, *Being and Time*, 145-146; idem, *Raboty i razmyshleniia raznykh let*, 12.

of Dasein. In Schleiermacher, the hermeneutic circle was a technical device for the scholarly, philological interpretation of a written text, a description of the sequence of steps in such interpreting: first there is a preliminary, already pre-interpretively existing notion of the meaning of the text as a whole; then, on the basis of this preliminary understanding of the whole, we engage in interpreting the first part of the text; as a result, our notion of the whole changes. Hence, the first "hermeneutic circle" closes. Further, on the basis of the changed understanding of the whole, we turn to the second part, and so on, according to this algorithm. This applied algorithm of philological critique takes on fundamentally new significance in Heidegger's hermeneutic philosophy, where interpreting becomes one of the foundational existentials of Being as such (Dasein in the ontological aspect):

> Every interpretation operates within the fore-structure which we characterized. Every interpretation which is to contribute some understanding must already have understood what is to be interpreted. This fact has always already been noticed, even if only in the realm of derivative ways of understanding and interpretation, in philological interpretation. The latter belongs to the scope of scientific cognition. Such cognition demands the rigor of demonstration giving reasons. Scientific proof must not already presuppose what its task is to found. But if interpretation always already has to operate within what is understood and nurture itself from this, how should it then produce scientific results without going in a circle, especially when the presupposed understanding still operates in the common knowledge of human being and world? But according to the most elementary rules of logic, the *circle* is a *circulus vitiosus*. If this is so then the business of historical interpretation is thus banned *a priori* from the realm of rigorous knowledge.[158]

Heidegger here proceeds from how Dilthey conceived of hermeneutics as the foundation of the methodology of the "sciences of the spirit" or the historical sciences. From the point of view of traditional logic, the hermeneutic circle falls

---
158 Ibid., 147-148; idem, *Raboty i razmyshleniia raznykh let*, 14.

under the definition of an error in a "circle of proof." But the very principle of "proof" has force only in the sphere of precise mathematical science, which believes in the existence of a certain "objective," "true" meaning in the objects of the world to which the concepts of human cognition must correspond (the traditional metaphysical understanding of truth as *adaequatio*). Yet, in Aristotle, to whom Heidegger traced back this traditional treatment of truth, Heidegger also discovered a different, more profound understanding of truth as "unconcealment." The requirement of *adaequatio* loses its significance. Heidegger strives to show that an "objective" meaning which is independent of the observer-interpreter and which corresponds to our concepts *does not exist*:

> Meaning is an existential of Dasein, not a property that is attached to beings, which lies "behind" them or floats somewhere as a "realm between." Only Dasein "has" meaning in that the disclosedness of being-in-the-world can be "fulfilled" through the beings discoverable in it... This means: its own being and the beings disclosed with that being can be appropriated in an understanding or they can be confined to incomprehensibility.[159]

A being in and of itself cannot be meaningful or meaningless. Only Dasein imparts meaning to a being by attending to it or denying it attention and meaning. Therefore, interpretation in the human sciences, "revolving" in the hermeneutic circle, takes on a much deeper significance for man as a being living in the world: interpretation does not reveal meaning that *is simply already there (from where?)*, but carries out the creative work of filling the world with *completely new meaning*, which is to say that the world is created as a world of meanings in such interpreting.

What about the natural sciences? They also carry out this work and move around the very same "hermeneutic circle," but they do so in pursuit of different tasks and using different means. If we think about it, then it is indeed in the natural sciences, with their goal of practically transforming the

---

[159] Heidegger, *Being and Time*, 147; idem, *Raboty i razmyshleniia raznykh let*, 14..

world, that the creative, active character of human cognition is manifest most of all. If scientific cognition were only passive *adaequatio* (the perceptive, speculative side of the productive power of imagination in Kant's *Critique of Pure Reason*), then how could any creative use of this knowledge (the "spontaneous," "creative" character of the power of imagination) be possible in practice? Insofar as projecting is the existential mode of Dasein's being in general, the corresponding means of cognition by the hermeneutic circle takes on universal significance with Heidegger. The natural sciences always treat the human sciences haughtily, yet they themselves turn out to be in a position of "catching up": it is only a lack of comprehension of projecting at the core of these sciences that creates the illusion of "objective truth." Heidegger will have much to say about this, as well as its consequences for modern European science and technology, in his works after the Turn.

In *Being and Time*, Heidegger calls interpretation "taking care." This "circumspective understanding" and interpretation is called *ermeneia*, from which the term "hermeneutics" is derived. This kind of interpreting is contrasted — not absolutely, but as only one extreme point on a certain "scale" — to abstract theoretical judgment that is separated from life, i.e., "metaphysics," which is to be overcome.

Before Heidegger, interpretation was primarily concerned with texts. Insofar as a sign was understood to be a bearer of meaning, and given that there was presumed to be an author or creator who once and for all endowed this meaning, interpreters were supposed to strive with all their might to disclose this meaning. If meaning is an existential of Dasein, and not an "identity" belonging to a sign, then *absolutely any objects* to which the "concerned" human being is capable of imparting meaning, anything that might be *significant* for the human being, are signs and are therefore objects of hermeneutic interpretation. In actuality, all the objects of everyday human life, all the "events" ("fulfillments") of temporal human existence, as well as the word, as part of the daily course of *homo legens* (the "reading human"), are objects of interpretation. This expansion of the possible circle of objects of hermeneutic interpretation, already employed by Heidegger in the *Hermeneutics of Facticity* lectures, is the main theoretical prerequisite for the possibility of a "hermeneutic philosophy," that is, a philosophy that hermeneutically examines all the phenomena of human being-in-the-world (*in-der-Welt-sein*) as well as all the problems which traditional metaphysics, according to Heidegger's conviction, had left unsolved and allotted as the inheritance of hermeneutics as metaphysics retreated before the barely opened foundation of the "creative power of the imagination."

§6. The Hermeneutic Solution to the Problem of Grounding Metaphysics in *Kant and the Problem of Metaphysics*

Reconstructing the Methodological Ground

Heidegger's *Kant and the Problem of Metaphysics* is a vivid example of the application of the hermeneutic method to the history of philosophy. Heidegger is often reproached (with rather rigorous argumentation) for his "subjectivism" in outright distorting Kant's thought and attributing to Kant things which he never said, never implied, etc. All of these reproaches carry weight from the point of view of the traditional (classical) concept of truth and the notion that the history of philosophy is a science whose intent is to "reflect" the actuality of philosophical thought as adequately as possible.

But *within* Heidegger's philosophizing, there are sufficient grounds for this indeed rather specific approach to Kant and to the history of thought in general, that is, to closely reflecting the History of Being. Heidegger exposes the ambiguity of the traditional ideals of historical interpretation: on the one hand, there is the task and concrete goal (achievable to one degree or another) of interpreting and disclosing what Kant *actually* said or wanted to say. This notion of "objective meaning" is put in line among other "objects" of history and the "object of objects" is constituted, that is, a view of history. But, on the other hand, Heidegger points to the seemingly obvious truth that *any interpretation is conditioned by a number of preconditions*, whether biological, psychological, cultural, and linguistic, which determine not only the form but also the content of interpretation. One could protest: the form, yes, but not the content. However, if we follow Heidegger, *the border between form and content is itself conditional and mobile*: the content of a text is not an "objective" meaning that is independent of its form (even if it is *relatively* independent).

In *Kant and the Problems of Metaphysics*, Heidegger evidently tends towards freedom of creative interpretation. This was predominantly connected with the fact that Heidegger's Dasein retained, despite all of his critique of the Cartesian "subject," traits bearing a certain affinity to this concept. In this work, Heidegger is still on the way from his discovery of the nature of meaning to fully overcoming subjectivity. Here he still believes in the freedom of the interpreter to create meaning. The text, of course, is part of this creativity, acting as an interlocutor rather than merely as material, but the creativity is carried out by the subject, that is, the interpreter.

The main idea of this course, which Heidegger delivered in the winter semester 1927-28, arose two years before, in the winter of 1925-26, when he was finishing work on *Being and Time*. Yet, the content of the *Kant and the Problem of Metaphysics* lectures turns out to be not so much a development of the ideas of *Being and Time* as it is a *search for a more formidable foundation* in accordance with the methodological principle of "estrangement," or moving back from obvious consequences to hidden premises. Therefore, Heidegger himself saw the analysis of metaphysics contained in this course as preparatory in relation to *Being and Time*: turning to the history of philosophy, particularly to Kant, serves to ground the relevance and justification of posing the problem of Being anew. Of course, the process of this grounding raises new problems, new tasks, and entails the introduction of new terminology.

The main "innovation" in Heidegger's conceptual apparatus that appears in this course is the concept of "metaphysics" and its corresponding problematic. The task of this course is "interpreting Kant's *Critique of Pure Reason* as a laying of the ground [*grundlegung*] for metaphysics and thus of placing the problem of metaphysics before us as a fundamental ontology."[160] Heidegger elaborates:

> Fundamental Ontology means that ontological analytic of the finite essence of human beings which is to prepare the foundation for the metaphysics which "belongs to human nature." Fundamental Ontology is the metaphysics of human Dasein which is required for metaphysics to be made possible... It is true that metaphysics is not a building or structure that is at hand, but is really in all human beings "as a natural construction or arrangement" [Kant, *Critique of Pure Reason*].[161]

Thus, the main concept of the work, "metaphysics," is interpreted in a completely non-traditional sense. To be more precise, here we find Heidegger speaking of, as it were, three "metaphysics":

1. Traditional metaphysics — that from which Kant departed in his "ground-laying."
2. "Fundamental ontology," that is "the metaphysics of human Dasein which is required for metaphysics to be made possible," or fundamental ontology as the "ontological analytic of the finite essence of human beings," i.e., the project of "hermeneutic ontology" developed in *Being and Time*. This "metaphysics" should serve to "carry out" or "prepare the ground" for the third "metaphysics."

---

160 Heidegger, *Kant and the Problem of Metaphysics*, 1; idem, *Kant und das Problem der Metaphysik*, 1.

161 Ibid.

3. The metaphysics that belongs to human nature, the "natural construction or arrangement" that will be disclosed in full only in Heidegger's later works. Such is the "standing out into the Nothing" (*Hineingehaltenheit in das Nichts*), existing, the capacity of man as a being among other beings to respond to the "call of Being," the fundamental twofoldness of man.

By following the course of Heidegger's interpretation of the *Critique of Pure Reason*, we can once again see in living enactment Heidegger's hermeneutic method and the results it brings.

Heidegger interprets the traditional concept of metaphysics by turning to historical data:

> It is known that the initial, purely technical meaning of the expression μετὰ τὰ φυσικά (the collective term for those of Aristotle's treatises that were arranged [in sequence] after those belonging to the *Physics*) later became a philosophically interpreted characteristic of what is contained in these rearranged treatises. This change of meaning, however, is not as harmless as people ordinarily think. Rather, it channeled the interpretation of these treatises in a specific direction, and thereby the interpretation determined what Aristotle treated as "Metaphysics." Nevertheless, we must ask whether what is brought together in the Aristotelian *Metaphysics* is "metaphysics."[162]

Thus, what was initially only an auxiliary expression for ordering the Aristotelian corpus in a certain way subsequently became the ground for interpreting this division as the doctrine of what is "beyond physics." Heidegger believes that this interpretation does not grasp the essential in Aristotle's thought: "In subsequent Scholastic philosophy (Logic, Physics, Ethics), there was no discipline or framework in which to insert precisely what Aristotle strove for here as πρώτη φιλοσοφία, as authentic philosophy or philosophy of the highest order. μετὰ τὰ φυσικά is the title of a fundamental philosophical difficulty."[163]

---

162 Ibid., 4; idem, *Kant und das Problem der Metaphysik*, 5.
163 Ibid.; idem, *Kant und das Problem der Metaphysik*, 6.

Thus, from the very beginning, traditional metaphysics has been deprived of the possibility of seeking its own grounds by referring to Aristotle or, even more so, to Plato. Its grounds must be sought within itself. "Two themes have determined the development of the above-mentioned Scholastic concept of metaphysics, and at the same time they have increasingly hindered the possibility that the original problematic can be taken up once again."[164] It is important to understand these themes, or motives, in order to possibly find a means for neutralizing them, along with the narrow "Scholastic" concept of metaphysics, and to make way for a more original, broad, and at the same time grounded notion of metaphysics. As for the first motive:

> One theme concerns the division of the content of metaphysics and arises from Christianity's devout interpretation of the world. According to this interpretation, every being that is not divine is created: the *Universum*. In turn, the human being has a special place among the created beings to the extent that everything depends on the salvation of the human soul and its eternal existence. Therefore, according to this world- and Dasein-consciousness, the totality of beings is divided into God, Nature, and humankind, and to each of these spheres respectively is then allied Theology (the object of which is the *summum ens*), Cosmology, and Psychology. They constitute the discipline of *Metaphysics Specialis*. In contrast, *Metaphysica Generalis* (Ontology) has as its object the being [*Seinde*] "in general" (*ens commune*).[165]

As for the second motive:

> The other theme that is essential for the development of the Scholastic concept of Metaphysics concerns its type of knowledge and its method. Since its object is the being [*Seiende*] in general and the highest being in which "everyone takes an interest" (Kant), Metaphysics is science of the highest dignity, the "queen of the sciences." Accordingly, the type of knowledge it has must also be the most rigorous and the most binding. This requires that it be assimilated to an appropriate ideal for knowledge, as

---

164 Ibid., 5; idem, *Kant und das Problem der Metaphysik*, 7.

165 Ibid., 6; idem, *Kant und das Problem der Metaphysik*, 7-8.

"mathematical" knowledge is reputed to be. It is rational in the highest sense and *a priori* because it is independent of chance experiences, i.e., it is pure science of reason. Thus the knowledge of its principle divisions (*Metaphysics Specialis*) become a "science established on the basis of mere reason."[166]

Thus was formed the traditional, classical concept of metaphysics which Heidegger defines in Baumgarten's words: "Metaphysics is the science which comprises the first principles of human knowledge," or as Heidegger alternatively formulates: "Metaphysics is the first science in so far as it comprises the decisive grounds for what human knowing represents."[167] For the sake of convenience, Heidegger proposes another definition: "Metaphysics is the fundamental knowledge of beings as such and as a whole."[168]

Here Heidegger introduces the "ontological difference" between beings and Being that is the cornerstone of the fundamental analytic of Dasein. In the traditional understanding of metaphysics, according to Heidegger, Being was not addressed, only "beings as such and as a whole." However, this "definition" of metaphysics "can only have value as an announcement of the problem," which raises the following questions: "In what does the essence of the knowledge of Beings by beings lie? To what extent does this necessarily open up into a knowledge of beings as a whole? Why does this point anew to a knowledge of the knowledge of Being?"[169] "Thus," Heidegger writes, "'Metaphysics' simply remains the title for the philosophical difficulty."[170]

As we can see, Heidegger sees in the traditional understanding of metaphysics the fundamental problem that is to be worked through in *Being and Time*: the problem of

---

166 Ibid.; idem, *Kant und das Problem der Metaphysik*, 8.
167 Ibid., 3; idem, *Kant und das Problem der Metaphysik*, 7.
168 Ibid., 5; idem, *Kant und das Problem der Metaphysik*, 8.
169 Ibid.; idem, *Kant und das Problem der Metaphysik*, 9.
170 Ibid.; idem, *Kant und das Problem der Metaphysik*, 8.

the relationship between ontic and ontological knowledge. Was this problem really contained in traditional metaphysics, or is it only Heidegger who sees it there? I think that Heidegger is presenting the opportunity to see previously hidden aspects in long-since well-known questions. The deceptive impression is to be had that Heidegger's assertions, like the utterances of an oracle, arise as if "out of nothing," whereas underlying them is the deep work of thought.

In *Kant and the Problem of Metaphysics* and *Being and Time*, Heidegger traces ontic knowledge, the cognition of beings as it is carried out in the sciences, back into the fold of ontological knowledge, that is, back into the interpretation of beings through the fundamental comprehension of their Being. This ontological knowledge precedes any ontic-scientific knowledge, otherwise the latter would be left groundless. The main concepts of all the sciences contained in their postulates and axioms should be rooted in the preceding comprehension of the "disposition-of-being" of man in the world. This comprehension radically differs from logic, which only studies and systematizes the present, coincidental state of science.

Metaphysics is engaged in cognizing beings as such and as a whole. Such being(s) can in no way be perceived sensorily; knowledge of them must be pure, *a priori*, i.e., not derived from sensorial cognition. The problematic nature of metaphysics lies in the question of whether there are grounds for the suprasensible, *a priori* knowledge that it claims. For Heidegger, however, the problematic character of traditional metaphysics does not mean that it should be discarded. To the contrary: constant attempts at overcoming metaphysics have ended in failure, have been inconsistent and ineffective; therefore, before the task of overcoming metaphysics is posed, it is necessary to first clarify the question of the inner possibility of this science. "Thus arises the task of a ground-laying in the sense of an essential determination of metaphysics."¹⁷¹

Hence, Heidegger's task is not to "clarify the question of the inner possibility of metaphysics," but rather only to interpret the motives that drove Kant to take up the problem of "grounding metaphysics" in his *Critique of Pure Reason*. In the ensuing lectures, Heidegger will "follow" Kant, reinterpreting him in the language of the "fundamental analytic of Dasein." Only at the very end, in summating the outcomes of the Kantian ground-laying, will Heidegger express his own point of view on the limitations of Kant's results.

Heidegger argues that the ground of metaphysics, in terms of the determination of its inner possibility, should primarily aim at the finite goal of metaphysics: to define the essence of *Metaphysica Specialis* as a certain exceptional kind of knowledge of suprasensible Being. However, the question of the inner possibility of this knowledge requires a preliminary resolution of the more general question of the inner possibility of rendering beings as something evident at all. Hence, "ground-laying is now elucidation of the essence of a comporting toward beings in which this essence shows itself in itself so that all assertions about it become provable on the basis of it."¹⁷² At first glance, the model for this comportment towards beings is mathematical natural science. Heidegger poses the question and then turns to Kant's *What Real Progress has Metaphysics made in Germany since the Time of Leibniz and Wolff?*:

> Is there an "indication" of what makes such a comporting possible? In actual fact: [it is] the method of the natural scientists. Upon them "a light broke... They realized that reason has insight only into what it produces itself according to its own design [project,

---

171 Ibid., 6; idem, *Kant und das Problem der Metaphysik*, 8.
172 Ibid., 7; idem, *Kant und das Problem der Metaphysik*, 8. Behind this difficult formulation lurks the phenomenological principle of "to the things themselves," which Heidegger rediscovered in the Aristotelian understanding of truth as "unconcealment": when a being is unconcealed, all assertions about it become "provable."

Entwurf], that it must not allow itself to cling, as it were, to Nature's apron strings, but must lead the way with principles of its judgments according to permanent laws, and that it must constrain Nature to answer its own questions."[173]

But this preliminarily "projected" plan ("plan of Being," *Seinsplan*) outlined in the main concept and principal of each science, to which all questions of research should pertain, "is rather only a statement of the direction in which it, to be understood in its more fundamental universality, must first be sought."[174] Accordingly, what makes such a comportment to beings (ontic knowledge) possible is the "essence of the preliminary understanding of Being, i.e., of ontological knowledge in the broadest sense."[175]

I think that Heidegger here is "following through Kant's thought further than Kant did himself" (to paraphrase Heidegger's later saying about "following through Greek thought more consistently than the Greeks themselves"). Wherever Kant speaks of the active character of human cognition, there is no talk whatsoever of "ontological cognition," not to mention that such would precede any ontic cognition. Nor does Kant trace — as Heidegger wants to show — the limited scope of human cognition back to the finitude of human nature: for Kant, such is inherent to "all rational beings." But Heidegger claims the liberty to freely reinterpret the meaning of Kant's work: "Whether Kant himself achieves the full clarification of this problem remains a subordinate question."[176] Nevertheless, this "hermeneutic experience" proves to be valuable in its results and in many respects anticipates the philosopher's later ideas — for example, deepening the traditional understanding of truth in metaphysics as the *adaequatio* of knowledge and beings: "Ontic knowledge can

---

173 Ibid., 7; idem, *Kant und das Problem der Metaphysik*, 9.
174 Ibid.
175 Ibid.; idem, *Kant und das Problem der Metaphysik*, 10.
176 Ibid., 8; idem, *Kant und das Problem der Metaphysik*, 11.

only correspond to beings ('objects') if this being as being is already first apparent, i.e., is already first known in the constitution of its Being. Apparentness of beings (ontic truth) revolves around the unveiledness of the constitution of the Being of beings (ontological truth)."[177]

Heidegger then seeks to demonstrate that the essence of Kant's "Copernican revolution" in philosophy lies in its placement of the problem of ontology at the center.[178] All of the main concepts of the *Critique of Pure Reason* are translated onto the plane of the ontological difference between Being and beings, and accordingly between ontological and ontic knowledge.

(1) The question of the possibility of *a priori* synthetic judgments is interpreted to be the question of the possibility of ontological knowledge. According to Heidegger, Kant's formulation of the question grasps the essence of cognition in traditional terms as "judgment," but when it comes to synthetic knowledge: "This known what-Being [*Wassein*] of the being [*Wasgehalt des Seienden*] is brought forward *a priori* in ontological knowledge prior to all ontic experience, although it is precisely for this [ontic experience]."[179]

(2) In Heidegger's view, Kant used the term "transcendental philosophy" to designate the problem of traditional ontology: here "transcendence" is understood as "the constitution of the Being of the being," the "stepping-over [*Überschreiten*] (transcendence) of pure reason to the being, so that it can first and foremost be adequate to its possible object."[180] In this way, Heidegger interprets, "the legitimate interpretation of the sense of the 'Copernican Revolution' is renewed."[181]

---

177 Ibid., 8-9; idem, *Kant und das Problem der Metaphysik*, 12.
178 Ibid., 8; idem, *Kant und das Problem der Metaphysik*, 16.
179 Ibid., 9; idem, *Kant und das Problem der Metaphysik*, 13.
180 Ibid., 10; idem, *Kant und das Problem der Metaphysik*, 15.
181 Ibid., 11; idem, *Kant und das Problem der Metaphysik*, 16.

This interpretation fully illustrates the possibilities of the hermeneutic method. Approaching the interpreted text "without presupposition," hermeneutics reveals aspects which are otherwise not obvious. In interpreting Kant's *Critique of Pure Reason*, Heidegger discerns the main elements of *Being and Time*, though not fully developed in a sequential order, as we will see below. The point here is not that Heidegger "traces back" *Being and Time* to the philosophical tradition of Kant, as if skipping over all of 19th century philosophy. Heidegger could find the very same provisions in Aristotle, Descartes, Nietzsche, Dilthey, etc. Heidegger's hermeneutics is, as it were, "extra-historical": it views the entire history of philosophy as a singular line in the development of metaphysics and takes up this tradition as a whole. This does not mean that hermeneutics has no sources which have directly defined its formation. But, up to a certain stage in its development, hermeneutics has the form of "simply" interpreting, or "self-interpreting" philosophy. Properly new provisions are advanced only rarely and with extreme caution. In *Kant and the Problem of Metaphysics*, interpretation ceases to be merely "laying out" and becomes critique as soon as Heidegger passes to expounding the outcomes of the *Critique of Pure Reason*'s ground-laying of metaphysics. This outcome boils down to the following.

The productive power of the imagination is, according to Heidegger, the ground upon which rests the inner possibility of ontological knowledge, and hence *Metaphysica Generalis*.[182] The productive power of the imagination is the "spiritual capacity of man" that makes him not simply a being among other beings, but the one who stands in the world relatively freely, independently. As Kant put it: "The power of imagination (*facultas imaginandi*) [is] a faculty of intuition, even without the presence of the object."[183] In other terms: "The intuited

---

182 Heidegger, *Kant und das Problem der Metaphysik*, 120.

183 Immanuel Kant, *Anthropologie in pragmatischer Hinsicht* in *Werke*, vol. VIII, §28, 54, quoted in Heidegger, *Kant and the Problem of Metaphysics*, 90.

being itself does not need to be presenting [*anwesend*], and furthermore, the imagination does not intuit what it has taken in stride as intuition, as something really and only at hand, as is the case with perception for which the Object 'must be represented as present.'"[184] Thus, the power of the imagination can intuit, that is, perceive some kind of form even without the correspondingly intuited-perceived object being discovered as a being and itself having this form. Thus, in the power of imagination there lies, before all else, a "peculiar non-connectedness" to being(s): "It is without strings [*ist freizügig*] in the taking-in-stride of looks, i.e., it is the faculty which in a certain way gives itself such [looks]."[185] In this lies the creative or spontaneous character of the power of the imagination. But, in all its spontaneity, it also retains its intuitive, receptive character.[186] Hence:

> The productive power of imagination forms only the look of an object which is possible and which, under certain conditions, is perhaps also producible, i.e., one which can be brought to presence. The imagining itself, however, never accomplishes this production. The productive forming of the power of imagination is never even "creative" in the sense that it can likewise form just the content of the image [*Bildgehalt*] simply from out of the nothing, i.e., from out of that which has never before and nowhere been experienced.[187]

According to Kant, the productive power of the imagination "is not powerful enough to bring forth a sensible representation which previously was *never* given to our sensible faculty, but rather we can always point out the stuff of that same [representation]."[188] "That is why," Heidegger concludes,

---

184 Heidegger, *Kant and the Problem of Metaphysics*, 90, referring to Reicke, *Lose Blätter aus Kants Nachlass* (1889), 102.

185 Ibid., 91; *Kant und das Problem der Metaphysik*, 112.

186 Just as perception for Husserl both is and is not "constituting."

187 Heidegger, *Kant and the Problem of Metaphysics*, 92; idem, *Kant und das Problem der Metaphysik*, 127.

188 Quoted in Heidegger, *Kant and the Problem of Metaphysics*, 92. See Kant, *Anthropologie* §28; cf. idem, *Kritik der reinen Vernunft*, A124.

"with the decisive characterization of the essential unity of ontological knowledge, Kant expressly enumerates three elements: pure intuition (time), pure synthesis by means of the power of imagination, and the pure concepts of pure apperception."[189]

Heidegger's genuinely important conclusions enable a critical comparison of the first and second editions of Kant's *Critique of Pure Reason*. Heidegger shows that the ground that Kant "hit upon" in his grounding of metaphysics, namely, the productive power of the imagination, is pushed into the background in the second edition, yielding to the first two "basic cognitive faculties" of sensibility and reason, whereas in the first edition it was the transcendental power of the imagination that was deemed the common "root" of both of these "trunks." Heidegger writes:

> But what has actually resulted from the occurrence [*geschehen*[190]] of the Kantian ground-laying? Not that the transcendental power of imagination is the previously-laid ground; not that this ground-laying becomes a question of the essence of human reason. Rather, as a result of unveiling the subjectivity of the subject, Kant falls back from the ground which he himself had laid.[191]

The ground-laying of metaphysics passed onto the plane of "interpreting the subjectivity of the subject" insofar as the transcendental power of imagination, which Kant himself laid as the ground, is, according to his definition, the "basic faculty of the human soul" (or the heart, *Gemut*).[192] However, Heidegger asks: "Does this falling-back not belong as well to the result? What occurs therein? Perhaps an inconsistency

---

189 Heidegger, *Kant and the Problem of Metaphysics*, 95. Cf. Kant, *Kritik der reinen Vernunft* A8, B104.

190 That Heidegger here calls the Kantian ground-laying a *geschehen*, that is an "occurrence," "happening," "fulfillment," or "event," anticipates his later approach to metaphysics as the "history of the oblivion of Being" wherein every significant philosophical system can be interpreted as an "event" of this history.

191 Heidegger, *Kant and the Problem of Metaphysics*, 150; idem, *Kant und das Problem der Metaphysik*, 205.

192 Kant, *Kritik der reinen Vernunft*, A78, B103.

to which Kant should own up? Are the falling-back and the not-going-to-the-end just something negative? By no means. On the contrary, they make it obvious that with his ground-laying, Kant himself undermines the floor upon which he initially placed the *Critique*."[193] It turns out that Kant's falling-back from the ground he himself established — the transcendental power of the imagination — is, in an effort to preserve pure reason and maintain its proper foundation, the very same movement of philosophizing that reveals the groundlessness (bottomlessness) of metaphysics. Kant was led to the productive power of the imagination by the internal logic of his reasoning in pursuit of the grounds of metaphysics as "knowledge of a special kind." Due to its dual spontaneous-receptive character, the power of imagination is no longer suitable as an explanation for the connection and qualities of the two main "cognitive faculties." In time, however, Kant came to recognize that grounding the entire edifice of metaphysics, with its demand for mathematically rigorous cognition, on such an unsteady foundation as the imagination is very risky. The opinion might arise that all forms of sense perception, and thus the world as a whole, are illusory and arbitrary in nature. Kant acknowledged this danger in the first edition as well: "What that something is we soon discover when we consider that appearances are not things in themselves, but are rather the mere play of our representations, which in the end emerge from determinations of inner sense."[194] The pure, inner sense is nothing other than time. Thus, it is through the determinations of time that the "play space" is formed, and only within this space does the "playing out of the pure representations of objectivity" become possible. As a result, the notion of "encountering" being arises (we are already familiar with the term "encountering," *das Begegnen*, from the *Hermeneutics of Facticity* lectures). For

---

193 Heidegger, *Kant and the Problem of Metaphysics*, 150; idem, *Kant und das Problem der Metaphysik*, 205.

194 Kant, *Kritik der reinen Vernunft*, A101, quoted in Heidegger, *Kant and the Problem of Metaphysics*, 138.

Kant, it was inconceivable for metaphysics to be conclusively grounded in talk of a "play space" or "mutual playing out" of representations, and Heidegger indicates that this is an inevitable inconsistency within the Kantian ground-laying. Heidegger "corrects" this inconsistency in *Being and Time*, where all ontology unfolds and develops on the basis of different determinations of time.

Heidegger worked on the *Kant and the Problem of Metaphysics* lectures and *Being and Time* almost simultaneously, but at first glance, the link between these works may not seem very significant. In *Being and Time*, Heidegger hardly mentions "metaphysics." Rather, the work speaks of "fundamental ontology" or the "existential analytic of human Dasein," but nowhere does it indicate a connection between the "ontology" of *Being and Time* and the "metaphysics" of *Kant and the Problem of Metaphysics*. Only later, in his second volume on Nietzsche and in the introduction to "What is Metaphysics?", will Heidegger write that ontology is a later name for the essence of metaphysics.[195] In Petra Jaeger's opinion, Heidegger in *Being and Time* and the *Kant and the Problem of Metaphysics* lectures is writing mainly about ontology understood as the genuine essence of metaphysics that remains in need of grounding.[196] With reference to this definition, Jaeger concludes that Heidegger was already endeavoring to overcome metaphysics in *Being and Time*, where metaphysics is defined as having not thought through its own essence-space (*Wesensraum*), that is, Being as such.[197] In my view, this opinion reflects only part of the truth. Even if we were to consider, on the basis of Heidegger's later testimony, *Being and Time* as having "metaphysics" in mind whenever it speaks of "ontology," we still cannot say that the work set

---

195 Martin Heidegger, *Wegmarken* (Frankfurt am Main: Vittorio Klostermann, 1967), 207.

196 Petra Jaeger, *Heideggers Ansatz zur Verwindung der Metaphysik in der Epoche von Sein und Zeit* (Frankfurt am Main: Peter Lang, 1976), 242.

197 Ibid., 38.

out to overcome metaphysics, or that this overcoming was a collateral result of the Dasein analytic.

We can attempt to reconstruct the steps of Heidegger's breakdown of the problem of metaphysics thusly:

1. The interpretation of Kant's *Critique of Pure Reason* as an attempt at grounding *traditional metaphysics* ("knowledge of beings as such and as a whole");

2. Heidegger's conclusion upon analyzing this attempt: traditional metaphysics in Kant's guise arrived at the *human being*, at concrete Dasein, as the only ground, but then "fell back" from it;

3. Heidegger conversely undertakes to carry out this ground-laying at which Kant halted;

4. This ground-laying unfolds as "fundamental ontology" in *Being and Time*, which shapes "Metaphysics-2." "Metaphysics-1" is "removed" and subjected to "destruction";

5. "Metaphysics-3", which is more of a figurative term, is the basic structure of the human being in which Heidegger finds the grounds for Metaphysics-2.

The only thing that allows us to speak of any "overcoming of metaphysics" in *Being and Time* is the "destruction of the history of ontology," that is, the destruction of traditional metaphysics. The ground for the latter is the fact that not a single historical ontology ("Metaphysics-1") has sufficiently clarified the question of the meaning of Being. The direct aim of *Being and Time* is to construct a Metaphysics-2 which should "serve to carry out" Metaphysics-3 as the "natural capacity in all humans."

The result of Heidegger's reflections expressed in *Kant and the Problem of Metaphysics* was the conclusion that traditional metaphysics is groundless. The question of the inner possibility of the type of knowledge that traditional metaphysics aspired to claim is therefore supposed to be clarified by way of the fundamental analysis of Dasein: this task is posed at the end of the lectures, which offer only a brief outline of the Dasein analytic intended to ground traditional metaphysics. In *Being and Time*, to the contrary, positing the groundlessness of traditional metaphysics, or more precisely the "unclarity of the question of Being in historical ontologies," serves as the starting point for constructing and developing the Dasein analytic. Nowhere is it mentioned that this analytic is supposed to ground something; to the contrary, the "history of ontologies" is subjected to destruction. It thus becomes clear that Heidegger initially saw fundamental ontology as a grounding of traditional metaphysics, which served as a point of departure. However, when the new ontology was developed, the need for traditional metaphysics had already fallen by the wayside, and the history of metaphysics came to be subject to destruction. Perhaps it was to prevent this changed relation to tradition from becoming too shocking that Heidegger used "ontology" instead of "metaphysics" in *Being and Time*, only to later recognize that they are, in fact, one and the same.

Having an idea of the hermeneutic method out of which Heidegger's fundamental ontology developed, we can understand the inner logic of the change in relation to traditional metaphysics in *Being and Time* in comparison to the *Kant and the Problem of Metaphysics* lectures. The point is that hermeneutics, like phenomenology, is first and foremost a method, and it can lead to definite theoretical postulates only over the course of the interpretation of certain philosophical texts. The fact that the hermeneutics of facticity was not further developed in Heidegger's works is, in my view, testimony to the insufficiency of the hermeneutic method in and of itself for the construction of a philosophy. The *Hermeneutics of Facticity* lectures' attempt to create a "hermeneutic philosophy" is more telling as an intention than an actual result. In order for hermeneutics to generate definite, positive theoretical material, it must first carry out the interpretation of already existing philosophical texts. This does not mean that hermeneutics is philosophically fruitless; rather, it generates genuinely *new* knowledge over the course of interpreting sources, but without sources interpretation has no meaning. Heidegger evidently felt this way, because after the first attempt to create a "hermeneutic philosophy" in the *Hermeneutics of Facticity* lectures, he once again, in 1924 and 1925, returned to interpreting philosophical sources. From the Dilthey-Yorck correspondence acquired in 1923, he took the principle of "historicality" which would be key for *Being and Time* (redefined as "temporality"). According to Kisiel, the winter semester of 1925-26 was marked by the discovery of the importance of Kant's doctrine of the schematism of pure rational concepts for the problem of temporality, which would become essential for *Being and Time* (we have already had the occasion to follow the course of Heidegger's interpretation of Kant's *Critique of Pure Reason*). In addition, Heidegger continued to work with Plato and Aristotle: the *Plato's Sophist* lectures during the 1924-25 winter semester and the "Truth and Human Dasein: Aristotle, *Nicomachean Ethics*" lecture from 1-8 December. The "phenomenological interpretation" of philosophical sources led Heidegger to one discovery after another. Perhaps the last impetus was the discovery of the "genuine outcome" of the Kantian groundlaying of metaphysics: the central role of the productive power of the imagination and Kant's "falling-away" from it. External circumstances also insistently demanded that Heidegger present himself as an independent philosopher with a serious published work: the ministry in Berlin twice turned down his candidacy for the position of ordinary professor at the University of Marburg's philosophical faculty. All of these circumstances, both external and internal, came together when Heidegger wrote *Being and Time*, a work that finally put him outside the current of phenomenology.

In *Kant and the Problem of Metaphysics* and *Being and Time*, which exemplify Heidegger's comprehensive approach to the problem of metaphysics before the Turn in the 1930s, there is still no call to "overcome metaphysics" in the traditional sense of the term, but the main outcome of the preliminary "grounding" turns out to be "groundlessness," which does not resolve the problematic character of metaphysics. Metaphysics, in its search for its grounds, arrives at man, at the "faculty of the human soul [/heart]," that is, the power of imagination. But metaphysics as such cannot fully affirm itself on this ground, and thus falls before it. Heidegger is more decisive on this front, as he undertakes to construct a "metaphysics of human Dasein" which can no longer be identified with "metaphysics" in the traditional sense of the word. Rather, it is a *questioning* of human being. This "questioning" is one of the main principles of the hermeneutic approach to both written sources and philosophical problems. The method of questioning will be characteristic of the entirety of the philosopher's work, which once again confirms the hermeneutic character of Heidegger's philosophizing as a whole. In *Kant and the Problem of Metaphysics*, Heidegger first speaks of a *"pre-conceptual* understanding of Being." The method of questioning that starts with and proceeds after this work is employed by Heidegger in order to obtain a "pre-conceptual understanding":

> Within every mood wherein "something is this way or that," our Being-there [Da-sein] becomes manifest to us. We thus understand Being, and yet we lack the concept. For all its constancy and breadth, this preconceptual understanding of Being is for the most part completely indeterminate. The specific manner of Being, e.g., of material things, of plants, animals, human beings, numbers, is known to us, but this knowledge is unrecognized for what it is. Furthermore: the Being of the being, which is understood preconceptually in its full breadth, constancy, and indeterminacy, is given as something completely beyond question. Being [*Sein*] as such comes into question so seldom that it appears as if there "is" nothing of the sort.[198]

---

198 Heidegger, *Kant and the Problem of Metaphysics*, 159; idem, *Kant und das Problem der Metaphysik*, 217.

Moreover, the *Kant and the Problem of Metaphysics* lectures already house passages which are more characteristic of Heidegger's work after the Turn, where the philosopher hermeneutically "plays up" the ordinary use of German words to bring into relief certain premises that will subsequently be substantiated as demonstrable or obvious. For example, from the use of the German word for "being," *Sein*, in the form of an auxiliary verb, "is" (*ist*), Heidegger draws a conclusion which we have already discussed:

> With the question concerning Being as such, we are poised on the brink of complete obscurity. Yet it is worthwhile not to evade this prematurely, but to bring the full peculiarity of the understanding of Being closer to us. For as impenetrable as the obscurity is which shrouds Being and its meaning, still it remains certain that, at all times and in the entire field of the openness of beings, we understand what Being is in order to concern ourselves with the what-Being and the so-Being [*Was- und So-sein*] of beings, in order to experience and dispute the that-Being [*Daß-sein*], in order to decide about the true-Being [*Wahr-sein*] of the being, and in order to mistake it. In every expressing of a proposition, e.g., "today is a holiday," we understand the "is," and equally what Being is [*dergleichen wie Sein*]. In the cry "Fire" [we understand] the following: "Fire has broken out [*Feuer ist ausgebrochen*], help is needed [*Hilfe ist nötig*], he who can save himself — who can can bring his own Being [*bringe sein eigenes Sein*] to safety — should do so!" But at the same time, if we do not express ourselves in particular about the being and if instead we relate to it silently, we understand its characteristics of what-Being, that-Being, and true-Being [*Was-sein, Daß-sein, und Wahr-sein*], which function with one another [*eingespielten*], although in a veiled way.[199]

In this "playing upon" and "letting play out" of various manners of "-being" (*-sein*) — as well as in the last sentence, where the English translation glosses over the sense of *eingespielten* as "playing well together"— we see the method and special style of "playing up" ordinary word usage. This approach will become one of the main, most characteristic devices in Heidegger's hermeneutic repertoire following the

---

199 Ibid.

Turn: he will derive from such word usage not only certain philosophical comprehensions, but even the very grounds for philosophical substantiations. At this point, meanwhile, such "play" remains only an auxiliary means for solving the task of "grounding metaphysics."

Some time after the release of *Kant and the Problem of Metaphysics* and *Being and Time*, Heidegger will develop his new understanding of "metaphysics," one that is increasingly wrested away from the traditional understanding of the word. Insofar as an understanding of Being comes about before concepts and is not expressible in them, Heidegger's style of philosophizing will increasingly become a "questioning" through which human perception and thinking are supposed to be liberated from the conditioned, pre-given conceptual structure that does not encapsulate the preliminary "understanding of being(s)." According to Heidegger, the destruction of the conceptual structures of thinking should help man *gain an experience of Being* as a kind of "emptiness," "impenetrable darkness," and "groundlessness."

To follow through the evolution of Heidegger's notion of the possibility of an adequate grasp of the being of beings in the categories of metaphysics, we can distinguish three main stages:

1. Interpretation is true if it originates out of a preliminary grasp of Being; in other cases it is violent;

2. Interpretation is always violent, but this violence can be justified by the methodical character of interpretation as a hermeneutic circle; however, not all violence is justified;

3. Interpretation is never justified, since in the "projection" it creates there is a vague pre-understanding of Being that is already veiled by the intelligible and conceptualizable clarity of beings.

The *Kant and the Problem of Metaphysics* lectures mark the transition from the second to the third stage, which will characterize the entirety of the further development of Heidegger's philosophizing after the Turn. Although Being is here comprehended *only out of beings*, it is understood *before* the conceptual grasp. Between the non-conceptual understanding of Being and the conceptual interpretation of beings lies a whole sphere of *meanings* which are not strictly confined within concepts. The conceptuality of interpretation *covers over* Being, since it has force and interest only *within* the plane of beings, that is, in the derivative projections of "projecting." Although Being lies at the core of conceptuality, it is given in a very derivative and dependent form. In his quest for a more *primordial* understanding of Being, Heidegger will subsequently attempt to create a "non-conceptual" language.

§7. The Existential Hermeneutics of Nothing in the Works of 1929 ("What is Metaphysics?" and *The Fundamental Concepts of Metaphysics*)

The hermeneutics of *Being and Time* that Heidegger called the "fundamental analytic of human Dasein" was a successful attempt at applying the interpretive method to major metaphysical questions, grounding metaphysical categories and foundations not in the form of a comprehensive discourse or apodictic derivation from self-evident *a priori* premises, but in the form of a deepened understanding of the very possibilities for thought that are borne by one or another metaphysical concept, such as "Being," "time," "being(s)." These "possibilities for thought" refer to the potential for imbuing existing forms of concepts, shaped by their history and traditions of understanding, with the meaning that is relevant to our Dasein and to our concrete existence in the world. In accordance with some sort of unspoken agreement between the philosopher and his readers and listeners, metaphysical categories are considered to be more "grounded" the more comprehensively and deeply the meaning within them is "unveiled" (or, more accurately, "inlaid") over the course of interpretation. This "agreement," which was typical of the philosophical situation of the time in Germany, conditioned a favorable opportunity for translating the entirety of philosophizing into another dimension. Traditional metaphysical questions, and first and foremost, the question "Why are there beings at all, and why not far rather Nothing?" (the 1929 formulation), thereby become the object of hermeneutic investigation, revealing meanings that are otherwise completely incompatible with the traditional understandings of metaphysics.

After *Being and Time,* Heidegger increasingly felt the restricting impact of the old load of the metaphysical history of interpretation bound up with the concept of "Being." Therefore, the further development of hermeneutic philosophy becomes bound up above all with interpreting "Nothing." Following Hegel, Heidegger acknowledges the dialectical identity of "Being" and "Nothing," but at this stage in the development of hermeneutics, the "Nothing" seems to be more suitable for "displaying" the "emptiness" that is experienced in the "pre-conceptual grasp" of Being.

> In the clear night of the nothing of anxiety the original openness of beings as such arises: that they are beings — and not nothing... The essence of the originally nihilating nothing lies in this, that it brings Da-sein for the first time before beings as such. Only on the ground of the original manifestness of the nothing can human Dasein approach and penetrate beings.[200]

In the preceding we already discussed two aspects of Dasein's projecting of the world indicated in *Being and Time*: on the one hand, Dasein is always breaking out of its boundaries, constituting what are for it new "possibilities" (transcending), while on the other hand, in the ensuing projecting, it nevertheless remains itself (existentially). Although Heidegger will arrive at the existential oneness of human being in his later works, the works before the Turn exhibit an emphasis on the opposite, that is, on transcending,

[200] Heidegger, "What is Metaphysics?" in *Pathmarks*, 90-91; idem, *Vremia i bytie*, 22.

on getting ahead of and going beyond one's boundaries, or, in the words of the *Kant and the Problem of Metaphysics* lectures, "metaphysics as a natural disposition of human beings."

> Da-sein means: being held out into the nothing. Holding itself out into the nothing, Dasein is in each case already beyond beings as a whole. Such being beyond beings we call *transcendence*. If in the ground of its essence Dasein were not transcending... then it could never adopt a stance toward beings nor even toward itself. Without the original manifestness of the nothing, no selfhood and no freedom.[201]

On the other hand, it turns out that the Nothing is opened up to us only in rare instances. The criterion for a true "experience of the Nothing" is what Heidegger calls "originary anxiety": "Yet what does it mean that this original anxiety occurs only in rare moments? Nothing else than that the nothing is at first and for the most part distorted with respect to its originary character. How, then? In this way: We usually lose ourselves altogether among beings in a certain way."[202] If the philosopher's task is to, unlike the ordinary person, preserve the constancy of thinking, then the philosopher should dwell in a state of constant anxiety. Heidegger later adds other native emotions — "unyielding antagonism," "stinging rebuke," "galling failure," "merciless prohibition," "bitter privation"[203] — as criteria of a genuine experience of the "nihilating of the Nothing." If we set aside the negative character of these experiences, the emotional saturation and sharpness intrinsic to them — qualities which Heidegger's hermeneutic interpretation emphasizes — impart color, sound, awe, and vitality to the interpreted metaphysical categories (such as the Nothing). By contrast, the average person is left without any suspicion as to the "far-fetched" thinking of these characteristics. "Antagonism," "rebuke," "failure," and "bitter privation" are not metaphysical

---

201 Ibid.
202 Ibid; idem, *Vremia i bytie*, 23.
203 Ibid., 92-93.

categories, but they are drawn into the circle of hermeneutic interpretation of the metaphysical category of the Nothing. From the point of view of traditional metaphysics, there is nothing more absurd than answering the question "What is Being?" by frightening the audience with the experience of an "originary anxiety." But metaphysics, according to the opinion already established here, has dissipated in its own impotence, in its inability to find the ultimate ground of its own possibility, and now metaphysical questions are to be resolved by completely different methods.

Yet another example of the hermeneutic resolution of this problem is Heidegger's answer to the question of what "metaphysics" is and what "philosophy" is:

> Going beyond beings occurs in the essence of Dasein. But this going beyond is metaphysics itself. This implies that metaphysics belongs to the "nature of the human being." It is neither a division of academic philosophy nor a field of arbitrary notions. Metaphysics is the fundamental occurrence in our Dasein. It is that Dasein itself... Philosophy — what we call philosophy — is the getting under way of metaphysics, in which it comes to itself and to its explicit tasks. Philosophy gets under way only by a peculiar insertion of our own existence into the fundamental possibilities of Dasein as a whole. For this insertion it is of decisive importance, first, that we allow space for beings as a whole; second, that we release ourselves into the nothing, that is to say, that we liberate ourselves from those idols everyone has and to which they are wont to go cringing; and finally, that we let the sweep of our suspense take its full course, so that it swings back into the fundamental question of metaphysics that the nothing itself compels: "Why are there beings at all, and why not far rather Nothing?"[204]

This response to the question "What is philosophy?" is quite telling, but it still calls for interpretation. What does it mean to "get metaphysics under way" and "allow space for beings as a whole" — does this mean that there is some kind of immobile structure or mechanism of metaphysics that needs

---

[204] Heidegger, "What is Metaphysics?" in *Pathmarks*, 96; idem, *Vremia i bytie*, 26-27.

to be turned on? What will this movement itself be? And in what space does it get underway? The "answer" generates many more questions than there were at the outset. For traditional metaphysics, such an answer would be completely absurd. Here, however, in hermeneutics, the main component of philosophizing is questioning, the movement from question to a "response" behind which lurk many new questions — this is the movement into which metaphysics must be brought underway, and metaphysics here is the capacity, rooted in the human essence, to go beyond in transcending and to come into a certain relation to oneself and to beings as a whole. The space in which this movement of questioning takes place is the space of interpretation, or meaning. Philosophy, according to Heidegger, should move in this space of meaning — it *is* this movement. Any metaphysical category, in this case the Nothing, is thereby transformed from an ordinary nomenclature for a certain rubric of a metaphysical problem into a path along which thought moves hermeneutically, with each step opening up new, vital meanings as well as old ones in a new way. Thus, here we have a de facto mature hermeneutic philosophy that possesses not only a developed method, but also positive theoretical results (*Being and Time*). The last step towards the autonomy of this hermeneutic philosophy, a step that logically stems from the whole course of its development, will take place over the course of the Turn in the 1930s: liberation from the old metaphysical problematic ("grounding metaphysics," "why are their beings rather than Nothing") and reaching a new, problem-filled domain that is more suitable to hermeneutics itself.

After 1926 and before the Turn, Heidegger spoke of "Being" as identical to the "Nothing," and even more of "Nothing" than of "Being," and this has even served as a reason to accuse Heidegger of nihilism. This nihilism has been perceived in Heidegger's demand that we "freely release ourselves into the Nothing." Such reproaches testify to the difficulties of receiving Heidegger's texts, especially those following *Being and Time*. Before the Turn, Heidegger's "Nothing" is only an attempt to find a more adequate term, instead of the "Being" of the preceding works, to avoid the metaphysical tradition prevailing over the word "Being" that has engendered the many connotations which Heidegger warns against. "Nothing" is not bare negation or negativity. Historico-philosophical parallels of such can be seen in Meister Eckhart's *Ungrund*, Dionysius the Areopagite's "radiant darkness," the "emptiness" (*śūnyatā*) of the Buddhist Mādhyamikas, or even in modern physics, in the "creative vacuum" of Akimov-Shipov's theory. In the latter, all beings are waves on the surface of a vacuum. With Heidegger, we could say that all beings are "waves" running across the surface of the Nothing. Heidegger undertakes to recognize the way in which this Nothing is present in the grounds of human existence. Here, the above-discussed "violence" of hermeneutics reaches its culmination, for what is most frightening of all for "everyday Dasein" turns out to be that which is closest to it, closer even than it is to itself. However, following this culmination comes a "discharge," an interpretive transition to another dimension that is less resistant: this is the passage to the interpretation of poetry and language as such. In the early 1930s, this Turn gets underway in Heidegger's philosophizing.

III
HEIDEGGER'S PHILOSOPHY OF LANGUAGE

§1. The Essence of the "Turn" in Heidegger's Philosophy: Prerequisites and Consequences

The "Turn" (*Kehre*) is a term that appears in studies of Heidegger's philosophy which discern an evolution in the philosopher's views. In this respect, it figures as a "technical term" in Heidegger studies designating a certain boundary or period of time over which Heidegger's philosophizing underwent a radical transformation, whereby the questions, tasks, method, and, most importantly, the very language of Heidegger's works changed. In the narrow sense, the Turn can be dated rather definitively to 1935-36. In the broader sense, the movement of the Turn had already begun in 1930-31. A crucial role in this Turn was played by the three years Heidegger spent living in the province, beginning in 1933, when he unsuccessfully tried to incarnate the principles of his philosophy in the life of the University of Freiburg, of which he was elected Rector in April 1933. After recognizing this failure and resigning, Heidegger secluded himself in a ski hut in the mountains, which he left only for short spans of time to deliver lectures, talks, and negotiations with publishers. According to Heidegger himself, living in nature amidst the majestic mountain landscape and ordinary villagers exerted a powerful influence on his philosophizing. Heidegger penetrated the solidity and regularity of laborious rural life, but this should come as no surprise. What is surprising is how his philosophizing proved capable of transforming into something akin to the labor of the peasant, "tilling the fields of thought." Heidegger writes:

> And this philosophical work does not take its course like the aloof studies of some eccentric. It belongs right in the midst of the peasants' work. When the young farm boy drags his heavy sled up the slope and guides it, piled high with beech logs, down the dangerous descent to his house, when the Herman, lost in thought and slow of step, drives his cattle up the slop, when the farmer in his shed gets the countless shingles ready for his roof, my work is of the same sort. It is intimately rooted in and related to the life of the peasants.[205]

Over three years of life in the province, far away from the problems of the city, including the problems of university philosophy, Heidegger rethought everything that he had hitherto said and wrote. Evidently, his striving to "ground metaphysics," to ground critical reason, which is by its very nature groundless, now turned out to have been but futile commotion. The aspiration to make thought invulnerable to critique consumed all of his attention and energy, which meant that genuinely decisive problems were left in the shade.

Speaking of Heidegger's "rural philosophizing" after the Turn is a calm assertion indifferent to criticism. Peasant work is a calm assertion inasmuch as it is accompanied by awareness of the invested efforts and a feeling of responsibility: if I don't do this, then no one will. Such is the law of the creator and the pioneer. For many of the readers and evaluators of Heidegger's works who remained in the cities, and for whom *Being and Time* from five years prior was a revelation and answer to the pressing questions of the time, the Turn of the 1930s was unintelligible and inexplicable. Many expected the announced continuation of *Being and Time*, but Heidegger disappointed these expectations. Moreover, his philosophizing became something completely different. It seemed to many as though Heidegger "froze" in a pose of superiority over any argumentation and let himself sink down into ritually staged thought-poetry. The impression was that Heidegger,

---

205 Martin Heidegger, "Why do I stay in the provinces?", trans. Thomas Sheehan, in Thomas Sheehan (ed.), *Heidegger: The Man and the Thinker* (Chicago: Precedent Publishing, 1981), 28; idem, *Raboty i razmyshleniia raznykh let*, 219.

having won fame for himself, became proud and settled into posing as a prophet proclaiming things in the name of Truth itself, which remained known to him alone. Such was the outward appearance of the Turn.

Internally, the Turn was, in my view, the consequence of a deep crisis that Heidegger experienced as a philosopher and as a person over the 10 months he spent as Rector of the University of Freiburg in 1933-34. Heidegger's predecessor was undesirable to the Nazis, and they had him removed for forbidding "Jewish posters" from being displayed around the university. In a situation of raging emotions in ideology and the Nazis' increasing control over all aspects of life, Heidegger consciously took the very risky step of positioning himself as a *"Führer* of students and teachers." Ever since Plato, who risked his life to travel to the Dionysius tyrants of Syracuse, philosophers have tended towards a self-oblivion bordering on recklessness whenever it comes to the possibility of incarnating the ideas they've nurtured. The substantial affinity between the Nazis' ideology and Heidegger's philosophy did not extend beyond their common aspiration for "blood and soil," yet it was perhaps this affinity that made Heidegger's promotion to the position of rector possible. Exhilarating opportunities seemed to open up for transforming the university on a new, non-metaphysical basis.

Since the Middle Ages, the European university has been a stalwart of traditional (originally Aristotelian) metaphysics, which found embodiment in the Scholastic system of education, the structure of faculties, the principles of teaching, etc. Heidegger's approach to this Scholastic system was something analogous to the standpoint of the Renaissance Humanists: they became participants in this system, for there was no other, yet they did everything to transform it from the inside, to humanize it, to bring it back to the soil of the real, vital needs of the integral human being.

For the sake of such possibilities, Heidegger made concessions to the official ideology in his speech upon accepting the position, "The Self-Assertion of the German University." He "justified" labor and military duty for students as "equiprimordial" with scholarly activity, and this would later serve as the grounds for stripping Heidegger of the right to teach after the Second World War until 1951. Although his calls for "struggle," "unity," and "self-assertion" could be understood as coming close to the Nazis, the inner meaning of all of this becomes, in Heidegger's words, "self-examination": "It is up to us whether, and to what extent, we concern ourselves with self-examination and self-assertion, not just in passing, but starting from its foundations..."[206] Indeed, this is a vivid example of the "double game" that Heidegger engaged in for the sake of his idea of reforming the university:

> The faculty is a faculty only if it becomes capable of spiritual legislation, and, rooted in the essence of its science, able to shape the powers of existence that pressure *it* into the *one* spiritual world of the people. The student body of a certain department is a student body only if it places itself in the realm of this spiritual legislation from the start and thus tears down departmental barriers and overcomes the staleness and falseness of superficial professional training.[207]

This program really did stem from the whole course of Heidegger's thinking up to the Turn: knowledge had been divided into "disciplines" under the reign of the "metaphysical" approach to beings, and this division did not conform with the "preliminary grasp of Being itself," and hence it led to a fundamentally superficial interpretation of, and approach to, beings. The university is the "citadel of metaphysics," but, at the same time, it is also the focal point of the scientific-spiritual potential of society. Heidegger opted for

---

206 Martin Heidegger, "The Self-Assertion of the German University" in Gunther Neske and Emil Kettering (eds), *Martin Heidegger and National Socialism* (New York: Paragon House, 1990).

207 Ibid.; idem, *Raboty i razmyshleniia raznykh let*, 229.

this "double game" in order to liberate this scientific-spiritual potential and give it space to "legislate in the domain of the spirit." "Superficial professional training" itself is based on the "unclarity of the question of Being" in traditional metaphysics: in such a framework, a certain relation to beings does not demand depth of thinking, but rather is perceived externally as a "given," and scientific knowledge is only the professional ability to treat this givenness with practical success. It is difficult to imagine what Heidegger realistically proposed instead of such "professional training" divided into disciplines. What we see in his "Self-Assertion of the German University" speech is more pathos and impulse than any concrete program of action. And it very soon turned out that developing such a concrete program on the basis of Heidegger's ideas would be impossible. Implementing such a program would require *changing* every member of the university, both students and teachers, and such change would have to be fundamental, i.e., they would need to be made into "philosophers" in the genuine sense of the word. But not every professional "philosopher" would be a suitable member of such a university. The epiphany came within 10 months: after recognizing the unrealistic prospects of his program for reforming the university, remaining in the post of rector became pointless for Heidegger, and so he resigned.

This moment meant a profound, inner crisis of Heidegger's philosophizing. Passing through the fire of ideological passion, this philosophizing was both purified and transformed. Heidegger's philosophical "insight into essence" recognized in the atrocities of the ruling Nazi ideology certain traits of the very same "metaphysics" (in the traditional sense) whose grounding had hitherto been the main task of his hermeneutics: (1) the "unclarity of the question of Being," (2) adherence to a "pre-given project that has not been thought through," and (3) a general lack of profundity of thinking. Therefore, changing the approach to metaphysics became the main content of the Turn now underway in

177

Heidegger's philosophizing. We can distinguish the following "dimensions" in this Turn:

(1) A changed understanding of metaphysics: for Heidegger, metaphysics now became the event of the "oblivion of Being" in the onto-history of European mankind.

(2) Accordingly, the approach to traditional metaphysics also changes: Heidegger passes from "grounding," even in the sense of "re-moving," to outright "overcoming."

(3) A new understanding of Being: Being is no longer transcendent, but immanent. We should no longer "hold ourselves out" into the Nothing, into Angst, in order to experience Being. Being is already within us, where "we are always already abiding" even though we can never reach it. Man is the "shepherd of *Being*"; he is, of course, separated from beings by the "ontological clearing (rift)," but this clearing itself constitutes the *inner* dimension of human existence, or *existing itself*.

(4) Rejecting the methodological structure of *logical grounding* and passing to *interpreting* in pure form.

(5) Working out a *special terminology* to express the "non-conceptual" comprehension of Being.

(6) The new objects of interpretation are: (a) *natural language*, whereby language itself is now defined as the "house of Being," and (b) the *poetry* of selected poets — Hölderlin, Stefan George, Trakl, etc. An anticipatory indication that language and poetry are the sphere of the fullest disclosure of the being of Dasein was already attested in the *Prolegomena to the History of the Concept of Time*: "The discoveredness of Dasein, in particular the disposition of Dasein, can be made manifest by means of words in such a way that certain new possibilities of Dasein's being are set free. Thus discourse, especially poetry, can even bring about the release of new possibilities of the being of Dasein."[208]

---

[208] Heidegger, *History of the Concept of Time*, 272; idem, *Prolegomeny k istorii poniatiia vremeni*, 286.

(7) Heidegger's aim is now not a "conceptual grasp" of Being, i.e., dividing up the meaning of Being into concept-significations, but a non-conceptual *experience of Being*. The objects of this pivot could already be noticed in Heidegger's works in 1929, such as when he spoke of the "experience of Nothing."

Having encountered in Nazism a manifestation of "metaphysics" in its worst sense, Heidegger changed his approach to using the terms of traditional metaphysics within his own philosophizing: terms like "Being," "nothing," and "ontology" were hitherto imparted with non-metaphysical, hermeneutic meaning in order to show that hermeneutics is capable of giving answers to the questions before which metaphysics turned out to be impotent; now, however, not only the "history of ontology," but also the terminology of ontology itself, and along with it the "basic question" of metaphysics — "Why are there beings at all instead of Nothing?" — would be subjected to "destruction." In 1936, Heidegger began collecting his notes for what would later (in 1954) be released under the title "Overcoming Metaphysics." In 1935-1936, the philosopher first faced the task of "overcoming metaphysics" and "removing metaphysics," whereas before the point had been "ground-laying" (*Grundlegung*). Although this "grounding" really was an overcoming in relation to traditional metaphysics, the variation of "fundamental ontology" that Heidegger advanced in *Being and Time* to replace the old metaphysics was by no means coincidentally called the "metaphysics of human Dasein," just as metaphysics was called the "natural capacity in all humans." Until the Turn, Heidegger's philosophizing had remained in its own main intentions *"metaphysical"* — if we understand "metaphysics" in the broad sense as any doctrine that proceeds from the premise that *Being is transcendent* in relation to beings (regardless of whether the question of Being is "clarified" or not). Before the Turn, Heidegger spoke of Being in the spirit of metaphysics as something beyond beings and beyond man as a "special kind of being" who is "held out into the Nothing" (i.e., "into Being"). The main human capacity consists in being able to "go beyond itself," "get ahead of itself," "break forth out of its own limits" towards Being, and therefore take up an approach to beings as a whole and to oneself. After the Turn, Heidegger did not speak of "Being" at all for some time, and when this notion appears again in the *On the Way to Language* lectures, his approach is already completely different. In order to gain an experience of Being, it is necessary to traverse a long path of thinking, but Being itself is always here and the path to it is the path leading to where "we are already always abiding." In other words, Being is interpreted as immanent (if it is legitimate at all to apply such a characterization from traditional metaphysics).

After the Turn, Heidegger defines "metaphysics" as the "oblivion of Being" in favor of beings, an "oblivion" that is fateful for all of Western European civilization. In 1962, at the seminar on his lecture "Time and Being," Heidegger expressed this thought in the following way:

> Metaphysics is the history of the formations of Being, that is, viewed from Appropriation [*Ereignis*], of the history of the self-withdrawal of what is sending in favor of the destinies, given in sending, of an actual letting-presencing of what is present. Metaphysics is the oblivion of Being, and that means the history of the concealment and withdrawal of that which gives Being.[209]

Moreover, according to Heidegger's own testimony,[210] it was in 1936-38 that he introduced the term *Ereignis*, a term that would become fundamental to all of his ensuing philosophizing. This term was the result of developing the dimension of his hermeneutic method which we have already discussed: creating his own terminology to express specific

---

209 Heidegger, *On Time and Being*, 41; idem, *Razgovor na proselochnoi doroge. Izbrannye stat'i posdnego perioda tvorchestva*, ed. A.L. Dobrokhotov (Moscow: Vysshaia shkola, 1991), 184.

210 Ibid., 43; idem, *Razgovor na proselochnoi doroge*, 185.

semantic content. Many of the fundamental premises of Heidegger's later philosophy are "encrypted" in condensed form in the term *Ereignis*. This term became the first "stone" (if we do not count Dasein) that Heidegger laid at the foundation of the new "non-conceptual" language he was thinking through. This term occupies the central place in the works he wrote "at his desk" in the pre-war and wartime years.

The substantive turn in this philosopher's thinking was accompanied by a change in the language of his works, as well as a change in his approach to language in general. Heidegger had undertaken bold "language experiments" long before the Turn, and such is indeed a characteristic trait of his philosophizing as a whole. Examples of this include Heidegger's philosophical reconceptualization of the word Dasein," which in the natural German language means simply "life" or "existence," as well as the Heideggerian "invention" of "*Verweisungszusammenhang* ("context of references") in *Hermeneutics of Facticity*. Working with language was an organic part of Heidegger's hermeneutic method from the very beginning, and perhaps it was these unique experiences with language that facilitated his advance and the success of his ideas in the 1920s, especially with the release of *Being and Time*. Before the Turn, Heidegger spoke of a "pre-conceptual understanding of Being" (*Kant and the Problem of Metaphysics*). After the Turn radically changed his approach to "metaphysics" in general, Heidegger ultimately abandoned the development of "fundamental ontology" and the "metaphysics of the human being" in order to focus on "rethinking language" (the natural German language as well as its various dialects). Ultimately, hermeneutics took on the form of working through terminology. Like a peasant adjusting his plough and tinkering with his tools, Heidegger worked through interpreting the meanings of words slowly, thoughtfully, and tirelessly. Socrates said that a philosopher needs leisure in order to follow any thought to its end, and politicians and orators lack such a possibility, since they need results by a given deadline. Heidegger strove to fully *understand* what meaning one or another word *can* bear. The "concepts" of metaphysics are merely words whose speakers did not manage to fully think them through, hence these words and the discussions where they are used are rendered superficial. A serious thinker, according to Heidegger after the Turn, should think through all terminology anew. All the efforts of hermeneutics in his later period were dedicated to this, no matter what was being said in interpretation.

The early 20th-century interest in language was a characteristic trait of the entire epoch. Not only philosophers, but also poets and authors turned to language not merely as a means of communicating information or conveying thought from one person to another, but as a self-sufficient source of meanings, a kind of depository in which centuries of the thoughtful activity of a people have left grains of enduring wisdom. In the wake of Nietzsche's words that "God is dead," groundlessness became the decisive characteristic of human existence (or "attunement" in Heidegger's terms). Hence, feelings of "alarm," "concern," "thrownness," and "forsakenness" came to the fore. Starting with the Renaissance, when faith ceased to be a sufficient basis for mutual understanding, interest in the problems of language, understanding, and interpreting rose to the point that such would never fade away again (from Petrarch and Francis Bacon to Schleiermacher, Wilhelm von Humboldt, etc.). A convergence between thinking and poetry began to emerge: the beauty and perfection of lingual form became increasingly significant criteria for the truth of an expressed thought. With the "renaissance" of Hölderlin and Kierkegaard in the early 20th century in, among other places, Stefan George's school, language took on even greater significance in terms of understanding the fundamental relationship between man and the world. The role of language in cognition also came to be acknowledged by positivist scholars and philosophers (Avenarius). Thus, in the early 20th century, the problematics of language and understanding were already quite developed. During the Turn, Heidegger went further than others perhaps only in terms of the boldness with which he inserted the problem of language into the very center of the entire philosophical problematic, whereby poetry was taken as a source and ground for philosophizing, and language itself in its natural form became a matter of thinking, reworking, and transformation.

Word and Meaning after the Turn

Meaning is the capacity of a text to influence consciousness, to awaken thought therein, and this capacity comes into being in none other than the very real process of interaction between the "form" of a text and thinking consciousness. It is, therefore, evidently possible to formulate a methodological principle of hermeneutics that is similar to Heisenberg's "principle of indeterminacy": in order to know the *meaning* of a text, it is necessary to sacrifice its form, and conversely, if we want to preserve the form, we cannot even *pose the question* of its meaning. For the one speaking (or writing), the form (the word) is a projection of meaning into a pre-established language field; for the one understanding, meaning is the effect on thought produced by this form. Thus arises a dialectical triad:

Meaning-1 // Word // Meaning-2

Meaning-1 and Meaning-2 can never coincide, firstly because the "substance of consciousness" (Meaning-1) which interacts with the word of the one who is understanding (Meaning-2) never coincides with the author (Meaning-1), even if they are the same person only a moment later. Secondly this is because Meaning-1 is itself an effect of forms which might not be fully known to the interpreter (or even the author himself).

Any interpretation is then *"presupposed"* in form as well as content, i.e., it is conditioned by the unrepeatable context of the life of the interpreter. Accordingly, the aspiration to present one's interpretation as "objective" risks giving one's personal peculiarities the status of being universal, since such an aspiration tends to conceal (including from the interpreter himself) one's "contribution" to the interpreting, one's own lot in the authorship of meaning. "Objective" interpretation is the interpretation of *das Man*, that is, the subject that wants to present itself as "average," as a "generally significant" person. In order to avoid this, it is necessary not to close one's eyes to the presuppositional nature of interpreting, and instead attempt to be conscious of these presuppositions and remove them through reflection. Is this doable, and if so, how? What is needed is not to pretend that one is interpreting "without presuppositions," but instead to *"put into play" one's own pre-understanding as an equally legitimate element of the interpretation.*

There is a "relation of indeterminacy" operative in the text being interpreted just as much as there is in the text expounding interpretation: interpretation yields fruit only to the extent that the "objective" form of the text is "removed" in the interpretation, i.e., reinterpreted. Accordingly, the main methodological problem of hermeneutics at this stage is *defining the optimal correlation* of form and meaning, tradition and creativity, necessity and freedom (that is, responsibility): to what extent is a text capable of, and in need of, being reinterpreted in order to gain new meaning without being torn too far away from the meaning that the author himself had in mind when writing the text?

Now it is the word that leads man out of being closed-off in his own Dasein: if hitherto in search for the grounds of his own "project" man was supposed to endlessly delve deeper into *himself*, now he discovers already within himself a certain level at which the division into "I" and "not I" ("you") is no longer operative — this is the "intersubjective" level, that is, the level of language. The problem of intersubjectivity can be solved in only one way: by means of "annihilating" the subject, and this annihilation is possible only by way of language.

The word is a *ploy*, an instrument for capturing meaning. The word "*casts itself*" into a domain full of meaning (where it "makes sense") and draws towards itself, concretizes, and compacts this meaning. Meaning remains, as before, the force of influence of the word-sign (of the other) or the thing-body (*sema-soma*, cf. Plato's *Cratylus* 400c); the word casts itself into the domain full of this force and strives to exhaust it. By means of the word, we "as-sign," "ap-propriate," and "as-similate" this influence, that is, we make it "self."[211] In order to express all of these meanings with one and the same root, Heidegger employs *eigen* in the verbal sense of "to make one's own."

But we do not obtain the word by ourselves alone. Its form carries traces of its use by many generations of speakers, just as the form of an axe handle expresses the traces of millions of hands of countless generations of woodworkers and carries their warmth. We obtain the word already "warm," sometimes even "hot" from use, and the philosopher's ordeal (the ordeal of dialectic in Plato's *Cratylus* and the ordeal of philosophy in Deleuze and Guattari) is to continue to mold, sharpen, and refine the form of the word.

At the same time, it is necessary to *follow the word* rather than violate it, to not treat it as Carroll's Humpty Dumpty did: "'When *I* use a word,' Humpty Dumpty said in rather a scornful tone, 'it means just what I choose it to mean — neither more nor less' ... 'The question is,' said Humpty Dumpty, 'which is to be master — that's all.'" Heidegger

---

211 The Taoist comparison of word to a weir (a trap for catching fish) has exactly the same meaning: "A weir is used to catch fish. When a fish is caught, the weir is forgotten... Words are used to express meaning. When meaning is grasped, the words are forgotten" [based on the Russian translation in V.V. Maliavin, *Zhuangzi, Laozi* (Moscow: Mysl', 1995), 237].

calls this the uncovering of "the riches that language holds in store for us, so that these riches may summon us for the saying of language."[212]

The word as such is the most valuable heritage of any culture: it embodies the continuity of culture, and it is the object, means, and result of culture as *cultivating*. Texts are important only inasmuch as they give the word its "natural habitat," let it "come into play" and sparkle with all of its inlaid potencies. Therefore, according to Heidegger, it is necessary to interpret language itself and words themselves more so than texts — not the static shells of words, but words' usage, the word as a "gesture," "ploy," and "grip" of thought.

The word is the holy vessel of meaning. All the religions of the world share the commandment that God's name shall not be used in vain: the name of God is the vessel of everything holy that contains all the best and most supreme feelings of many generations of believers, all gathered drop-by-drop into this vessel. One reckless move is enough to spill or knock over this vessel.

The same can be said of other words of human speech which designate ideals and values: "love," "friendship," "honor," "mother" — each usage of one of these words either adds its drop of meaning to the common cup or squanders and even pointlessly destroys this common heritage. Moreover, ordinary words like "house," "tree," and "dog" can be uttered appropriately, thereby reinforcing and elevating the word as well as their culture; conversely, one can ruin the embodiment of the best feelings and thoughts of our parents. But destruction can only be justified by subsequent creation.

It is also for this reason that one should not artificially transfer a word from the environment in which it arose and

---

212 Martin Heidegger, *On the Way to Language*, trans. Peter D. Hertz and Joan Stambaugh (New York: Harper Collins, 1982), 91; idem, *Gesamtausgabe* [GA] 12, *Unterwegs zur Sprache* (Frankfurt am Main: Vittorio Klostermann, 1985), 186.

developed into another domain, imparting it with artificial, superficial meaning. Any movement of thought expresses itself in changing the meanings of words, but this change should be like organic growth, drawing on past meanings, absorbing them, and giving them new life in new form. Just as "nature does not make jumps," so is any rift in the tradition of a word's usage harmful to its meaning. When torn away from its roots, the word becomes a splinter carried away on waves of coincidences, a toy for momentary needs and moods (including mentalities).

One vivid example of this is the word "culture." In its original meaning, it applied to cultivating, primarily the cultivation of land. From the hermeneutic point of view, the development of this word should consist in gradually expanding the possible objects of cultivating — the human body, emotion, thought, the human race, and so on — as well as the corresponding method of cultivating along with the essence of the very process of cultivation. The original "inner form" of thoughtful care, of concerned cultivating, should be preserved in all the new meanings of this word. Now, however, "culture" is usually defined through the concept of "information" in contrast to biological nature, but the concept of "information" is itself "homeless," has no "existential filling," and therefore makes "culture" just the same. It is no surprise that definitions of culture are multiplying without limit, with no end in sight.

If the word is a "gesture," a "hint," then language (as "speech," *Sprache*) and speaking is an *indication*, a call, calling man to constantly "make one's own" (*eignen* — *Ereignis*) and "gather" (*legein* — *logos*). Since what is one's most "own" is Being, language is the "house of Being" and a call to Being.

Before Heidegger's Turn, the subjective instance nevertheless dominated in the understanding of meaning: meaning is the force of influence of a thing (a sign) on me, and the conclusion was drawn that any meaning is my meaning, meaning for me, and that objective meaning does not exist. After the Turn, substantially different conclusions are drawn from this understanding of meaning, foremost among them being that the "principle of indeterminacy" as we formulated it for meaning and text (as the interpreting and the interpreted) can be expanded to the "author" (as the interpretation and the interpreted text). In other words, in order to "come to know" meaning, an author must enter into interaction with a text, but this necessarily implies that he himself must *change*, become other, sacrifice his old essence or position so as to *come to know* the meaning of the text. The author wields no privilege over his own text; like any reader, he is placed before a choice: *either come to know meaning, or preserve himself.*

The word sprouts through the subject, breaking through his rigid boundaries like a plant shoot emerging through asphalt. The "death of the subject" discloses man to the world: his consciousness is no longer the "black box" that Descartes came out with. Perhaps the "iconic" turning point was the discovery of X-rays: upon seeing his body "from the inside," man understood that both "outside" and "inside" are not absolute for consciousness, i.e., man's body divides the world into "inside" and "outside" only relatively. Just as we are permeated by fields and rays when we breathe, drink, and eat, so too is human consciousness permeated by substance, meaning, light, and the life fluids of the world which are neither produced by nor belong to us.

Now the word is not simply a projection, a shade of meaning. The word is the *"condensation point" of meaning* (every meaning, like every gas, has its "dew point"). Whenever man "gives birth" to meaning, at the same time dying in "birth pangs" — for example, when he first learns what love is — he is astonished to discover that there is usually already a word ready for his newborn meaning (e.g., "love"), which is ready to encompass and appropriate it (*eignen*). What does this mean? Not only that many have loved before me and that I have finally become like everyone else: this would be only another way of fleeing from oneself into *das Man*, into averageness. Here it is revealed that man is "not like everyone"; instead, he is everyone and everything. Hence, as for Nicholas Cusanus, man is one or another unfolding of the Absolute. Just as the word is a "gesture," a "hint," a "call," *so too is man himself a gesture*: a gesture of Being — whether a beautiful one or not so much. There are forces operating in this gesture which are not limited, hindered, or exhausted by the body or consciousness. Man usually does not even suspect that he is a gesture, what this gesture is, what forces call through this gesture, and whom and whither they call.

After the Turn, the schema of Meaning-1—Word—Meaning-2 no longer works, as Meaning-1 and Meaning-2 presupposed two independent subjects, the likes of which cannot be distinguished or established. Now the relation between word and meaning can be imagined differently:

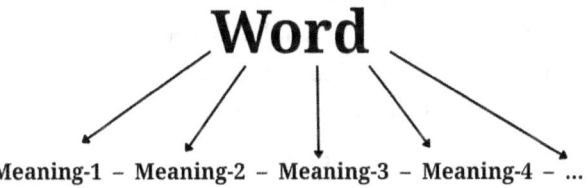

Meaning-1 – Meaning-2 – Meaning-3 – Meaning-4 – ...

This multiplicity of meanings is infinite, but they fill in a certain direction without crossing or superimposing themselves upon each other. This direction is not closed, and its interpretation will consist in moving from meaning to meaning in the direction that resounds in the word. This movement — in the space of meaning — is a *change in the one who is moving*. In changing, we also change the word, not in form, but in sound, in the associations it will provoke in the listener. *In this movement of thought lies philosophizing* — like the movement of a plow through the field of language, adding yet another furrow. This movement, which discloses ever deeper layers of the word's resonating, is *self-consciousness*, knowledge of the deeper layers of ourselves. Thus, it can be said that *self-consciousness is self-changing*.

The hermeneutic method is operative only on the condition that any remnants of "subjectivity" are overcoming in the notion of Dasein: if Dasein understands itself as an "isolated monad," then meaning will not be subjective, since it arises in interaction with an object while remaining individually unrepeatable. This would mean not only that man must retire to seclusion on the peaks of his own truth, like Nietzsche's Zarathustra, but, even more importantly, it would follow that meaning will be incommunicable in general: Meaning-1 not only could never be identical, but could never even be comparable to Meaning-2. If any understanding is possible, it could only be based on an accidental coincidence of interests. Therefore, it is wholly natural that for Heidegger, as well as for Sartre, who was even more invested in the vein of the "subjective" gnoseological standpoint, that non-alienated relations between people — that is, genuinely human relations of love and cooperation — would turn out to be impossible. Sartre imprinted this feeling of the world in his famous formulation that "hell is other people."

The Turn in Heidegger's philosophizing became a point of acknowledgement and discovery of the *intersubjectivity and supra-subjectivity of the creativity of meaning*, and therefore of the whole of human life.

For the sake of sufficiently treating the topic of the Turn here, it needs to be said that this term is used by Heidegger himself in the context of his philosophizing. Perhaps it was the case that Heidegger considered it necessary to offer a philosophical interpretation of this term after critics had already deemed a certain stage in his philosophizing a "turn." The context in which this interpretation is offered is built on an altogether specific terminology that requires special interpretation — for now, we can only share a quotation from the work "The Turning," which contains terminology that we already know:

> As the danger, Being turns about into the oblivion of its coming to presence, turns away from this coming to presence, and in that way simultaneously turns counter to the truth of its coming to presence. In the danger there holds sway this turning about not yet thought on. In the coming to presence of the danger there *conceals* itself, therefore, the possibility of a turning in which the oblivion belonging to the coming to presence of Being will so turn itself that, with *this* turning, the truth of the coming to presence of Being will expressly turn in — turn homeward — into whatever is.[213]

Here the Turn is interpreted in the "ontological" sense as overcoming the "oblivion of Being." The possibilities for interpreting Heidegger's later hermeneutics are extremely complicated by the specificity of its terminology: the interpretation of one term is impossible without involving others, each of which, in turn, requires interpretation. Therefore, here we can only point to the possible connection that Heidegger implied between the "Turn" in his philosophizing in the 1930s and the "turning" towards Being from its "oblivion." By using one and the same term in reflecting on the development of his own philosophizing and in pondering the "fate of Being" of Europe, perhaps Heidegger was pointing towards a kind of deep analogy: at a certain stage, he carried out this "turning" towards the truth of Being; now the task of his philosophizing is to bring others to this "turn." This, however, is only one presumption.

After the Turn, chronology is no longer as important to analyzing Heidegger's philosophizing. His work proceeds in several directions in parallel as different aspects of one and the same work. Generally speaking, the regions of Heidegger's philosophizing after the Turn are the following:

1. Understanding Being in its historicity (through the "traces" of Being)

---

213 Martin Heidegger, "The Turning" in *The Question Concerning Technology*, 41.

- the philosophy of history as the "onto-history of Europe," the history of the *events* that occur on the deep levels of Being itself (not on the levels of the "collective unconscious" or "mentalities");
- the history of philosophy seen as part of the philosophy of history insofar as the events in the onto-history of European mankind are reflected and expressed most "properly" in philosophy.

Accordingly, the topics of Heidegger's later works become:
- *overcoming metaphysics* as the essence of the modern era in onto-history;
- *interpreting philosophical texts*: Heraclitus, Parmenides, Plato, Descartes, Hegel, Nietzsche, etc.
- modern European science and technology (the "Enframing" and "world picture")

2. Understanding Being "in and of itself":
- *interpreting language itself*, since "language is the house of Being";
- *interpreting poetry*, since language most fully "speaks itself forth" in poetry, speaking forth its essence as "Saying" which gives word to Being and therefore founds beings.

§2. Heidegger's Hermeneutics after the "Turn": Creating a "Non-Conceptual" Language

We already saw in the case of the *Hermeneutics of Facticity* lectures just how important of a role the development of a special terminology plays in the hermeneutic method. The creative interpretation of terms is an indelible part of the hermeneutic method. Heidegger formulates this as a special methodological principle only in his post-war work *On the*

Way to Language, where he calls such the method of the "reflective use of language": "But the reflective use of language cannot be guided by the common, usual understanding of meanings; rather, it must be guided by the hidden riches that language holds in store for us, so that these riches may summon us for the saying of language."[214] The non-reflective, "common, usual understanding of meanings" bears the imprint of repeated, superficial usage that does not touch the deep significances of a word which go beyond momentary interests. Accordingly, the ordinary meanings of words are not suitable for deep philosophizing. On the other hand, if we turn to well-known cases from the history of philosophy in which there were attempts at creating a reflective terminology, then, according to Heidegger, we find ourselves under the power of the *conceptual* means of representation. In the logical sense, a "concept" differs from a "word" of natural language in that its meaning is generally, clearly, scientifically defined according to a common convention among scholars. An array of concepts then forms a certain system of scientific views — a "paradigm" in the sense understood by Kuhn, Lakatos, and Feyerabend. This "paradigm" (Avenarius' "apperceptive") is superimposed onto sensorily perceived experience, conditioning one or another understanding of it. In *Being and Time*, Heidegger called this "fore-structure" or "project." Up to the Turn, Heidegger considered "project," as well as "metaphysics" itself, to be an indelible characteristic of human Dasein. "Project" was understood in a sense related to the "categorial intuition" of phenomenology, i.e., "fore-seeing" conceptual content in the data of sensory experience. Thus, in *Being and Time*, conceptual means of representation were attributed to the very essence of Dasein as "interpretation":

> What is held in the fore-having and understood in a "fore-seeing" view becomes comprehensible through the interpretation. The interpretation can draw the conceptuality belonging to the beings

---

214 Heidegger, *On the Way to Language*, 91; idem, GA 12, 186.

to be interpreted from these themselves, or else the interpretation can force those beings into concepts to which they are opposed in accordance with their kind of being. The interpretation has always already decided, finally or provisionally, upon a definite conceptuality...[215]

As is evident here, the conceptual means of representation is still seen as the only means of knowledge, of "grasping" beings. The only danger that Heidegger sees in this means of cognition is the possibility of "violence" upon beings. Obviously, this "violence" is still interpreted within the classical understanding of "truth" as the "correspondence" (*adaequatio*) of concepts to beings. "Non-corresponding" concepts are "violently imposed." However, long before the release of *Being and Time*, from no later than 1919-1920, Heidegger knew another understanding of "truth": "unconcealment," *a-letheia*. Heidegger discovered this understanding of truth among the ancient Greeks over the course of his deepening interpretation of Aristotle, and he was astonished at how close it was to the phenomenological "insight into essences."

Heidegger himself, however, was not yet ready to formulate all of the consequences that follow from such an understanding of "truth." One of them is the pre- and supra-conceptual character of grasping truth: concepts are static, they "work" only within the frameworks within which they are formulated; but it is only the word as *logos*, and not concepts, that can, as per Heidegger's interpretation of Aristotle, make something manifest, present, "unconcealed." Heidegger derives the Greek *logos* from the verb *legein*, "to gather," and interprets it as a kind of primordial "gathering saying" that not only designates but *creates* what is said in it.

In *Kant and the Problem of Metaphysics*, the materials for which were prepared in the period when *Being and Time* was emerging, Heidegger first spoke of the "non-conceptual character of understanding the being of a being": "With every

---

[215] Heidegger, *Being and Time*, 145-146; idem, *Raboty i razmyshleniia raznykh let*, 12.

mood wherein 'something is this way or that,' our Being-there [*Da-sein*] becomes manifest to us. We thus understand Being, and yet we lack the concept."[216] From this point on, in the context of the "ontological difference," Heidegger speaks of a "conceptual means of representation" only in relation to ontic cognition: the "fore-structure" on which conceptual content is based does not correspond to any "preliminary grasp of the being of a being." In other words, the derivative convention among scholars or philosophers on the definitions of concepts is determined by many factors and, perhaps, even reflects the structure of human perception in general, but it nevertheless remains only a derivative convention that is "imposed" upon a being insofar as it is not preceded by a clear understanding of this being's "disposition-of-being" (*Seinsanlange*). This disposition-of-being is "clarified" without the use of concepts. The problem is how one can achieve such a "clarification of Being" (*Erlichtung*) and, at the same time, avoid an involuntary return to the ordinary, conceptual means of perception — this becomes the main problem of hermeneutics after *Being and Time*, both before and after the Turn. Heidegger rejects hermeneutic variants of resolving this problem one after another as insufficiently consistent. The experience of overcoming these difficulties also found expression in *On the Way to Language*: "the metaphysical manner of forming ideas is in a certain respect unavoidable... That is what Kant saw clearly, in his own way...," because "the mode of conceptual representation insinuates itself all too easily into every kind of human experience."[217]

Experience — this is the goal that becomes the alternative to conceptual means of understanding. Heidegger's 1929 works set the task of gradually advancing the questioning to arrive at an "experience of the Nothing": "For the last time

---

[216] Heidegger, *Kant and the Problem of Metaphysics*, 159; idem, *Kant und das Problem der Metaphysik*, 217.

[217] Heidegger, *On the Way to Language*, 25; idem, GA 12, 110.

now the objections of the intellect would call a halt to our search, whose legitimacy, however, can be demonstrated only on the basis of a fundamental experience of the nothing."[218] The attempt at aiming for a "non-conceptual understanding" of the Nothing was expressed here by describing the state of "originary anxiety," when "beings as a whole slip away, so that precisely the nothing crowds around."[219] The difficulty of such an approach lies in that anxiety "only seldom springs, and we are snatched away and left hanging."[220] On the whole, the experience of a non-conceptual grasp of Being turns out to be practically unachievable; after all, if it does come about, then it is against our will and unexpected. All that hermeneutics achieves up to the Turn is raising the question, the answer to which can only be further questioning. "The question of the nothing puts us, the questioners, ourselves in question."[221] Thus, the principle of the movement that is ongoing in questioning was established — this is the "way" that will be developed after the Turn. At the point of the Turn, Heidegger evidently realized that a non-conceptual understanding of Being cannot be achieved by means of questioning as long as the answers to the questions that have been posed thus far remain within the existing terminology, which is "permeated by conceptuality." Endless questioning can make us less dependent on the conceptual means of representation, but it can never lead to a positive result, i.e., to an experience of the non-conceptual understanding of Being (or the "Nothing"). In order for this experience to be expressed in words, Heidegger sets the task of working out his own "non-metaphysical" terminology in which the "terms" would not be "concepts." The prerequisites for this were already there: in *Hermeneutics of Facticity* and in *Being and Time*,

---

218 Heidegger, "What is Metaphysics?" in *Pathmarks*, 87; idem, *Vremia i bytie*, 20.
219 Ibid., 89. idem, *Vremia i bytie*, 21.
220 Ibid., 93. idem, *Vremia i bytie*, 24.
221 Ibid., 96. idem, *Vremia i bytie*, 26.

"Dasein" was not at all a "concept" in the metaphysical sense, nor were "care," "curiosity," "unconcealment." The terminology of Heidegger's hermeneutics differs from the "concepts" of metaphysics by a whole range of essential attributes:

1. Concepts are the result of the *superficial usage of words*. Heidegger, to the contrary, poses the task of a "reflective use" of language, one that thinks meditatively or, more precisely, hearkens to the richness of meanings inlaid (like a "treasure") in the resonance of the roots of the words of natural language (the "inner form" in Potebnya's doctrine).

2. The content of a concept in metaphysics is defined in accordance with the place in the metaphysical picture of the world, or "project," that this concept occupies: individual concepts are defined by each other, from more common ones to the most universal ones. In hermeneutics — as Heidegger saw it, at least — a term is interpreted without starting from one or another "plan" or "project," but *"presuppositionlessly,"* in accordance with the *possibilities* that are already inlaid in the very structure of the word.

3. A concept is considered to be more perfect the more unambiguously it expresses the meaning that is inlaid in it (in its definition); in hermeneutics, a term is considered to be more perfect and of greater gravity the more polysemiously it can be interpreted.

4. Concepts are *static* and do not grasp becoming; they constitute a result of convention among scholars that assumes the status of a *paradigm* of science; in hermeneutics, every term is only a *way*, a designation of the *movement* of interpretation and the direction of this movement.

5. A concept presupposes an *objectively significant meaning* which needs to be communicated, as far as such is possible, without distortions; a hermeneutic term does not presuppose an objective meaning, but rather enables Dasein to, over the course of its interpreting, impart as many different meanings as possible — not arbitrary ones, but meanings which correspond to the direction inlaid in the "inner form" of the word.

6. Unlike metaphysical concepts, Heidegger's terms are not connected to each other *logically* or *theoretically*, but by the kinship of their *"inner form"*; in order to underscore this kinship, Heidegger modifies the prefix from the common root, e.g: *Sein* and *Da-Sein*, *Ver-nehmen*, *Hin-nehmen*, *An-nehmen*, etc. This is a very characteristic trait of Heidegger's hermeneutics which has since found application in Russian texts imitating Heidegger.

7. The "concepts" of metaphysics serve the aim of a clear *understanding* of an object; Heidegger's terms, to the contrary, are most often expressly *"unclear"* — indeed, the often encountered "unclearness" of Heidegger's texts is not always justified; often enough, the deep meaning would not suffer from more simple formulations. But Heidegger is fundamentally against the demand for "clarity." According to Heidegger, one of the most severe consequences of the "oblivion of Being" in metaphysics is that man is used to obtaining truths in "readymade," i.e., "dead" form. The entirety of the metaphysical system of education is based on this "vicious" principle — the Scholasticism of European universities that was retained in its core as well as its main traits from the Middle Ages to the 20th century (and, let us add, into the 21st century). Such a system of education has led us to nearly completely lose the capacity for the creative thinking, or thoughtful creating, of conversing with Being "in its language." Unlike the concepts of metaphysics, a hermeneutic term does not "express" a ready meaning; it can be thought through, but this requires effort on the part of the listener-reader, while the term itself serves only as a starting point for interpretation. Heidegger is often reproached for "esotericism" on this point. Indeed, in esoteric philosophy, a symbol does not *express* meaning, but

rather "*conceals*" it or, more precisely, is the door and path through which one can achieve as much as one is capable of. Heidegger's "terms," however, cannot be called "symbols" in the full sense of the word.

In dealing with this kind of terminology, we inevitably encounter certain difficulties in interpreting Heidegger's hermeneutics after the Turn. In defining one term by another, we end up so involved in the "hermeneutic circle" that any independent reflection becomes impossible. The works of some scholars (Mikhailov, Podoroga[222], and others) creatively use Heidegger's hermeneutic method and terminology, including in cases where the discourse is explicitly about hermeneutics in the historico-philosophical context. These works represent a philosophical interest more so than a historico-philosophical interest. Indeed, in Heidegger's wake, the boundaries between historico-philosophical discourse and properly philosophical discourse cannot always be sharply defined. Heidegger's philosophy is, above all, a language, and this language, just like the conceptual language of metaphysics, too easily "creeps into" works dealing with hermeneutics. As this happens, however, hermeneutics becomes closed into its own sphere, one that can only be understood from within. Insofar as the tasks of historico-philosophical interpretation somewhat differ from the tasks of interpretation in Heidegger's philosophical hermeneutics, it seems to me that it would not be appropriate to immediately delve into working with Heideggerian terminology within the Heideggerian problematic itself, by leaping into the "hermeneutic circle," which in this case really is like a *circulus vitiosus*; instead, therefore, let us endeavor to disclose the philosophical content of hermeneutics by proposing an interpretation of the main Heideggerian terms.

---

[222] V.A. Podoroga, "*Erectio. Geo-logiia iazyka i filosofstvovanie M. Khaideggera*" in Motroshilov (ed.), *Filosofiia Martina Khaideggera i sovremennost'*.

§3. Language and Being

Language as the "House of Being"

What does the definition "language is the house of Being" mean? In his "Letter on 'Humanism,'" Heidegger writes:

> But what "is" above all is being. Thinking accomplishes the relation of being to the essence of the human being. It does not make or cause the relation. Thinking brings this relation to being solely as something handed over to thought itself from being. Such offering consists in the fact that in thinking being comes to language. Language is the house of being. In its home human beings dwell. Those who think and those who create with words are the guardians of this home. Their guardianship accomplishes the manifestation of being insofar as they bring this manifestation to language and preserve it in language through their saying.[223]

Being is one of the meanings generated by Dasein's care — perhaps the first and primordial meaning, but still only a meaning like all others. As follows, the assertion that "language is the house of Being" can be derived from the premise that "language is the sphere of meaning." And meaning, according to Heidegger, is none other than a moment, a point, an aspect of the *event of understanding*. Understanding comes to be in language; therefore, language can be called the "sphere of understanding," the "abode of understanding": communing with language means entering into the realm where understanding is possible, where understanding "eventfully comes into its own" (*ereignet*).

The house — properly speaking, the walls and roof — is the border that separates the inner and the concealed from the chaos of the elements. Likewise, language is more like the border guard of understanding and meaning than their substance and bearer. Just as the emptiness within a house allows for one to inhabit it, so does the "emptiness" within language, the spillages of ambiguity and the play of

---

[223] Heidegger, "Letter on 'Humanism,'" trans. Frank A. Capuzzi, in *Pathmarks*, 239; idem, *Vremia i bytie*, 192.

indeterminacies, allow for understanding to "dwell" within it, allowing meaning to come into its own.

Language is the *event* of understanding, the moment-points of which are meanings. Insofar as this event unfolds organically as *history*, it can be said that language is the *memory* of all the events of understanding that have happened within it. Of course, this is an *effective* history — memory remains the ruling element in the present as well (what Gadamer calls "effective-historical consciousness," *wirkungsgeschichtliches Bewusstsein*). Plato's depiction of memory as a dove (*Theaetetus* 197c-d) is, albeit ostensibly a good joke on the everyday notion of memory, not suitable here. In this case, memory is the ruling element that compels the soul to yearn for the unearthly and to fall into the frenzy of love when all "present-at-hand" and "ready-to-hand" beings no longer satisfy the suffering soul.

Each and every time we aspire to be understood, we *recall* past events of understanding. Insofar as the Event (*Ereignis*) is *prior* to time (as the dimension of meaning and value), nothing hinders us from *communing* here and now with the sphere of understanding and the *event* of language by way of recollection. Here, "recollecting," even when effective, does not mean returning to the past, but rather the ascent from sign to meaning. Anything can figure as a sign: first and foremost, I myself, then "another," then, in order, the things of the "surrounding world," the signs of things and thoughts, and finally, thoughts themselves — everything calls for understanding, needs to be thought through, to be given meaning, and the main meaning among others is the meaning of "Being."

The "Call of Being"

The "*call of Being*" is a very important and profound symbol of Heidegger's philosophizing. Being is forgotten by man, but, nevertheless, it dwells as possibility in the very source of the human being. In a certain sense, Being is closer to man than man is to himself. Therefore, it is the "call of Being" that serves as the only pledge for man to remain man. If the "call of Being" ceased for even an instant, beings would instantly seize man, and man would lose his "special standing" among beings. "Man [is] the message-bearer of the message of the two- fold's unconcealment"[224] and thus the 'unconcealment of the two-fold' is the 'truth of Being'. Man is "used by the two-fold" so that its message can be heard by man; in this message, the two-fold puts forth (promises, grants) itself to man, which means that "man stands in hermeneutical relation," for this relation "brings the tidings of that message."[225]

Generally speaking, one of the characteristic traits of metaphysics is that wherever it uses imagistic language, we find ocular, luminous symbolism. Plato's idea of the good is the sun, the other ideas are forms ("looks"), and knowledge is the clear seeing of what there is. Preferring sight to other senses is to some extent bound up with the very essence of metaphysics. In Heidegger as well, Being has "ocular" characteristics: "unconcealment," "clearing," "clarity"; Being "hurts the eyes" like a "sudden flash," and so on. This, in my opinion, testifies to the "metaphysical heritage" in Heidegger's philosophizing, the inevitable conditioning of overcoming by that which is to be overcome. But what is of interest here is that the symbolism of hearing, listening, and sound starts to play an increasingly important role in his later hermeneutics. *Being and Time* spoke of Dasein's "fundamental attunement" and various "moods" which correspond to the existentials of "care," "curiosity," and so on. Then awareness of Being as a certain primordial "attunement" (*Stimmung*) that "sets" (*bestimmt*) and "tunes" (*einstimmt*) the nature of man through its sound becomes more significant for Heidegger. Auditory

---

224 Heidegger, *On the Way to Language*, 41; idem, GA 12, 128.

225 Ibid., 33, 40; idem, GA 12, 118, 128.

symbolism, like the symbolism of light, is well developed in Indian philosophy based on the Vedas. According to this teaching, the primordial vibration of the mantra *AUM* (*OM, OUM, AOUM*) lies at the core of Being. This vibration wields a creative power that is sufficient for the world to emerge out of nothing. The main vibration is preserved as the main tone, the "background sound" of the "world symphony," and every created being is a certain modification of *AUM*, co-vibrating with it and receiving the energy of its existence thanks to this co-vibration. In his later hermeneutics, Heidegger's "Being," in its essence (the "main tone") and in its relation to beings ("attunement," "resonance"), is similar to the Indian understanding of *AUM*. We can continue this parallel: according to the *Bhagavad Gita* (XVIII, 61), "God dwells in the heart of all beings, turning everything like on a potter's wheel, the *māyā* of the three *gunas*." Heidegger's "Being" also lies within every being as its being-possibility, and Being is closer to man than man himself. In Vedānta, God constantly appeals to man, who is otherwise captivated by beings, from within his own heart, giving tidings of himself. In Heidegger, this corresponds to the "call of Being," the "hint" (or "gesture") and the "promise" (*Zusage*) in which Being "promises itself" to man. Through its main tone, through its main vibration resounding from within the very core of the human being, Being "attunes" man so that he represents a harmonious resonance in all his manifestations. It is demanded of man that he "hear the call of Being," "bear the tidings of Being," and "find himself in a hermeneutic relation to Being." According to Heidegger, this "hermeneutic relation" is not a static relationship in the sense of a proportion or correspondence, but a dynamic "re-lating" or "re-laying," a "carrying." "Hermeneutic" means "interpretive." According to ancient Greek myths, Hermes brought people the tidings of the gods or relayed their conversations he had overheard, but because the language of the gods was unintelligible to humans, Hermes had to reinterpret and translate everything into human language. Hermes was the "converter," the "transformer," the "translator" who conveyed the otherwise overwhelming energy of the divine vibrations to humans in accessible form. That "man by his nature is in a hermeneutic relation to Being" means that the essence of the human being lies in transforming the vibrations of Being (or the "divine"). Man's presence in the circle of beings disclosed to him is so important for beings because man is the only being among others capable of transforming the "primordial tone" of Being into a form that is accessible to beings. Man is not the creator of beings or Being, but he is the necessary *intermediary*, the herald between the poles of the two-fold. And man's "scope of usage" is the distance between poles which man, in his capacity of interpreting, is able to transform and overcome.

Heidegger's hermeneutics can also be seen as closely resembling the Russian tradition of religious philosophy, if we interpret it as a kind of "metaphysics of the heart." For Heidegger, the nature of language is Saying, which founds a being; that which is said in Saying is Being. Heidegger describes this "Being" as that which is closer to man than man himself, i.e., it belongs to the very essence, to the very heart of the matter, to man's *heart*. Turning towards Being, that is, towards one's essence, to the heart — this is what Heidegger demands in all of his interpretations, i.e., that one turn to it, return to it, and dwell with it. The task of hermeneutics is to reveal Being itself in the Saying, in the word that is said, and in the being that is "founded" or "established" by this Saying. Therefore, hermeneutics questions and "hearkens" what is said, tries to catch in the variegated polyphony of beings the main harmony, the main tone belonging to Being. This main harmony is almost always deeply hidden, drowned out by the striking polyphony of beings, but without it, words themselves — like reality itself — lose meaning. Without it, all of our words, feelings, and life itself become superficial, like a thick shell which, after being used once, is thrown away forever. Hermeneutics gives back to words that which the legacy of metaphysical, conceptual thinking has covered over: their "rootedness in Being," to speak Heidegger's language, or their "heartfelt resounding" (*serdechnoe zvuchanie*), to speak the language of Russian philosophy.

But "rootedness in Being," when examined in the terms of Russian philosophy, also suggests that in the heart, which should resound in all spoken words, *God dwells*. It is because "God dwells in the heart of all beings" that God says *himself* in the word that gives Being to beings. Therefore, man is man only insofar as he can become a co-participant of this act of divine creation.

"Saying"

As in the case of the "emanation" of the world from the One in Plotinus, for Heidegger there is no dynamic in the sense of a transmission of energy or anything else in the "hermeneutic relation" between man and Being. "Emanation" simply describes the relation between different levels of Being. Likewise, the "hermeneutic relation" in which man dwells does not "transfer" anything. There is still a certain dynamic role at play in this relation, but it is a different kind of dynamism. Heidegger embeds this dynamism into the interpretation of a term that is otherwise uncommon in modern German, *Sage*, "Saying." "Saying" is connected to "name," "word," and "speech." But Saying is not "speech," for speech (*Sprache*, *Sprechen*) is at once greater and smaller than Saying. In German, *Sprache* means both "speech" and "language," although there is a special word for designating "speech" as "discourse" or "talk," *Rede*. In the Ukrainian language, for example, *mova* means both "language" and "speech," whereas in Russian and English these are different lexical units. Heidegger actively uses this peculiarity of the

German language: if he were to have written in Russian or English, he would have needed to discuss the special point that "speech" and "language" are one, which is not obvious. As language (*Sprache*), speech is the "house of Being" and therefore contains all being-possibility in the form of all of the inexhaustible possibilities — for such is being-possibility — of speaking in language. As "speaking" (*Sprechen*), speech is lesser than Saying, because it revolves within the sphere of already established, verified beings. Saying is the coming into being of the "hermeneutic relation" of man and Being: if man manages to "stand in the clearing of Being," to let the voice of Being "attune" itself, then in Saying he obtains the possibility *of giving word to Being*, i.e., "giving Being the floor [to speak]." The word harbors a certain fundamental vibration of sound and at the same time equips it with a certain sonar form that distinguishes the word from the one "attunement of Being." As always, Heidegger's definition of "Saying" is in need of interpretation: "'To say' [*sagen*], related to the Old Norse '*saga*,' means to show: to make appear, set free, that is, to offer and extend what we call World, lighting and concealing it. This lighting and hiding proffer of the world is the essential being of Saying."[226] If the fundamental vibration or tone of Being is the ground (*Grund*), that is the earth, the soil, then the word is, to issue a comparison through Hölderlin's imagery, the bud of a flower growing out of the earth. Heidegger greatly underscores this "earthly" character of the being of Saying:

> It is much more important to consider whether, in any of the ways of looking at the structure of language we have mentioned, the physical element of language, its vocal and written character, is being adequately experienced; whether it is sufficient to associate sound exclusively with the body understood in physiological terms, and to place it within the metaphysically conceived confines of the sensuous. Vocalization and sound may no doubt be explained physiological as a production of sounds. But the question remains

---

226 Heidegger, *On the Way to Language*, 92; idem, GA 12, 210.

whether the real nature of the sounds and tones of speech is thus ever experienced and kept before our eyes. We are instead referred to melody and rhythm in language and thus to the kinship between song and speech. All would be well if only there were not the danger of understanding melody and rhythm also from the perspective of physiology and physics, that is, technologically, calculating in the widest sense. No doubt much can be learned this way that is correct, but never, presumably, what is essential. It is just as much a property of language to sound and ring and vibrate, to hover and to tremble, as it is for the spoken words of language to carry a meaning. But our experience of this property is still exceedingly clumsy, because the metaphysical-technological explanation gets everywhere in the way, and keeps us from considering the matter properly. Even the simple fact that we Germans call the different manners of speaking in different sections of the country *Mundarten*, modes of the mouth, hardly ever receives a thought. Those differences do not solely nor primarily grow out of different movement patterns of the organs of speech. The landscape, and that means the earth, speaks in them, differently each time. But the mouth is not merely a kind of organ of the body understood as an organism — body and mouth are part of the earth's flow and growth in which we mortals flourish, and from which we receive the soundness of our roots. If we lose the earth, of course, we also lose the roots... When the word is called [by Hölderlin] the mouth's flower and its blossom, we hear the sound of language rising like the earth. From whence? From Saying in which it comes to pass that World is made to appear. The sound rings out in the resounding assembly call which, open to the Open, makes World appear in all things.[227]

This "sound rising like the earth...from saying" does not equate Saying to earth or the common ground of everything, Being; rather, it says that everything rooted in the earth grows through Saying, for Saying is the power of growth and is the growth itself of all growths, and that which grows in the soil of Being is the world.

---

227 Heidegger, *On the Way to Language*, 98-101; idem, GA 12, 193-194.

§4. The Relation of Thing and Word in Heidegger's Later Hermeneutics

Heidegger defined this relation over the course of his philosophical interpretation of a single poem by Stefan George, entitled "*Das Wort*"[228]:

Wunder von ferne oder traum Bracht ich an meines landes saum	Wonder or dream from distant land I carried to my country's strand
Und harrte bis die graue norn Den namen fand in ihrem born —	And waited till the twilit norn Had found the name within her bourn —
Drauf konnt ichs greifen dicht und stark Nun blüht und glänzt es durch die mark...	Then I could grasp it close and strong It blooms and shines now the front along...
Einst langt ich an nach guter fahrt Mit einem kleinod reich und zart	Once I returned from happy sail, I had a prize so rich and frail,
Sie suchte lang und gab mir kund: «So schläft hier nichts auf tiefem grund»	She sought for long and tidings told: "No like of this these depths enfold."
Worauf es meiner hand entrann Und nie mein land den schatz gewann...	And straight it vanished from my hand, The Treasure never graced my land...
So lernt ich traurig den verzicht: Kein ding sei wo das wort gebricht.	So I renounced and sadly see: Where word breaks off no thing may be.

The final line of this poem captures, in poetic Saying, that which, in Heidegger's view, thinking has forever struggled with: the relation between word (name, sign) and thing. The German *sei* is a conjunctive or imperative from *sein*, "to be," which means that the latter phrase can be translated as "Nothing (no thing) is to be where the word is missing." At the first rung of his interpretation, Heidegger simplifies this phrase to "Where the word is missing, no thing is [*kein Ding ist*]," i.e., the name that names a thing is absent.

---

[228] Translation from Heidegger, *On the Way to Language*, 140. It bears noting that George took the poetic "liberty" of writing the names of nouns in lowercase, whereas nouns in German are always written with a capital letter.

Meaning otherwise lies here, on the surface, as something is named. The hermeneutic analysis begins as soon as we attempt to clarify what is really meant by the words "word," "thing," "name." Heidegger remarks that word and name are united in George's poetic experience, an indication of which is contained in the second strophe:

> And waited till the twilit norn
> Had found the name within her bourn

But, according to Heidegger, "word" and "name" are understood here not in the way that we usually understand them, i.e., as a designation that equips something with an oral or written sign, a cipher. Rather, here they have the meaning they do in expressions like "in the name of the king" or "in the name of God," where they signify a command or request. Let us note to ourselves, Heidegger says, and not rush to understand the words "norn," "bourn," and "treasure" as ordinary signs. "We have become very slovenly and mechanical [*rechnerisch*] in our understanding and use of signs."[229] Further, there is no "thing" where the word is missing. "Thing" is understood here in the traditionally broad sense, implying an "ever-present" Something that in one way or another *is*. In this sense, God is also a "thing." "Only where the word for the thing has been found is the thing a thing. Only thus is it. Accordingly we must stress as follows: no thing *is* where the word, that is, the name is lacking. The word alone gives being to the thing."[230] Now Heidegger comes to the word *sei*, "[not] to be," which is not ordinarily used this way in everyday German. In German, this word is usually used in indirect speech; therefore, we can presume that it is by means of indirect speech that the last strophe expresses the content which we have just examined, namely: that is *not* something where the word is missing. But George, as Heidegger notes, is very selective about punctuation, and in

---

229 Heidegger, *On the Way to Language*, 61; idem, GA 12, 153.
230 Ibid., 62; idem, GA 12, 154.

indirect speech he could have made do without the colon. This means that the colon has some kind of other meaning: "...we must be careful not to force the vibration of the poetic saying into the rigid groove of a univocal statement, and so destroy it."[231] The poet experienced a definite relation between word and thing, and as a result of this experience, he came to a renunciation, the content of which is expressed in the final line of the poem. In this line, "may [not] be" (*sei*) is appropriate not only as a conjunctive, but also as an imperative, a command which the poet now follows, and to which he will henceforth always be subject.

> If so, the "may be" in the line, "Where word breaks off, no thing may be," would mean: do not henceforth admit any thing as being where the word breaks off. In the "may be" understood as a command, the poet avows to himself the self-denial he has learned, in which he abandons the view that something may be even if and even while the word for it is still lacking.[232]

The poet has *undergone an experience* of the word as that which first brings a thing to ordinary existence as a thing, to presence (*Anwesenheit*). But, at the same time, the word is a "possession" that has been entrusted to the poet as a poet. The poet has undergone the experience of poetic calling in the sense of a "commanding call" to the word as the source of Being. "The poet, then, ought to rejoice at such an experience, which brings to him the most joyful gift a poet can receive. Instead, the poem says: 'So I renounced and sadly see.'"[233] Heidegger interprets this "sadly" in the following way:

> That sadness, however, is neither mere dejection nor despondency. True sadness is in harmony with what is most joyful — but in this way, that the greatest joy withdraws, halts in its withdrawal, and holds itself in reserve... The poet could never go through the experience he undergoes with the word if the experience

---

231 Heidegger, *On the Way to Language*, 64; idem, GA 12, 157.

232 Ibid., 65; idem, GA 12, 158.

233 Ibid., 66; idem, GA 12, 159.

210

were not attuned to sadness, to the mood of releasement into the nearness of what is withdrawn but at the same time held in reserve for an originary advent.[234]

This passage represents an altogether characteristic model of Heidegger's style after the Turn. Heidegger is often criticized for "esotericism," intentional unintelligibility, etc., but such criticism misses the main task of Heidegger's hermeneutics: undergoing an experience of language (*mit der Sprache eine Erfahrung machen*) by way of thinking through what is said in poetic "Saying." Heidegger strives to speak in such a way that language itself "speaks" in his speaking, because only in this way can thinking "enter into conversation" with poetry, in which language says itself. No one demands such direct, unambiguous "intelligibility" from music, representative art, or poetry. Heidegger insists on thinking's right to "unintelligibility" and "non-conceptualism." Thinking that is void of concepts does not claim to be immediately intelligible; to the contrary, here thinking paves the way along which man can arrive at an experience of everything that is otherwise expressed in concepts in the language of metaphysics. Hence, Heidegger's *On the Way to Language* lectures try to bring man to *experience* the essential Being of language that manifests itself here in the relation between word and thing.

Moreover, the notion of the relation between word and thing that is gained in this unordinary way is significant not only for hermeneutics, but for philosophy in general. Heidegger formulates the main question of metaphysics, that is, of philosophy from Plato to Nietzsche, thusly: "Why are there beings at all instead of Nothing?" Heidegger believes that metaphysics cannot give a definitive answer to this, as the answer lies beyond metaphysics. In his *Introduction to Metaphysics*, philosophy is defined as questioning, as a constantly renewed posing of this question, but obtaining a final answer to this question would mean the end of

---
234 Ibid.

philosophy. In Heidegger's later hermeneutics, this main question is never explicitly posed, yet it is the captivation by this fundamental *metaphysical* question that led the philosopher to turn to interpreting poetic "Saying." And it is precisely in interpreting the work of poetry that Heidegger finds a fully credible answer to the main question of metaphysics, the credibility of which lies in the directness of the poetic experience. Although Heidegger no longer poses the metaphysical question in this formulation in his works after the Turn, it is obvious that the notion of the relation between word and thing that is gained as a result of hermeneutic interpreting really is an answer to this question: *there are beings instead of Nothing just as there is a fitting and therefore sufficient word that in each and every moment upholds a being as a being in its simple Being.*

With such a resolution to the problem of the relation between word and thing, a connection can be drawn between Heidegger and a greatly revered religio-philosophical tradition whose sources are lost in the depths of the ages in the mysterious East. The Gospel of John's "In the beginning was the Word" was already a later, mature expression of the common conviction of many, many sages and thinkers of antiquity. According to Hermetic tradition, God created man so that he might share with Him the joy of creation and crown the act of creation by giving a name to everything. The event of "world" comes about in the heart of the human being, and every being acquires its own Being, i.e., is completed in its creation, through its participation in this event. Every thing that "touches the nerve" of man, his heart, plucks a note in the world symphony of the event, and it is this note that is expressed and consolidated in the word.

The "substance" of the word is the "scream," pain, and protest of a being that is melted down into God in man's heart. This pain is from the fissure of the Nothing (according to Sartre) and penetrates the monolith of a being "in itself."

The language of "essential poets"[235] mints words out of this "golden substance" and releases them into circulation. In the era of paper and even electronic money, we have long since forgotten about the substance of words. The task of hermeneutics is to bring "memory of Being" back to man.

Up to the Turn, Heidegger understood metaphysics as an act of transcendence, going beyond the confines of beings and coming to fruition in the ground of the human being. After the Turn, to the contrary, the human being is defined by what is found in the "hermeneutic re-lation" to Being. Just as Hermes, as the ancient Greeks thought, carried tidings of the divine truth to people, so too does man carry within himself the truth of Being: in his very essence, man is constantly going beyond the being that he himself is, heading towards Being; but Being itself, in turn, *needs* man and requires that he give to Being the word in which his "Being" and "tiding" can be transmitted into the world. Man is man inasmuch as he gives to Being this word and carries it, i.e., finds himself in an essential re-lation to Being. It is the word that captures the unconcealment (*a-letheia*) of Being and first gives a thing the possibility to be — to be that which it "is."

According to Heidegger, it is precisely such a "feeling" — if we are to refrain from calling it an "understanding" — that was inherent in the ancient Greek perception of language as *logos*. However, this perception did not contain any indication as to *who* the subject of language as *logos* is, or whether the act of the primordial naming of beings in their essence is accessible to all. The interpretation of the work of poetry testifies to the fact that this subject is, above all, the poet. "But what endures is founded by poets" are Hölderlin's words so often cited by Heidegger. Any person who accepts the being that is established in poetic saying is participating in

---

235 The "essential" (*Wesentliche*) poets, according to Heidegger, are those in whose poetry the "essence of poetry" itself "takes the word," i.e., says itself. Therefore, it would only be half correct to translate this characterization of "essential" as "significant."

this act of founding. As Hölderlin wrote: "Full of merit, yet poetically, man dwells on this earth."

Thus, Heidegger not only consolidates the philosophical status of hermeneutics (albeit understood in a non-traditional sense of the term), but puts hermeneutics at the center of the entire gnoseological and ontological problematic. The act of "naming," understood as interpreting the "call of Being," that is, as a hermeneutic act in the broad sense, now becomes not only the foundation for the possibility of knowing anything whatsoever, but also the condition for the possibility of the existence of the very object of knowledge: the thing, determined in its essence. Therefore, in this approach, insofar as the whole of actuality can be seen as a "text," the question arises of just how much this reality can be called "objective" if, at first glance, it is established in an *arbitrary* poetic saying. Heidegger writes:

> The poet names the gods and names all things with respect to what they are. This naming does not merely come about when something already previously known is furnished with a name; rather, by speaking the essential word, the poet's naming first nominates the beings as what they are. Thus they become known *as* beings.[236]

Does this mean that every poet creates the real (substantial) word in accordance with his own poetic arbitrariness? An indication of the answer to this question is already contained in what we said above: man himself, including the poet, of course, is defined in his essence by way of his relation to Being, namely, by the way in which he gives to Being the word in which Being can reveal its truth to the world.

> But when the gods are originally named and the essence of things comes to expression so that the things first shine forth, when this occurs, man's existence is brought into a firm relation and placed on a ground. The poet's saying is not only foundation in

---

[236] Heidegger, *Elucidations of Hölderlin's Poetry*, 59; idem, "Gel'derlin i sushchnost' poezii," trans. A.V. Chusov, *Logos* 1 (1991), 42.

the sense of a free bestowal, but also in the sense of the firm grounding of human existence on its ground.[237]

Human Dasein, as a being among beings, albeit of a special kind, is first "illuminated" in the poetic saying in which Being says itself and thus allows beings, including Dasein, to be. Therefore, the seeming arbitrariness of the poet in founding beings boils down to an attentive heeding of the "call of Being": only inasmuch as the poet rises up to such a heeding is he authentically a poet, one who is admitted into the "Beingful" act of the naming of beings. Only thanks to the fact that at the core of any poetic saying there lies One and the Same — Being — does understanding between people become possible on the strength of their mutual involvement in Being through language ("language is the house of Being"), and only thanks to this does that which comes into being in this understanding become real, that is, "objective," "substantial," "thingly" actuality.

Let us return to Heidegger's interpretation of Stefan George's poem "The Word." Up to this point, the object of this fruitful interpretation has been the final strophe, or rather, even just its second line. This is unsurprising since, after all, George's final line expresses the crystallization of the sum of his dramatic experience of the relation between word and thing. However, despite the rich results of this interpretation, Heidegger does not believe his aim to have been achieved, for his goal here is to arrive at the possibility of enabling his listeners to undergo an experience of language. Therefore, Heidegger continues his hermeneutic, experiential exposition. The poet has, indeed, gained a living experience of language. But how? How did he do so, and how can we follow him? Heidegger sees the corresponding indication in a single word in the final strophe, one that has not yet been subject to interpretation (and here we shall even leave out Heidegger's particular interpretations of the

---
237 Ibid.

words "*so lernt ich*," "*gebricht*," "*traurig verzicht*" in the senses and varying translations of "learning a lesson," "breaking off," "renouncing," "sadly seeing"). The line begins "So I..." How "so"? The answer is contained in the first six strophes. At first, the poet defines the relation to language which he had before the experience. Heidegger writes:

> At first, and for long, it seems as though the poet needed only to bring the wonders that enthrall and the dreams that enrapture him to the wellspring of language, and there in unclouded confidence let the words come forth to him that fit all the wonderful and dreamlike things whose images have come to him. In a former time, the poet, emboldened as his poems turned out well, cherished the view that the poetic things, the wonders and dreams, had, even on their own, their well-attested standing within Being, and that no more was necessary than that his art now also find the word for them to describes and present them.[238]

It is not difficult to see that the relation to language expressed here coincides with our ordinary notion of the role of words and the relation between words and things. This means that both the poet and we ourselves, striving to arrive at an experience of language, start from the same point.

> But in the end the moment comes for Stefan George when the conventional self-assured poetic production suddenly breaks down and makes him think of Hölderlin's words:
>
> > But what endures is founded by poets.
>
> For at one time, once, the poet — still filled with hope after a happy sail — reaches the place of the ancient goddess of fate and demands the name of the rich and frail prize that lies there plain in his hand... The goddess searches long, but in vain. She gives him the tidings:
>
> > "No like of this these depths enfold."
>
> There is nothing in these depths that is like the prize so rich and frail which is plainly there in his hand. Such a word, which would let the prize lying their plainly be what it is — such

---

[238] Heidegger, *On the Way to Language*, 67-68; idem, GA 12, 161.

a word would have to well up out of the secure depths reposing in the stillness of deep slumber [*so schläft hier nichts*].²³⁹

But no such word turned up, and the rich treasure in his hands, so it seems, did not attain the being of a thing, i.e., it did not become "a poetically secured possession of the land."

Such was the path on which the poet gained his experience of language. Aiming to gain a similar experience, we must arrive at it along our own path. In general, the notion of "path" or "way" occupies one of the central places in Heidegger's hermeneutics. It is obvious that the notion of *Tao* from Chinese philosophy had an influence here. This is understandable: after all, according to Heidegger, metaphysics was the fate and heritage of Western European civilisation, and overcoming metaphysics means that philosophical thought can go out to meet the broader layers — both in actuality and those which have not been fully thought out — of Eastern philosophy, or more precisely, Eastern wisdom (the notion of "philosophy" that arose in Western European thinking is only fully applicable to the latter). The notion of "way" for Heidegger, like the *Tao* for the Chinese, is not simply a passage from one place to another. For Heidegger, "way" is the movement of thought in its hermeneutic relation to Being:

> All is way. These lectures make their way within the neighborhood of poetry and thinking, underway on the lookout for a possibility of undergoing an experience with language... The way allow us to reach what concerns us, in that domain where we are already staying. Why then, one may ask, still find a way to it? Answer: because where we already are, we are in such a way that at the same time we are not there, because we ourselves have not yet properly reached what concerns our being, not even approached it.²⁴⁰

Here we can also establish a direct connection with Indian wisdom, which knows that "God abides in the heart of all beings, turning them as on a potter's wheel, by the *māyā* of

---
239 Ibid., 68-69; idem, GA 12, 161-162.
240 Ibid., 92-93; idem, GA 12, 187.

the three *gunas*." Here "God" plays the same role as "Being" in Heidegger: he is closer to man than man is to himself, and constantly gives man signs, hints, and indications so that man might come to himself, i.e., to where God is always awaiting him. These signs and hints are the whole of actuality around man, the whole "veil of *māyā*," but in order to unveil the meaning of the divine call (Heidegger's "call of Being") encoded in these hints, man must interpret them — this corresponds to the task of Heidegger's hermeneutics. The creative power of the word has always been known in the East: in India, this corresponds to the universal mantra *AUM*; let us also recall the Biblical "In the beginning was the Word." Further obvious parallels could be cited, for, after all, Heidegger strove to return to the primordial roots of Western European thinking, and these roots lead on the whole and in full back to the East. Accordingly, the demand that thinking be rooted in the "soil," i.e., in Being, should not be taken as some kind of *Pochvennichestvo*[241], nationalist ideology, or other such farces.

The Kinship of Thinking and Poetry

And so, in order to undergo an experience of language itself, thinking proceeds along the way that runs through the neighborhood... of what? Poetry, of course. A very important role in founding the relationship between poetry and thinking is played by "Saying": "The nearness that brings poetry and thinking together into neighborhood we call Saying"[242]; "poetry and thought, each needs the other in its neighborhood."[243]

---

241 *Pochvennichestvo* was a socio-literary movement that took shape in the 1860s. Established by Apollon Grigoryev, Fyodor Dostoevsky, and Nikolai Strakhov, this current advocated turning to the "soil" (*pochva*) of Russian tradition, developing "original" (*samobytnaia*, "self-being") Russian culture, and bringing the Russian people to consciousness of their special "mission" in world history — but without the anti-Western rhetoric that was typical of the Slavophiles.

242 Heidegger, *On the Way to Language*, 93; idem, GA 12, 188.

243 Ibid., 70; idem, GA 12, 163.

The poet gained his experience of language in this poetic "magical country," in whose distant outskirts dwells the Norn, the ancient goddess of fate.²⁴⁴ The Norn peers into her well and searches the depths for the name that she might bring up. "Word, language, belongs within the domain of this mysterious landscape in which poetic saying borders on the fateful source of speech."²⁴⁵ Thinking must follow the poet into this magical country, to the fateful source of Saying, so that it might come to the source of the existence of beings, to Being itself. Fortunately, thinking does not have to "go" anywhere to this end: it is always already in the mysterious landscape, in the neighborhood of poetry. "The neighborhood of poetry and thinking is not the result of a process... The nearness that draws them near is itself the occurrence of appropriation by which poetry and thinking are directed into their proper nature."²⁴⁶ The "authentic attitude of thinking," Heidegger writes, "is a listening to the grant [of the being that is founded in poetry], the promise of what is to be put in question... it comes to a focus in listening to the promise that tells us what there is for thinking to think upon."²⁴⁷ This "listening" is a "heeding," an "attending to," a "giving thought to." In Russian, we translate Heidegger as saying that thinking is *vnimanie*, which in everyday language means "attention." In Russian, the words *vnimat'* and *vniat'*, i.e., "to hear," "to hearken," "to heed," are consonant with the word *priniat'*, "to accept," "to take in": to *vniat'* means not simply to pay attention to something, but to accept it, to take it with heart and soul, to take it up and put it on par with what is one's ownmost. This is the sense in

---

244 In Russian, "fate," *sud'ba* or *rok*, bears a connection with *sud*, "court," *recheniem*, "pronouncement," and *izrechenie*, "dictum" or "sentence," i.e., fate is bound up with the word.

245 Heidegger, *On the Way to Language*, 67; idem, GA 12, 160-161.

246 Ibid., 90; idem, GA 12, 185.

247 Ibid., 71, 75; idem, GA 12, 169. See also the omitted passage cited in the asterisk footnote in the English edition of *On the Way to Language*, 91.

which Heidegger interprets the German *Vernehmen*.²⁴⁸ What thinking "heedfully takes in" (*vnimaet*) in attention is the being(s) founded in poetic saying, the hints at the being of the being(s) established by "naming." As Hölderlin wrote:

> Yet us it behooves, you poets, to stand
> Bare-headed beneath God's thunderstorms,
> To grasp the father's ray, itself, with our own hands,
> And to offer to the people
> The heavenly gift wrapt in song²⁴⁹

The essential being of poetry is the founding of beings in saying, which can be called the "offering of the heavenly gift." But this gift is *concealed* in the song, and the essence of thinking lies in heeding (*vniat'*) this gift, accepting it in such a way that the gift is opened up in thinking, is appropriated and "eventfully comes into its own" (*ereignet*). This is the meaning of the thesis that thinking and poetry abide in essential kinship and in each other's neighborhood.

Thus, Heidegger's interpretation of George's poem, drawing in poetic passages from Hölderlin, discloses the fundamental hermeneutic relation: the relation between word and thing. This result itself is obtained hermeneutically: the concealed indication of this relation is found in the interpreted works themselves. This, evidently, is what is meant when Heidegger's defines hermeneutics as "the attempt first of all to define the nature of interpretation on hermeneutic grounds"²⁵⁰: hermeneutics discloses the fundamental principle on which interpretation is based in the interpreted works themselves. Perhaps it is in this specific manner that Heidegger achieved the fulfillment of Husserl's normative "presuppositionlessness."

---

248 See the further discussion of these terms in §6 below. In *History of the Concept of Time: Prolegomena*, *vernehmen* has been translated as "apprehending," "perceiving," and "coming to awareness," in *Introduction to Metaphysics* as "apprehending," in *What Is Called Thinking?* as "taking-to-heart," and in *Zollikon Seminars* as "receiving-perceiving."

249 Heidegger, *Elucidations of Hölderlin's Poetry*, 72-73.

250 Heidegger, *On the Way to Language*, 11; idem, GA 12, 93.

On the one hand, Heidegger's hermeneutics, although having a rather peculiar relation to what is traditionally understood by the term "hermeneutics," can and should be perceived only in the context of his entire philosophy; on the other hand, the results gained therefrom are of general philosophical significance. The posing and partial solution of the task of constructing a certain "hermeneutic actuality" should be recognized as the main result of Heidegger's hermeneutics. With Heidegger, by virtue of his specific understanding of the act of interpretation that is inlaid at the very basis not only of gnoseology, but also ontology, hermeneutics takes on a fundamental philosophical status.

What does it mean that Being "uses" man in order to carry its call, first and foremost to himself, and only secondly to all other beings? Whence does this call originate? The call of Being originates in the depths of the "soil" — the depths of the past into which our ancestors have departed. We cannot allow for their lives to end up meaningless, but they might very well turn out meaningless if all the ages of labor, feats, and struggle lead to a worthless us. "By their fruit you will recognize them" (Matthew 7:16). The Jews' exodus from Egypt imparted their preceding exile and Egyptian captivity with meaning, just as Easter justified Christ's suffering on the cross. From a hermeneutic point of view, Christ liberated the righteous patriarchs of the Old Testament by imparting meaning to their lives through his own feat.

Past generations depart and their forms die only to become the soil for the birth of the new. All that is left is the burning of their spirit, the burning of their aspirations, dreams, and ideals, and that which remains constitutes the foundation of the continuity of life and true immortality. This fire fills up language as the event of meaning and "shoots" or breaks up out of the depths of lingual consciousness into the sprout of the word. The word is born as man — from Being.

Just as parents do not create their child's soul, man does not create the *meaning* of a word, that is, its capacity to influence consciousness. Man lets the word resound and pronounces it, but it is *through* the word and *through* man that the imperfect past *draws* towards perfection, the sinful towards redemption, the meaningless towards the meaningful, or more accurately, the old meaning towards its self-resurrection in new, clearer, fuller meaning. In this call, it is not only the voice of past generations that calls, but the voice of all of "natural history," the voice of all of mute nature that requires man to give it the word and fill its existence with meaning.

But what does it mean that this message is addressed to man? Man is two-fold in his essence: he lives between the poles of the two-foldness of Being, and therefore he must be the "distant echo" of the call of Being. This means that man, in order to be man, must bear some kind of message. This message ("tiding") of Being is what establishes the essence of man as man, and thus it is always already addressed to man. If man forgets his true essence and purpose, then the call of Being shall remind him.

It follows that "to bear the message" of Being means to interpret, to translate from one "tone" to another, to raise or lower the pitch of the "call of Being." The essence of man lies in his transforming the sound of Being into the sound of beings.

We can now offer a clearer answer to the previous question: What brings the parts of the Event together into one? The word (as *Logos*), as the sound that carries up from the depths of Being, as the tone (vibration) in which different overtones and modulations can be distinct and can come into relief. The Event comprises everything vibrating together, everything resonating in response to the foundational tonality of the "essential Word" that is said.

§5. "Interpreting Actuality" after the Turn

After the Turn, one of the most important directions of the hermeneutic method's application remains, as was the case in the early *Hermeneutics of Facticity* lectures, the *interpretation of actuality*. But now the understanding of actuality and the approach to its interpretation are essentially different. This is not the actuality of the "everyday existence" of Dasein, but a certain "poetic dimension" in which the things in everyday human life are seen in their primordial meanings, which are concealed not only from metaphysical, conceptual comprehension, but also from everyday, superficial talk. Only the encounter between poetry and thinking in the act of interpretation can illuminate a "thing" in its genuine meaning.

It could even be said that this poetic "interpretation of actuality" is some kind of "method." In a certain sense reviving Pythagorean numerology, the closest example of which would be Nicholas Cusanus's doctrine of "conjectures," Heidegger introduces a kind of "numerical code" for comprehending the being of things: the "Fourfold" (*Geviert*) of earth and sky, divinities and mortals. Heidegger uses the Fourfold, which was presented in the lecture "The Thing" given at the Bavarian Academy of Fine Arts on 6 June 1950, as an interpretive device. Here, the "object" of interpretation is once again, as in the 1923 *Hermeneutics of Facticity* lectures, "actuality," but now it is the actuality of particular things rather than "particular Dasein." A jug is at the same time a thing and a symbol. Heidegger sees in this symbol the oneness of four: earth and sky, mortal and immortal. They cannot be brought under one common category: they are neither "four notions" nor "four hypostases," etc. They are so different from each other that they do not permit any unification under any kind of common "rubric." However, being together in this difference, they constitute a certain mystical oneness, like the Pythagorean Tetractys or Nicholas Cusanus's "four unities."

Present in the jug, as in any "substantial" thing, are, firstly, earth and sky:

> The spring stays on in the water of the gift. In the spring the rock dwells, and in the rock dwells the dark slumber of the earth, which receives the rain and dew of the sky. In the water of the spring dwells the marriage of sky and earth. It stays in the wine given by the fruit of the vine, the fruit in which the earth's nourishment and the sky's sun are betrothed to one another. In the gift of water, in the gift of wine, sky and earth dwell. But the gift of the outpouring is what makes the jug a jug. In the jugness of the jug, sky and earth dwell.[251]

In its outpouring, the jug involves both mortals and immortals, depending on to whom its content is dedicated: "To pour a gush, when it is achieved in its essence, thought through with sufficient generosity, and genuinely uttered, is to donate, to offer in sacrifice, and hence to give... In the gift of the outpouring dwells the simple singlefoldness of the four."[252]

The Fourfold is not intrinsic to the jug alone, nor does it distinguish it among other things. It cannot be said that the interpretation has revealed the Fourfold within the symbol of the jug as some kind of hidden meaning. Rather, the Fourfold unites the jug with all other *genuine* things; the Fourfold confirms the genuineness of a thing in view of how its very own irreplaceable meaning is opened up within it, e.g., the "jugness" of the jug, the "hearthness" of the hearth, etc. The necessity of genuineness in this criterion arises insofar as the world around us is increasingly filled with empty, untrue things.[253] This is a world of "things...

---

251 Heidegger, "The Thing" in *Poetry, Language, Thought*, 170; idem, *Vremia i bytie*, 320.

252 Ibid., 170, 171; idem, *Vremia i bytie*, 320, 321.

253 See Rainer Marie Rilke's letter from 13 November 1925: "To our grandparents, a "house," a "well," a familiar steeple, even their own clothes, their cloak *still* meant infinitely more, were infinitely more intimate—almost everything a vessel in which they found something human already there, and added to its human store. Now there are intruding, from America, empty indifferent things, sham things, *dummies of life...* A house, as the Americans understand it, an American apple or a winestock from over there, have *nothing* in common with the house, the fruit,

shifting their existence more and more over into the vibrations of money."²⁵⁴ Empty and untrue things are the spawn of metaphysics, modern European science, and technology, whose "projects" are in no way consonant with the "main tone" of Being. The Fourfold is a challenge to metaphysical thinking. Since Parmenides' time, the Western mind has been busy with the "technical" apprehension of beings, whereby the dominant principles have been Oneness, Twoness, and Threeness. The oneness of Being is the necessary condition constituting the universe, and that which cannot be counted does not exist. Hence the successes of modern science and technology — but these successes are perhaps too successful for a living, organic being like man ("Our life is limited, but knowledge is unlimited. It is dangerous for the limited to follow the unlimited" — *Zhuangzi*²⁵⁵). Twoness is the polarity of truth and falsehood, idea and actuality, correctness or correspondence and incorrectness or non-correspondence. According to Cusanus, for example, twoness is the equivalence (identity) between the One and itself, that is, correspondence, correctness, trueness. The Three, as in the Trinity, is the peak to which metaphysics could only rarely raise itself, the Connection (the third hypostasis according to Cusanus) of the One and the Other, Being and Nothing, light and dark, the becoming and the self-unfolding of the world of forms, the World Soul of Plato and the Neoplatonists, which takes in ideas as the principles of things from the intellect of the Demiurge. Metaphysics, including Christian metaphysics, stopped at these three foundations. After the Turn, Heidegger poses the task of overcoming metaphysics in everything. In resolving this task, he puts forth a new numerical ("numerological") code for Being. In some respects, this code is like Pythagoras' Tetractys. It is depicted in the

the grape into which the hope and thoughtfulness of our forefathers had entered..." — from *Briefe aus Muzot*, quoted in Heidegger, "What Are Poets For?" in *Poetry, Language, Thought*, 110-111.

254 Ibid.

255 Based on L.D. Pozdneeva's Russian translation of *Zhuangzi*, Chapter III.

form of an equilateral pyramid with a triangular base — a tetrahedron. In Pythagoras, the monad (unit) — the tip of the pyramid — symbolized the incomprehensible Principle of Principles, the Unsayable, the ground that is the triunity inherent in any creative act: the active principle, the passive principle, and the "event" of their meeting, including the act of cognition in creating meaning. But metaphysics "bracketed" the Incomprehensible and thereby eliminated the "ontological gap" between Being and beings, which gave rise to the "oblivion of Being."

The "fourfold," or tetrad, has since antiquity referred to the world of bodies which possess mass, are substantial, are cognizable by the senses, and are different from the One, the Intellect, and the Soul. The tetrad was never highly appreciated in metaphysics, since the world of things is the furthest removed and most distorted reflection of the truth, the level on which the truth is virtually indistinguishable. The categories of reason are inoperative here, and the mind feels out of its element, unconfident, defenseless, confused, and embarrassed. The Fourfold is not logical: earth and sky, divine and mortal are still understood separately in their polarity, but their unification as four does not proceed from rational grounds. Why these pairs instead of, say, "past and future," "outer and inner," etc.? This cannot be proven or understood rationally. It is completely obvious that it is written *poetically*, and therefore it is necessary to "take it in" (*vnimat'*). The Fourfold is "unproven," but it bears the direct cogency of an image. The pairs of opposites really could have been other ones, as could the whole course of interpretation, but such would only be different, not any more or any less "true." The Fourfold brings thinking to poetry. The poet is like God: in creating the world, he is completely free, but he bears full responsibility. In an era when man becomes the "poet" of actuality ("poet" in Greek means "creator") and creates his own artificial world to replace the old one, the Fourfold reminds man of the "poetic responsibility of the creator."

§6. Heidegger on the "Neighborhood" of Thinking and Poetry

Saying and attentive heeding are to be found in both thinking and poetry: in poetry, in attending to the divine and to saying it in the word; in thinking, in attending to the divine clothed in the form of a being, divulging and "appropriating" (*eignen*) this divine. Both poetry and thinking are essentially interpretive bearing, but poetry is the downward bearing of the "divine gift" that is "concealed in song," whereas philosophy is the upward movement of thought from beings to the truth of Being.

"Attending" (German *vernehmen*, Russian *vnimanie*)

As we have already heard, Heidegger associates thinking with *vernehmen* in the sense of "listening," "heeding," "giving thought to," "taking in," which we have translated with the Russian *vnimanie*, and this category is paired with "saying." The "authentic attitude of thinking," Heidegger writes, "is a listening to the grant [of the being that is founded in poetry], the promise of what is to be put in question... it comes to a focus in listening to the promise that tells us what there is for thinking to think upon."[256] This is a rare case in which Heidegger's thought finds an even greater correspondence in Russian than in German: as said above, *vnimat'* and *vniat'*, i.e., "to hear," "to hearken," "to heed," are consonant with the word *priniat'*, "to accept," "to take in": to *vniat'* means not simply to pay attention to something and thereafter remain indifferent, but to accept it, to take it with heart and soul, to take it up and put it on par with what is one's "own," to honestly respond to it, to accept it as a direction of leadership in life. This is the sense in which Heidegger interprets the German *vernehmen*. In modern German, the verb *vernehmen* means "to interrogate" (witnesses), but *vernehmbar* would in Russian be *vniatnyi*,

---

256 Heidegger, *On the Way to Language*, 71, 75, 91; idem, GA 12, 169, 186, 230.

that is, something that has been heard "distinctly," "clearly," "intelligibly." Heidegger associates *vernehmen* with *hinnehmen* ("receiving") and *annehmen* ("allowing"). The essence of thinking is *vernehmen* in the sense of "allowing attention to be given to that which is distinctly heard" ("*annehmen und hinnehmen als vernehmen*," "*der Mensch als das Wesen vernehmende*," i.e., "man as the 'receiving-perceiving' being" — this is one of the topics of the Zollikon seminars[257]). That which thinking listens and attends to is the being(s) founded in poetic saying, the hints at the being of the being(s) founded by "naming." Heidegger cites a verse by Hölderlin as confirmation of this[258]:

> *Doch uns gebührt es, unter Gottes Gewittern,*
> *Ihr Dichter! mit entblösstem Haupte zu stehen,*
> *Des Vaters Strahl, ihn selbst, mit eigner Hand*
> *Zu fassen und dem Volk ins Lied*
> *Gehüllt die himmlische Gaabe zu reichen,*
> *Denn sind nur reinen Herzens*
> *Wie Kinder, wir, sind schuldlos unsere Hände.*

> Yet us it behooves, you poets, to stand
> Bare-headed beneath God's thunderstorms,
> To grasp the father's ray, itself, with our own hands,
> And to offer to the people
> The heavenly gift wrapt in song,
> For only if we are pure in heart,
> Like children, are our hands innocent.

The essence of poetry is the founding of being(s) in saying, which can be called the "heavenly gift."

The poet founds a being in his Saying because he hears and heeds the call rolling forth from the depths (and heights) of Being better than others. Through the heart of the poet, Being lays down its road from the past into the future. Now ,"Being" in Heidegger takes on a meaning that

---

[257] See Heidegger, *Zollikon Seminars*, wherein *vernehmen* is translated as "receiving-perceiving."

[258] Heidegger, *Elucidations of Hölderlin's Poetry*, 72-73.

is very close to the meaning of the title of the first book of Moses in the Bible, which in Greek is *Genesis*, "becoming," but which was translated into Old Slavonic as "Being" (*bytie*) even before the Russian language acquired the entire web of metaphysical concepts.

But this gift of the founding of being(s) is *concealed* in the song, and the essence of thinking lies in heeding (*vniat'*) this gift, accepting it in such a way that the gift is opened up in thinking, is appropriated and "eventfully comes into its own" (*ereignet*). Now the specificity of man as a "special kind of being" takes on a new meaning: it is not "going beyond beings as a whole" in "ek-stasis," in experiencing the primordial angst of "being held out into the Nothing," but rather a peaceful, serious, and responsible attentiveness of heeding (*vnimanie*). Evidently, this heedful taking-in (*vnimanie*) is what Being requires of man. It is through his attentiveness (*vnimanie*) that man illuminates and renders unconcealed the circle of things of his lifeworld. It is in attending (*vnimanie*) that things come into presencing by man. Each and every thing can be likened to a flower that grows out of the fertile soil of the "primordial sound" of Being. But the flower, like the word, is not enough. The flower opens up to meet the sun so that its beauty and fragrance might attract the productive attention of the bee. The word remains only *a possibility*, even when embodied in sound, until it has been attentively, distinctly heeded (*vniato*), admitted into the heart, into the source of attending in the human being. In Russian, this kinship could be expressed by way of a play of words: "a thing [*veshch'*] is what is proclaimed [*vozveshcheno*]," i.e., a thing is that which has a word in whose resounding its essence is gathered. Furthermore, "a thing is what is lit up [*osveshcheno*]" by the radiant beam of attending (*vnimanie*) that takes this thing out of "concealment" into the "clearing of Being."

Attending (*vnimanie*) gives a thing its thingness. But attending itself needs the word in order to embody its mysterious, unsayable force in a visible image. Attending figures as "being-possibility," which requires a word, an essential word, from man, so that the "tiding of Being" can be borne.

The Russian word *vniat'* is an etymological calque of the German *vernehmen*. Also of interest is the Ukrainian word *uvaga*, which has the same meaning. The root *vaga* means "heaviness," "load," "weight," which is figuratively featured in the Russian word for "respect," *uvazhenie*. "To respect," *uvazhit'*, has the same meaning as *vniat'*. Similar connections can be found in other languages: in Sanskrit, *guru* means both "heavy," "weighty," as well as "respected one," "teacher" (cf. English "grave," meaning both "heavy" and "solid"). In a certain way, attending [*vnimanie*] can produce a weight, a heaviness in what it is directed towards. Without a doubt, paying attention [*vnimanie*] to something is a cause for its weightiness, its "gravity," and not vice versa: to *vnimat'* is to *uvazhivat'*, to make heavy (*utiazheliat'*), and after the weight has been produced, it draws new attention [*vnimanie*] to itself.

There are indeed a whole number of other terms which Heidegger brings into the context of his philosophizing, either by creating them himself or, as is more often the case, by imparting new meaning to the already existing words of the natural German language. Vladimir Bibikhin characterizes Heidegger's approach to language thusly:

> Every word of Heidegger's, taken by itself, resounds with a whole gamut of meanings that are inherent to this given word in the natural German language. Every thinker who starts upon the critique of language (Leibniz, for instance) ultimately returns to the natural sound of words. Heidegger is inseparable from what he says; the resounding word invokes within him all meanings, not only the ones that ordinarily arise to us in the ordinary context. Hence the difficulty of translating significant thinkers into another language: one must, perhaps, be a double of the

author in order to pour the content into the forms of another language and to not distort through such forms that which is to be said. Heidegger's speech "burns through" language and drains its body for the spirit; language can't stand the tension of the spirit, and in some instances of tension the very matter of language warps and is torn apart (or the visibility of its smooth matter is torn apart).[259]

The Newfound "Discovery" of the Imagination

Already in his *Kant and the Problem of Metaphysics* lectures, Heidegger had come to the conclusion that Kant's genuine discovery was the "groundlessness" of metaphysics: it turned out that the only common ground for the two trunks of knowledge — sensibility and reason — is the productive power of the imagination, which was found unsuitable to serve as the ground of metaphysics. This thought on the role of the imagination did not leave Heidegger, and after the Turn he became evermore definitively inclined to think that metaphysics must be content with the imagination as its only ground, for it has no other. To this end, metaphysics must take up a "new beginning," and it is not just any "imagination" that is to be embraced, but only poetic imagination, the imagination of the "essential" poets.

In Russian, the very word "poet" (*poet*) poorly corresponds to the role of poetry in Heidegger. This Greek word was "imported" to Russia to designate the art of composing verses, which in and of itself is sufficiently far removed from Being. In Rus', the "essential poet" was called a *pevets*, a "singer," because his verse was always a song (as per Hölderlin's verse, discussed by Heidegger, which says that the gift of poetry is "*ins Lied gehüllt,*" "wrapt in song"). But closest of all to Heidegger's understanding of the role of the poet is the Vedic *kaviḥ*, the "holy poet-prophet," of whom

---

[259] From the conspectus of a lecture course on Heidegger delivered by Bibikhin at the Faculty of Philosophy of Moscow State University.

it can by all means rightfully be said that he "stands bareheaded beneath God's thunderstorms." According to this marvelous Hindu analogy, the Vedas, the fruit of the creative works of the *kavayaḥ*, are the "goldmine" from which the philosophers and prophets of India have over all the ages drawn their ore (extracting it like miners in a mine), which they melted down in the crucible of their heart and and poured out as the gold coins of true teachings, releasing them into circulation. Every teaching is a golden coin of one or another state or era, but all of the gold in them, that which constitutes their value, comes from one source: in the final analysis, this source is the poetic inspiration of the poet-prophets, the *kavayaḥ*.

Heidegger's thinking fully concords with such a vision of the relationship between poetry and philosophy, and even allows it to be complemented with new strokes: the mysterious process of the "mineralization of the ore" takes place in the soul of the *kaviḥ*-poet when he places himself before the fire of the divine lightning storm. Truth is lethally dangerous in the instant when it first comes into contact with the primal element of human life (and just how much truth human nature can bear was the main experiment of Nietzsche's life). Through his *stiftende nennung*, his "affirming-establishing naming," the poet imprints the divine Fire. In the light of this analogy, Heraclitus' expression that "many ores are melted down by those who search, but little gold is found" can be understood as the philosopher's lamentation for his contemporary poets, who ceased to bear their lofty service and reduced poetry to "the most innocent of occupations." Hence the harsh condemnation that "poets tell many lies," a sentence that was incontestable for Plato as well as Aristotle.

§7. The "Hermeneutics of Language"

As a general rule, "hermeneutics" deals with discourse, whether written, oral, or conveyed through other signs. From the very beginning of the development of his hermeneutics, Heidegger considerably expanded the object of hermeneutics: first he spoke of "interpreting actuality," then of the "Dasein analytic," and then the subject of hermeneutic questioning became the "Nothing." In the wake of the Turn, it is as though Heidegger brought hermeneutics back to its "primordial object": written language. But this return comes about on a fundamentally different basis than that of the traditional interpretation of texts.

According to Heidegger, traditional hermeneutics understands language in accordance with two premises which are not called into question:

> First and foremost, speaking is expression. The idea of speech as an utterance is the most common. It already presupposes the idea of something internal that utters or externalizes itself. If we take language to be utterance, we give an external, surface notion of it at the very moment when we explain it by recourse to something internal.[260]

The second axiom of traditional hermeneutics is that "speech is regarded as an activity of man... Finally, human expression is always a presentation and representation of the real and the unreal."[261] Both of these premises, which understand language as outward expression and as human activity, are inoperative for Heideggerian hermeneutics. As has already been said with respect to Heidegger's early hermeneutics, the latter denies that anything (texts, speech, things) has an "objective" meaning that first exists within the speaker and is then expressed in speech. Meaning arises only in the creative act of interpretation, in "understanding"; meaning is neither external nor internal, it is a projection in which

---
260 Heidegger, "Language" in *Poetry, Language, Thought*, 190; idem, GA 12, 12.
261 Ibid.

the dichotomy of "outer vs. inner" does not actually apply. With some reservations, it could be said that "meaning" in Heidegger's hermeneutics is the very interaction of the outer and inner, but only if both merge into one within the domain of human presence. Thus, according to Heidegger, language is not a "human activity," for this formula presupposes that there is some kind of being called "human" which sometimes, whenever it wants, externally manifests its interior and opts to "speak." Rather, according to Heidegger, "We are always speaking, even when we do not utter a single word aloud."[262] Language belongs to the essence of man, or, as Heidegger puts it, "the essence of man belongs to language": "For man is man only because he is granted the promise of language, because he is needful to language, that he may speak it."[263] Thus, in Heidegger's hermeneutics, "language" takes on a completely different meaning than in traditional hermeneutics: "language is the house of Being." The main consequence of this rethinking of language is that the object of hermeneutics becomes language itself, not only written or oral discourse. This turn is not so obvious in German, since *die Sprache* means both "speech" and "language." Nevertheless, this turn is fundamental: in traditional hermeneutics, meaning is ascribed only to a text, discourse, or utterance, whereas now the task is within language itself, through interpreting the various cases of speaking in language so as to open up all kinds of meaning, i.e., to let language itself, as Saying, rather than words, to strike our nerves.

For traditional hermeneutics, this is awkward: meaning can be imparted to a text only by its author, but if the author does not do so, the text is meaningless. Language has no "author," hence it cannot have meaning. For Heidegger, to the contrary, meaning that has an author is always superficial and inessential, and his task is to "let language speak": "We leave the speaking to language. We do not wish to ground

---

262 Ibid., 187; idem, GA 12, 9.

263 Heidegger, *On the Way to Language*, 90; idem, GA 12, 185.

language in something else that is not language itself, nor do we wish to explain other things by means of language."[264] In other words: "We do not wish to assault language in order to force it into the grip of ideas already fixed beforehand... To discuss language, to place it, means to bring to its place of being not so much language as ourselves: our own gathering into the appropriation [*Ereignis*]."[265] What is this essence called "language" that Heidegger wants to hear? In Heidegger's texts we hear the expression "*Sprache spricht*," "language speaks," which is like many other cases where Heidegger artificially creates verbal forms out of the roots of nouns: "world worlds" (*Welt weltet*), "time temporalizes" (*Zeit zeitigt*), "essence essences" (Wesen west), "Nothing nihilates" (*Nichts nichtet*). Accordingly, *Sprache spricht* could be translated as "speech speeches," which in Russian would be *rech' rechet'*, provided that we understand *rech'* as simultaneously meaning "language," and not merely "speech" or "discourse." In propositions that grammatically possess a subject and verb, the subject and predicate can be singled out logically (for instance, "snow is falling," "the bell tolls"). The division into subject and predicate immediately takes us into the metaphysical, conceptual manner of thinking. Heidegger tries to avoid this by deriving the subject and predicate from one and the same root: *Sprache spricht*. What is expressed in this proposition is not an attribution of some attribute to the subject, but a bringing of the immobile form of the noun into movement signified by a verb (in German, "verb" is *Zeitwort*, that is "time word"). The noun corresponds more to metaphysics, because it designates some kind of constant "essence," even when it is a process that is being spoken of. Heidegger shows that the very emergence of metaphysics was bound up with the verb "is" turning into the noun "being" in Parmenides' philosophy. Heidegger carries out a reverse transition from nouns to verbs. Verbs existed prior, but only as what is said of nouns. Heidegger strives to almost entirely

---

264 Heidegger, "Language" in *Poetry, Language, Thought*, 189; idem, GA 12, 10.
265 Ibid., 188; idem, GA 12, 10.

remove nouns from his dictionary, or in the very least to blur the boundary between nouns and verbs. Therefore, expressions like *Wesen west* and *Sprache spricht* do not posit any "subject" of which something would be "expressed." "Language speaks" or "speech speeches" means an "event" (*Ereignis*) that happens of its own, an "act without an actor," a "summons of Being" to which man must hearken and respond. Thus, "listening to the speaking of language" and interpreting language itself means, according to Heidegger, endlessly moving around the hermeneutic circle of interpretation in order to undergo an "experience of language." Heidegger cites an ancient Greek adage: "What was entrusted to us in the beginning will become known last." In the "beginning," we have been "entrusted with" Being and language as the "house of Being," i.e., they rest in the very ground of our essence. Therefore, interpreting language is the way to ourselves, which has no end. "We would like only, for once, to get to just where we are already."[266]

In what direction does this interpretation of language as man's path to himself — the path of the speaking being — unfold in Heidegger's thinking? In my view, we can distinguish two directions of Heidegger's endeavor. Both directions began to be worked out intensely after the Turn, and neither of them excludes the other; rather, they complement each other. The first direction is "hearkening" to the sound of the roots of words: "the reflective use of language cannot be guided by the common, usual understanding of meanings; rather, it must be guided by the hidden riches that language holds in store for us, so that these riches may summon us for the saying of language."[267] By "hidden riches" Heidegger obviously means something like the "inner form" of the word as in Potebnya's theory, that is, a certain sound or combination of two or three sounds bearing an original "atom of meaning." Some ancient philosophers (predominantly from the Platonic

---

[266] Heidegger, "Language" in *Poetry, Language, Thought*, 188; idem, GA 12, 10.

[267] Heidegger, *On the Way to Language*, 91; idem, GA 12, 186.

tradition going back to Plato's *Cratylus*) and some 20th-century Symbolist poets believed that each individual sound carries a definite meaning. Different combinations of sounds mean that the meanings inlaid in them are brought together. Heidegger does not venture to analyze individual sounds, but he sees some original phonetic forms of the German language as thoughtful, and he even draws on the data of comparative linguistics.[268] In this respect, Heidegger sees language as the result of many centuries of the activity of thought. Whose thought? Not God's, not the Absolute Spirit's, nor the people's — rather, thought as an impersonal process which some significant thinkers follow to the extent their strength allows. The more a thinker commits himself to this impersonal fulfillment of thought, the more significant he is. Every word, in the time that it has been "granted" to be a "direct actuality of thought," undergoes significant evolution and becomes a living reflection of this evolution. What is valuable for Heidegger, however, is not this whole evolution, the last stage of which has proceeded under the signboard of metaphysics, but the most primordial layers of meaning that can be "heard" in the roots of current words. The entire terminology of Heidegger's hermeneutics is based on these original meanings, which condition the peculiarity that distinguishes this terminology from the "concepts" of traditional metaphysics.

The second direction in the "interpreting of language" is the interpretation of poetic works. Heidegger is often charged with having "poeticized thought," but the possibilities that this path of thinking opened up led him to ignore such reproaches. In Heidegger's texts we find a "justification" for making poetry into the main object of interpretation, but this justification itself is "poetic," and therefore is nothing more than a "pseudo-justification" for his critics. In brief,

---

[268] In "The Thing," for example, Heidegger compares German *giessen*, *Guss*, "gush," "pour," to the Indo-Germanic *ghu*, which means "to offer in sacrifice." Heidegger, "The Thing" in *Poetry, Language, Thought*, 170.

the course of this reasoning boils down to the following: Where can we seek the "speaking of language"? In the "spoken" (*Gesprochene*):

> The speaking does not cease in what is spoken. Speaking is kept safe in what is spoken. In what is spoken, speaking gathers the ways in which it persists as well as that which persists by it — its persistence, its presencing. But most often, and too often, we encounter what is spoken only as the residue of a speaking long past. If we must, therefore, seek the speaking of language in what is spoken, we shall do well to find something that is spoken purely rather than to pick just any spoken material at random. What is *spoken purely* is the poem.[269]

The latter statement, despite the preceding "justification," remains merely a "bare assertion," since it does not follow logically and it is unclear why poetry is "spoken purely." In "response" to this question, Heidegger proceeds to interpret Georg Trakl's poem "*Winterabend*" ("A Winter Evening"). And so, *why poetry?* Heidegger's "justification" takes us to the category of "saying": in the "sound of language rising like the earth... its earthyness... we pay heed again to the way in which we are everywhere under way within the neighborhood of the modes of Saying. Among these, poetry and thinking have ever been preeminent."[270] The category of "neighborhood" or "nearness" also plays a significant role in Heidegger's later hermeneutics. In an era when modern transport and means of communication have made everything uniquely close and yet exceptionally distant at the same time, Heidegger speaks of "nearness" in the old sense, when neighboring in space meant nearness to the human essence, and distance meant foreignness, the unknown.[271] This nearness

---

269 Heidegger, "Language" in *Poetry, Language, Thought*, 191-192; idem, GA 12, 13-14. My italics.

270 Heidegger, *On the Way to Language*, 101; idem, GA 12, 196.

271 "Yet the frantic abolition of all distances brings no nearness; for nearness does not consist in shortness of distance... What is least remote from us in point of distance, by virtue of its picture on film or its sound on the radio, can remain far from us. What is incalculably far from us in point of distance can be near to us.

is nearness in the "space of Being," in the place through which the path of "essential thinking" makes its way. In this place, "near" means "close to Being"; only those who are close to Being can be close to each other here. Those who are distant from Being will be far away from each other, even if they were in proximity to each other in space. Heidegger writes: "The neighborhood of poetry and thinking is not the result of a process... The nearness that draws them near is... that Saying in which language grants its essential nature to us."[272] Elsewhere, Heidegger says that poetry and thinking are "dwelling on distant peaks": just as two peaks rising up over an endless valley will be close to each other no matter the distance between them, so do poetry and thinking both rise over the sea of thoughtless speaking and are close to each other in their relation to Being. In Heidegger, thinking tries to outwardly liken itself to poetry, "grounding" its conclusions not in terms of authoritative evidence or logical argumentation, but through an "overflow of meanings" in the resounding of words.

Following Heidegger's interpretation further around the hermeneutic circle, we once again return to one of the main problems of hermeneutic philosophy, namely, the problem of the relation between word (sign) and thing. This relation "announces itself in a single word": "The word is *logos*. It speaks simultaneously as the name for Being and for Saying."[273] Thus, *logos* is defined by Heidegger as the "name of Saying" at the same time as it is, in the original sense, "language," "word," "speech." *Logos* unites poetry, thinking, and language. "Word, language, belongs within the domain of this mysterious landscape in which poetic saying borders on the fateful

---

Short distance is not in itself nearness. Nor is great distance remoteness... What about nearness? How can we come to know its nature? Nearness, it seems, cannot be encountered directly. We succeed in reaching it rather by attending to what is near." Heidegger, "The Thing" in *Poetry, Language, Thought*, 163-164.

272 Heidegger, *On the Way to Language*, 90; idem, GA 12, 185.
273 Ibid., 80; idem, GA 12, 174.

source of speech."²⁷⁴ Thinking must follow the poet into this mysterious landscape, to this "fateful source of speech," in whose depths Being is concealed. "Fortunately," Heidegger writes, in thinking "we do not need either to search for this neighborhood or to seek it out. We are already abiding in it. We move within it…"²⁷⁵ For, "poetry and thought, each needs the other in its neighborhood."²⁷⁶ The interpretation here incorporates the category of "attending" [*vernehmen, vnimanie*] discussed above. The essence of poetry is founding being(s) in saying, "offering up the heavenly gift." But this gift is *concealed* in the song, and the essence of thinking lies in heeding (*vniat'*) this gift, accepting it in such a way that the gift is opened up in thinking, is appropriated and "eventfully comes into its own" (*ereignet*).

To sum up, it can be said that Heidegger's philosophy of language after the Turn aspires to change the very meaning of philosophizing by turning it into a kind of "tilling of the field of thought." According to Heidegger, the previous manner of philosophizing, now defined as "metaphysics," is characterized by a superficial, conceptual means of thinking in which concepts are not premised upon a clear grasp of the "disposition-of-being" of beings. Heidegger sets the task of *overcoming metaphysics* by way of working through a "non-conceptual language" that is supposed to allow the philosopher to "undergo an experience" — an experience of Being, of Nothing, of language. This is an experience of "non-conceptual understanding" (in *Being and Nothingness*, Sartre, not without Heidegger's influence, considered such a means of understanding to be a "pre-reflective *cogito*"). To solve this task, Heidegger puts forth the method of the "reflective use of language," which, in essence, represents an interpretation of language as a bearer of mankind's

---

274 Ibid., 67; idem, GA 12, 160-161.

275 Ibid., 82; idem, GA 12, 176.

276 Ibid., 70; idem, GA 12, 163.

"collective memory" of the work of thought that has been carried out over the ages. This memory is concentrated in the roots of the words of natural language (what Potebnya called the "inner form of the word"). It is this interpreting of language itself that makes a non-conceptual experience of Being possible, for language itself, from Heidegger's point of view, is a manifestation of the "fundamental attunement" (*Grundstimmung*) of Being. It is from here that Heidegger derives the meaning of word (*logos*) as that which "gathers" (*legein*) and maintains a being as a being in its simple being. Insofar as the "guardian of the word" is man, it follows that man is responsible as the guardian of beings and the "shepherd of Being." The greatest lot of this responsibility falls to the "essential poets" who pronounce the "saying" in which "the word is first given to Being."

IV
HEIDEGGER'S PHILOSOPHY OF HISTORY

§1. The Problem of Time in Heidegger's Philosophy and his Philosophy of History

Man as an Historical Being

Humankind can be seen as one whole body not only in space, but also in time. In space, this would be the conquered and cultivated territory of land, sea, air, and underground resources. In time, this would be the totality of the events of human history. History in its essence, according to Heidegger, is *tradition*: insofar as history contains the labor and achievements of mankind in the past, there can be no genuinely new step forward until the achievements of *all of tradition* have been assimilated. For example, Modernity could take off only after the Renaissance recovered the forgotten treasures of ancient thought. But Greek antiquity is far from the entirety of history and does not exhaust all the achievements of mankind that call for assimilation. Heidegger wrote that turning to antiquity in our days should become a bridge for dialogue with the ancient culture of the East. Bringing all of the achievements of tradition, from the Egyptian initiations and the mystical insights of India to quantum physics and general relativity theory, together within today's so-called "spiritual" consciousness is paving the way for a new step in history.

Consequently, according to Heidegger, history is a dimension in the consciousness of man, but even more importantly, it is a *dimension of his being*. Man is the "reified memory" of all the past, not only his own, but of the world as a whole, and his essence, *essentia*, derived from his *existentia*, is existing in time, in the past, present, and future. This can be regarded as the "existentialist motif" in Heidegger. For Heidegger, however, this *existentia*, "presencing," or Being as essential presence, is not primary, but rather is derived along with time from the Event (*Ereignis*).

Insofar as the present is just as much an "ecstasy" of temporalizing as the past and the future, the human being can be called the *reified anticipation of the future* (the "bridge to the *Übermensch*," to literally quote Nietzsche), the projection of future tasks into the past evolution of life.

The Classical Understanding of Time and Heidegger's Critique

The classical understanding of time is bound up with the classical understanding of Being as that which truly *is*. Time is the totality of moments of now (*nuns stans*) in which the past and future are not (no longer or not yet) while the present is. But time, according to Heidegger, like Being, *is not*. Just as being "is not," but rather "essences" or "be-ings" (Russian *"bytiistvuet"*), so too is it the case that time "is not," but rather "temporalizes" (*zeitigt*).

Unlike its classical understanding, time for Heidegger is not linear and is not derivative of calculative operations. *Time is "three-dimensional,"* for the past, present, and future are three means of presencing (already in absence, now in presence, or still in absence), and even *"four-dimensional,"* since all of these means of presencing are thought from and within a certain primordial dimension: the dimension of *temporalizing*.

Time and Being are equiprimordial: Being as the presence of the presencing unfolds into and consists of three temporal modes of presence. Time constitutes Being, and Being constitutes time.

The Originary that unifies time and Being is the Event (*Ereignis*), where space-time and Being are given in inseparable unity.

The Concept of Time as Event (*Ereignis*)

Strictly speaking, the Event is *outside of time and Being*. In theology, the Event is comparable only to God. The Event finds its unfolding reflection in space-time. As Pascal said, "the crucifixion of Christ lasts for eternity, and there should be no sleeping during this time." The event of the "crucifixion of Christ" is, so to speak, on the noumenal, supratemporal plane, and its "beingful energy" affects all events within time from the very emergence of the universe, preparing the soil for its occurrence. To speak with the imagery of the metaphysics of light, we could say that the Crucifixion Event sends light from the supratemporal world into time, illuminating, proclaiming, and bringing into occurrence, into presence, into coming-to-be the thing-events that in turn lead, albeit in the immeasurably distant future, to the realization of the Crucifixion. The light sent by the Event is at once existential (bringing into Being), spiritual (illuminating spirit), intellectual (illuminating mind), and sensuous (emotional). The Light of the main, universal Event first constitutes time, Being, and space.

However, this does not rule out that the Event might disintegrate into smaller events, each of which would be the source of a particular light and existential tension, a "magnet of history." Such events might illuminate particular eras and, at a certain point of the space-time illuminated by them, their light might be focused to such a degree of concentration that it is embodied in one person with the maximal fullness and force — just as the Event of the Redemptive Sacrifice of God for the sake of man was incarnated in the life and death of Christ. Coming to be incarnated in space-time, this Event within beings illuminates the past and the future, imbuing them with meaning, beauty, life, and spirit.

In order for this light to reach as far as possible into the past as well as into the future, it is necessary for other events — whether human lives, the work of the elements, or something else — to enter the link of meanings from the past, as anticipation and preparation, and from the future, as the unfolding of the consequences and gratitude of beings summoned to Being by this Light. In order for space-time to not be rolled up like an old scroll, like the sky in the prophecy of the Apocalypse, it needs to be upheld by pillars of light, beacons of the spirit, servants of God who send each other the light of Being and meaning through time, from the past through the present into the future and from the future through the present into the past. The total Light of these beacons is the Light of the One Supreme Event of the Universe, transmitted in space-time from one beacon-focus to another through myriads of smaller fires, some fanning out and some gathering anew in the powerful focus of the Light.

§2. Event and Meaning

In the late 19th and early 20th centuries, the concept of "event" and semantically analogous terms became central to many philosophical systems of diverse tendencies. In the 1860s-70s, in the neo-Kantian school, the concept of the "subject" was reconceptualized in such a way that both "subject" and "object" ended up being two poles of a certain original reality, like the positive and negative poles of a magnet (an image proposed by Otto Liebmann). It subsequently became commonplace for philosophers to seek out a certain primal reality that precedes both subject and object and contains them as if in "collapsed" or "compressed" form. In Ernst Mach's empirio-criticism, this reality was the "neutral elements of experience," in William James' pragmatism "pure experience," and in Bertrand Russell "logical atoms." Both Heidegger and Ludwig Wittgenstein, seemingly independently, came to designate this supra-subjective and supra-objective reality, which, of course, they understood differently, as "event." In their wake, "event" came to occupy such a central and enduring place in the problematic of different tendencies that the philosophical situation of the mid-20th century could be called a "battle for the event". Concurring that it is precisely "event" that should be at the center of philosophical discourse, various philosophers debated what an event is, what its ontological and gnoseological status is, and how it can be rendered intelligible. Besides Heidegger's hermeneutics, this notion also occupied a central place for Alfred North Whitehead, who created an entirely distinctive form of "new metaphysics," "event metaphysics," as well as for Gilles Deleuze, who interpreted this term in a Postmodernist vein in his *Logic of Sense*.

In Heidegger, event and meaning are categories of the same order, almost identical. Both of them annul subject-object duality: while thought is inherently subjective, meaning is not; Being can be "objective," but an event can not.[277] Both event and meaning are real from the perspective where the observer is simultaneously the creator of the observed picture and a part of it.

Event is a form of the existence of meaning, a unit of meaning, an "atom," like Leibniz's monad or Democritus' atom. Insofar as there is no category in hermeneutic philosophy that is more primordial than meaning (even Being is one meaning which Dasein imparts to beings), event can be deemed an "*atom of the cosmos*" (if, like Democritus, we admit the existence of atoms that are "as big as the world").

An event is indelible not because it is impenetrable to other events, and not because it itself cannot be divided —

---

[277] In Russian, "event," *sobytie*, appears to be *so-bytie*, "with being," i.e., German *Mit-Sein*, but given that we are following Heidegger's thought as expressed in German, we shall leave this association, even though it virtually begs itself, outside of the "playing field."

it can; rather, it is because it loses meaning upon division, collapses into nothing, and therefore dividing it is *meaningless* and inappropriate, regardless of our intent.

Being and time "*come about*" (are gathered together) in event. Event gathers the world. But what gathers and maintains the parts of an event (the "subjective," "objective," and others)? What is the gathering *legein*? What is the spark which suddenly dashes between its parts? What grants the ground of its unity? Such cannot be the unity of the subject or the unity of the object, nor can it be spatial or temporal unity, since all of these concepts are derivative of the Event itself. In order to answer this question, even in part, let us examine the relation between event and *time*.

The peasant plowing his field in spring is the peasant from the future winter who wants to be well-fed, or an emissary of the latter. He is a *worker* from the future (not a "guest from the future"). One could, of course, protest: How can we, in the present, distinguish when we are "emissaries from the future" and when we are merely acting on the basis of our ideas about the future? After all, would the peasant be in error if he were sowing at the foot of a volcanic mountain and did not know that his crop would be destroyed by an unexpected eruption?

We are misled by the old division of time into past, present, and future, against which Augustine had enough to say. The event that we call "future" is supra-temporal or "always in the present" — in *its* present. The participants who find themselves *inside* an event experience it as unfolding in time, but, once again, in *its* — the event's — time. Then, when the participants get out of the event (and this is possible only through death, whether in the greater or lesser sense), they can try to grasp it in its totality. But the event "was," and was "always," integral; it *is* whole. This is precisely Augustine's understanding of *eternity* in its relation to time. In Heidegger's terms, we could express Augustine's thought very precisely in the following way: eternity is the "event (*Ereignis*) of the world."

Heidegger's innovation lies only in recognizing that events, like Leibniz's monads, are manifold: there are many events, including smaller ones that merge into larger ones and might *seem* to be limited within the time of the larger event. But *an event cannot be limited by any time*, just as volume cannot be limited by a line. Every event is a possible center of history, an event of events, in relation to which all of the past is pre-history and all of the future is the consequence, the unfolding. Therefore, just as in Leibniz every monad reflects the whole Universe, only with differing degrees of distinctness, *so does every event encompass all time and all of history, but in different perspectives and different degrees of "distinctiveness."*

Therefore, when the peasant is plowing his field in spring, he is not an "emissary" of a winter that still has yet to arrive — winter has already "onset" in his plow, along with summer and autumn. If the earth's axis suddenly turned and winter did not arrive as usual, and instead an eternal spring did, this would not mean that the peasant was wrong in his calculations for winter. It would only mean that the event of "winter" was limited to the premonition of the caring plower. The same goes for the sultry wind of the desert that usually forebodes a sandstorm: it can, of course, change, but it is *not only a sign*; it is already *part* of the storm, and in it, the storm has already begun to come about (just as Gorky's petrel, a bird which in Russian is called a *burevestnik*, a "storm-herald," is part of the storm, its outer frontline unit and reconnaissance agent).

Heidegger's "History of Being" sees only Events, not facts or incidents. The significance of historical Events is like the meaning of signs and things. Just as meaning is the articulated and differentiated meaning for outward expression, so is significance an event in its projection upon other events.

The connection between events in history is semantic, not causal, or more precisely, it is "significant," since the category of "causality" has application only within time, whereas the category of "significance," like "meaning," is outside of and above time.

Events form contexts, in which they fulfill the role of signs. They remain internally self-sufficient, but they are "drawn" towards each other (in semantic space) by greater events to which they are hierarchically subordinated (which they "enter," "become part of").

Signs obtain meaning only in context, from other signs. Events obtain significance only in history, from other Events.

Before the Turn, Heidegger already proceeded from the premise that a sign has meaning only in context. Now it bears clarifying that a word, as an Event, has meaning in and of itself, but has significance only in context.

Future Events might be significant for past Events to a greater or lesser extent, or vice versa. For example, the repentance of a sinner (as in the Biblical parable of the prodigal son) imparts meaning to past wanderings of the soul, i.e., it is significant for them; if there had been no repentance, they would remain meaningless. But the converse, i.e., that the repentance would obtain significance only from past sins, would not be true: repentance has its own, "irreducible" meaning whose context is broader than the sins preceding it.

The time of history is, once again, "intra-event time," and history itself is constituted by some great Event that opens up space for lesser Events to come about and become the subject of history. Therefore, history must have a beginning and an end — not because historians change or we lose interest in history, but because the event at the core of history is a whole, which means that it has its own limits. And we "historical people," moving within the time of a still greater Event, leave the Event of history through our own transformation, that is, death in the broad sense. Thus, history is fulfilled, which is to say that it is finished, for it has come about.

Heidegger endeavors to hermeneutically uncover the Events that lie at the core of, first, European history in general, and second, the history of the modern era ("New Time," *Neuzeit*) in particular.

Ereignis

In the modern German language, the word *Ereignis* means "event," and is synonymous with *Geschehen*, which means "event," "occurrence," "incident." This term drew Heidegger's attention because "event" pertains to history, and because "historicality," which the philosopher discovered in 1924 in the correspondence between Dilthey and Count Yorck, became a "guiding star" for Heidegger's philosophizing. Moreover, unlike *Geschehen*, *Ereignis* harbors the very significant root *Eignen*, which unites this word with a whole circle of words that share this root. In the lecture "On Time and Being" delivered in January 1962, Heidegger spoke of "bringing into view Being itself as an event." As always, Heidegger has to expend great effort on overcoming the ordinary metaphysical "hearing" of words: "In the phrase 'Being as Appropriation [Event],' the word 'as' now means: Being, letting-presence sent in Appropriation [Event], time extended in Appropriating [Eventing]. Time and Being appropriated in Appropriation [Event]."[278] Since Heidegger is here relying, even more so than in other cases, on the root *Eignen* ("appropriating," "owning") resounding in *Ereignis*, the Russian translation does not convey the "intrigue" at play in Heidegger's thinking, while the existing English translation outright puts "Appropriation" instead of "Event." In Russian, there is a potential interplay of meaning here between the word for "Being," *bytie*, and the word for "event," *sobytie* (*so-bytie*, "with-being," cf. *Mit-Sein*), which could also bring into play the Heideggerian notion

---
278 Heidegger, *On Time and Being*, 22; idem, *Vremia i bytie*, 404.

of "gathering" (*sobiranie*): "event" (*sobytie*) is "Being" (*bytie*) in gathering (*sobiranie*), i.e., "Being together." Since the term "event" occupies the place of the main subject of hermeneutic interpretation in the last period of Heidegger's works, this period is the most difficult to understand on the basis of translations. Here, Heidegger recognizes that "overcoming" is always conditioned by what is being overcome:

> To think Being without beings means: to think Being without regard to metaphysics. Yet a regard for metaphysics still prevails even in the intention to overcome metaphysics. Therefore, our task is to cease all overcoming, and leave metaphysics to itself. If overcoming remains necessary, it concerns that thinking that explicitly enters Appropriation [Event] in order to say It in terms of It about It.[279]

The term "event" has its own history in Heidegger's philosophizing: before *Ereignis* came to be put in the place of "Being" itself (as the subject of hermeneutics), Heidegger spoke of "events" in the "onto-history" (History of Being) of Western European mankind. The main "event" that has determined Europe's fate is the "oblivion of Being." The "events" of this history include the reconceptualization of the essence of truth in Plato's image of the cave, the victory of method that culminated in the philosophy of Modernity, the "death of God" in Nietzsche's philosophizing, and the "unbridling" of metaphysics amidst the dominance of modern European technology. Furthermore, we can also presume that Heidegger considered his own philosophy to be an expression of a certain "turn" in the onto-historical fate of the West, a turn towards thinking Being. It follows from the picture of the "History of Being" drawn by Heidegger that the "event" of Heidegger's philosophy wields significance of the same order as the event to which Plato's dialogues testify: the epoch of the dominance of metaphysics began back then, and now this era is ending. Western European history began back then, and now it is ending, passing into world history.

---

[279] Heidegger, *On Time and Being*, 24; *Vremia i bytie*, 406.

§3. The Emergence of Metaphysics and the Meaning of History

According to Heidegger, the very notion of history becomes possible only in the epoch of metaphysics, when Being (Event, *Ereignis*) has been forgotten, leaving only the collecting of exterior, secondary events ("incidents," *Geschehen*). Before the emergence of metaphysics, the main participants and creators of events were gods and heroes; in history, there are historical actors. Heroes know the omnipotence of the gods and follow their duty and nature, and even the gods follow the necessity of fate, whereas the actors of history carry out the expansion of their personality, which, if circumstances allowed, would be limitless. History is derivative of metaphysics (the oblivion of Being) because it is the indiscriminate collecting of accounts, which means that it does not take into account the ontological (existential, divine) dimension of events. History did not exist before metaphysics, for time was perceived in different perspectives, such as in the dimension of myths, legends, and tales.

For Heidegger, the beginning of history coincides with the "beginning of Europe." The essence of Europe is irreducible to geographical determinations, for it is an onto-historical category: the domain of space and the interlude of time are caught up in the whirl of the "Event of metaphysics" as the "oblivion of Being." For Heidegger, the "beginning of Europe" coincides both in time and in meaning with what Karl Jaspers defined as the "axial age" of world history. For Jaspers, the "axial age" is the moment of the emergence of history and is marked by three processes (or "Events" per Heidegger) which have defined the life of European mankind over the entire course of its history to the present. The main historical markers of the "beginning of Europe" (the "axial age") are:

- *in social life*: the collapse of the traditional tribal structures of society and their replacement by civil (legal) ones, a consequence of which was the formation of empires;
- *in religion*: the formation of monotheism, the crisis of ritual religion, and the development of the religion of moral self-consciousness;
- *in philosophy*: the emergence of metaphysics, the division between the speculative and sensory worlds, theoretical and practical orientations, and true knowledge and opinion;
- the emergence of *science* as a consequence of the metaphysical approach to comprehending actuality, the practical component of which, technology, emerges as a means of subjecting actuality to the metaphysical "project" (the "world picture").

The axial age is only the peak of the spiritual restructuring that took place in the three cultural centers of Eurasia – China, India, and Greece – all of which, however faintly, were engaged in interaction with each other. This spiritual restructuring initiated a shift in thought and in the conditions of material and social life. Over the course of 2,500 years, this movement spread and deepened to the point of becoming worldwide in breadth and conscious of its own essence in depth (in order to be conscious of the significance of the axial age, one needs to see it from a distance of 2,500 years).

The modern epoch also recognizes itself to be a new "axial age." Some have associated this with the astrological cycle of the procession of the Earth's axis (the past "axial age" coincided with the Spring Equinox entering the constellation of Pisces, whereas now it is entering the constellation of Aquarius). The significance of the threshold at which mankind stands now incomparably exceeds the "axial age" of antiquity, because never before in its history has mankind stood on the precipice of the real threat of the annihilation of life on the planet. Do we have any grounds for optimism? The emergence of the noosphere might, of course, proceed through various crises and turning points, but the logic of the development of nature suggests that development cannot break off on this level. In its actions henceforth, humankind on this planet must take into account not only momentary benefits, but far-reaching consequences and prospects, i.e., it must become the subject of planetary, cosmic, and self-consciousness. Mankind, awakening from the "oblivion of Being," must be conscious of its connection with all beings and its responsibility before them, and cease to be guided solely by whatever is "visible" on the surface of beings. Mankind must lead its life in accordance with the "call of Being." Of course, Heidegger does not clarify what expressions this might take on, since the event of the "oblivion of Being" is far from ending, and the "end of metaphysics" itself might make up an entire era, but in the depths of the onto-history of mankind, this event has already begun to yield to a new one. Accordingly, a new era has begun to "take the word" in the language of the "essential poets" and thinkers, and everyday human existence is inevitably tuning in to the "main tone" of the event resounding through it.

If history became possible only with the beginning of metaphysics, then it is obvious that the end of metaphysics should mean the "end of history." But, interpreting Heidegger's thought, in what sense can we speak of the "end of history"?

History is now ending because space-time has shrunk to such an extent that collecting data on events is no longer necessary, as an overwhelming amount of information and events are constantly bombarding humanity. On the other hand, the scale of events has become so fine-grained that even the death of the world will hardly hold as much significance for us as, for example, the Olympic Games did for the ancient Greeks.

Hence, it is necessary to take into consideration how the word "history" is used in several senses:

1. The past in general ("natural history," the history of the evolution of man, etc.).
2. The past as covered by written documentation (Jaspers).

3. History as a science that collects noteworthy facts and occurrences to satisfy the curiosity of future generations.
4. History as the unfolding of events, an unfolding which is not defined by man even though it consists of the sum of human actions ("getting caught up in history").
5. History as historical self-consciousness: man is conscious of himself in the context of a particular, unrepeatable era and is conscious of the impact of the past as well as the impact on the future.

History-1 cannot end as long as the world physically exists. History-2 cannot end because it does not exist "objectively," as it is a fiction of "historical consciousness." History-5 cannot end because it has not even begun for all people, only for rare thinkers who rise up to philosophically think the human past. History-3 and History-4 are tightly bound up with metaphysics because both proceed from the metaphysical preconception that an "event" is an instance, a fact, a recorded given that is accessible to all. However, *genuine and definitive Events are not universally accessible,* and yet it is these Events that are necessary to study first and foremost in order to understand the past. History-3 and History-4 will end when man wakes up, becomes conscious of the main Events, and becomes a conscious actor on this dimension, a "co-worker of evolution" (according to the Russian Cosmists, this is the main predestination of mankind, and its actualization is evolutionary inevitable).

What will become of the world after the end of history? Will it die? This, unfortunately, cannot be ruled out, but it is by no means predetermined by the end of history as such. Just as before the beginning of history, man will live in different dimensions of time (different forms of perceiving and experiencing time). Which dimensions? Heidegger leaves this question open.

§4. The Events of the History of Being and their Corresponding Epochs

1. The Beginning of Europe: Rethinking the Concept of "Truth" (*Aletheia*)

The concept of "truth" became one of the first objects of Heidegger's phenomenological interpreting on the basis of materials from various works of the Aristotelian corpus. This "concept" became the foundation for the corresponding "term" in Heidegger's hermeneutics. Heidegger began to think through this term in 1919, when he became Husserl's assistant and held, alongside lectures and seminars, a weekly circle that worked through Husserl's *Logical Investigations*. Heidegger writes that over the course of preparing for these sessions,

> I learned one thing — at first rather led by surmise than guided by founded insight: What occurs for the phenomenology of the acts of consciousness as the self-manifestation of phenomena is thought more originally by Aristotle and in all Greek thinking and existence as *aletheia*, as the unconcealedness of what-is present, its being revealed, its showing itself. That which phenomenological investigations rediscovered as the supporting attitude of thought proves to be the fundamental trait of Greek thinking, if not indeed of philosophy as such.[280]

Interpreting the Greek word for "truth" as "un-concealment" (*a-letheia*) is not justified from an etymological point of view. Instead, Heidegger approaches this word from a different point of view than that of scientific etymology. The latter proceeds from the ordinary metaphysical conviction that a word has an objective, inner structure reflecting the source and origin of the word which can be discovered insofar as one skillfully applies scientific critique. Heidegger does not claim to reveal a scientific etymology and objective

---

[280] Heidegger, "My Way to Phenomenology" in *Time and Being*, 79; idem, "Moi put' v fenomenologiiu", 207.

picture of the origin of the word. What is important to him is what semantic load the word *could have borne* in the thinking of the ancient Greeks. The word's participation in human thinking is often conditioned not by scientific etymology, but by its resounding and consonance alongside other words. In *aletheia* resounds *leta*, "concealing," and *a-*, its negation. Taken together, this consonance yields "unconcealment," "unhiddenness." It needs to be noted that Heidegger's interpretation of *aletheia* was guided from the very beginning by the developed phenomenological principle of the "self-manifestation of phenomenon," which was thereby "transferred" onto Greek soil. Such an interpretation of the Greek word subsequently turned out to be very fruitful and, on the whole, confirmed the intuitive insight that was initially unsubstantiated. Heidegger writes:

> The more decisively this insight became clear to me, the more pressing the question became: Whence and how is it determined what must be experienced as "the things themselves" in accordance with the principle of phenomenology? Is it consciousness and its objectivity or is it the Being of beings in its unconcealedness and concealment?[281]

Thus, it was a definitive rethinking of the old metaphysical concept of "truth" that ultimately led Heidegger to pose the question of "Being" instead of the "absolute consciousness" of phenomenology, to pose the task of constructing a "fundamental ontology," and to finally break with phenomenology.

The traditional understanding of "truth" as the correspondence between human concepts and actuality rotates within the sphere of the conceptual means of representation. *Aletheia*, unconcealment, is not achieved by concepts. Thus, out of the understanding of truth as unconcealment arises the demand for "undergoing an experience of Being" before and above any concepts. Thus arises the problem of "concealing and withdrawing": What is the cause of concealment, what

---

281 Ibid.

is this concealment, and how is it overcome? How did the transition from truth understood as "unconcealment" to the traditional metaphysical treatment of "correspondence," *adaequatio*, historically take place? The problem of the "concealing and withdrawing" of Being was already resolved before the Turn: in 1929, speaking of the "Nothing" in the same way he spoke about "Being" before, Heidegger wrote: "And yet [our] constant if ambiguous turning away from the nothing accords, within certain limits, with the most proper significance of the nothing. *In its nihilation the nothing directs us precisely toward beings.*"[282] Further: "the nothing is at first and for the most part distorted with respect to its originary character. How, then? In this way: We usually lose ourselves altogether among beings in a certain way."[283] In *On the Way to Language*, it is said that "nearness" bears a relation to "truth", for it is "that nearest nearness which we constantly rush ahead of, and which strikes us as strange each time anew when we catch sight of it. And which we therefore quickly dismiss again from view, to stay instead with what is familiar and profitable."[284] Man is constantly in a state of "two-foldedness," "captured by the ontological difference" between the ontic understanding of beings and the ontological grasping of Being. The "disposition-of-being" is such that "grasping" Being (or the "Nothing," "nearness," "unconcealment," etc.), in comparison to grasping beings, demands incomparably greater effort, for Being itself strives to evade, slip away, and conceal itself. The conceptual means of understanding to which man is ordinarily accustomed and which "too easily creeps into any experience" is not operative in ontological knowledge. The non-conceptual understanding, which does not rely on an unambiguous clarity of "concepts," demands that man himself put meaning into the words that might become "hints" pointing out the way to Being. The

---

282 Heidegger, "What is Metaphysics?" in *Pathmarks*, 92; idem, *Vremia i bytie*, 23. My italics.

283 Ibid.

284 Heidegger, *On the Way to Language*, 12; idem, GA 12, 94.

way is what stands in-between man and "grasping Being." The way not only demands man's own efforts in thinking, but also does not guarantee any result: moving along the pathway, man *might* discover something new, but everything depends on him alone, especially since this "path" has the form of a "hermeneutic circle" and is constantly returning to one and the same. Interpreting the "way" thus turns out to be inseparably linked to interpreting "truth," no less in relation to the difficulty of comprehending it. This is confirmed, among other places, in Heidegger's analysis of the moment in the history of thought when the decisive shift in the thinking of truth occurred. Heidegger sees this "pivot" in Plato's philosophy and its most definite expression in the *Republic*, in the famous "image of the cave." Heidegger's "Plato's Doctrine of Truth" is dedicated to interpreting this image.

Here, once again, the understanding of truth as "unconcealment," a concept Heidegger discovered long ago, is revealed: "The unhidden and unhiddenness designate at each point what is present and manifest in the region where human beings happen to dwell."[285] Truth thus turns out to be inseparably bound up with *man*. After all, it is man who establishes, like a center, the circle of all those things to which he "grants his presence." In Heidegger's early hermeneutics, this corresponds to the premise that only Dasein "has" meaning, while everything else "receives" meaning only insofar as Dasein has "attained understanding." The sphere of the "unhidden" is delineated by the limit of the reach of Dasein's "projecting" and "going beyond itself" in existing. Insofar as "Dasein is not *in possibility*, but existentially *is*," which is to say that the whole sphere of "projecting" is Dasein in its mode of existing, then truth as "unconcealment" belongs to the human essence.[286] The interpretation of the

---

[285] Martin Heidegger, "Plato's Doctrine of Truth," trans. Thomas Sheehan, in *Pathmarks*, 168; idem, *Vremia i bytie*, 351.

[286] Cf. Heidegger's interpretation of the dictum "Man is the measure of all things" in "The Age of the World Picture" in Martin Heidegger, *Off the Beaten Track*, trans./ed. Julian Young and Kenneth Haynes (Cambridge: Cambridge University Press, 2002).

Platonic "image of the cave" allows Heidegger to illuminate anew the problem of the "concealment" and "withdrawal" of that which is revealed in truth:

> But two factors are essential to the unhidden: not only does it in some way or other render accessible whatever appears and keep it revealed in its appearing, but it also constantly overcomes a hiddenness of the hidden. The unhidden must be torn away from a hiddenness of the hidden; it must in a sense be stolen from hiddenness. Originally for the Greeks hiddenness, as an act of self-hiding, permeated the essence of being and thus also determined beings in their presentness and accessibility ("truth"); and that is why the Greek word for what the Romans call *"veritas"* and for what we call "truth" was distinguished by the alpha-privative (ἀ-λήθεια). Truth originally means what has been wrested from hiddenness. Truth is thus a wresting away in each case, in the form of a revealing. The hiddenness can be of various kinds: closing off, hiding away, disguising, covering over, masking, dissembling.[287]

In the Platonic "image of the cave," concealment is depicted as the cave itself, which represents a determinate space of "unhiddenness" that is simultaneously demarcated from the rest of the world by its vaults. Heidegger believes that the "image of the cave" cannot be adequately and fully understood without employing the understanding of truth as "unconcealment." At the same time, however, the image itself shows that truth as *aletheia* no longer satisfies the needs of the cognitive mind. The circle of the "unhidden," in which beings might only open up the truth of their being to man, is here conceived as a cave enclosed on all sides. Indeed, Heidegger thinks, if Dasein constitutes the sphere of the reach of its "projection," then it can never escape this sphere, and therefore remains its prisoner. Everything that is incommensurate with Dasein will simply be "beyond" it, like the whole world for the prisoners of the cave in Plato's tale. There is an obvious, essential similarity here between

---

287 Heidegger, "Plato's Doctrine of Truth" in *Pathmarks*, 171; idem, *Vremia i bytie*, 353.

Heidegger's position up to the Turn and the view of truth held by the prisoners in the image of the cave. But it must be said that after the Turn, while retaining the main principle of understanding "truth" as "unconcealment," Heidegger made the position of human Dasein more "mobile": Dasein is constantly in a "hermeneutic relation to Being," "bears the tidings of Being," etc.

Heidegger associates the moment in which "truth" is reconceptualized from "disclosure" into the traditional metaphysical "correspondence" with the appearance of the principle of *paideia* in Plato's image of the cave. Paideia is the state of man's passage from one "sphere of the unhidden" to another one that is "more unhidden," "more true." For example, it is the passage from the shadows *to the things themselves* (in precise correspondence with Husserl's call to go "back to the things themselves"). Up to Plato (as well as for the early Heidegger), Dasein's attachment to and rootedness in its own "sphere of the unhidden" or "reach of its projection" seemed to be absolute. The image of the cave proclaims the possibility of passing from one sphere of unhiddenness to another, but this passage nevertheless turns out to be very difficult and even painful. Dasein's inner kinship with its "circle of the unhidden" is not disputed, but it follows that, in order to pass into the more unhidden, Dasein itself, in its very essence, must completely change. This change is carried out over the course of *"paideia."* Heidegger writes:

> The word does not lend itself to being translated. As Plato defines its essence, παιδεία means the περιαγωγή όλες της ψυχής, leading the whole human being in the turning around of his or her essence. Hence παιδεία is essentially a movement of passage, namely, from ἀπαιδευσία into παιδεία. In keeping with its character as a movement of passage, παιδεία remains always related to ἀπαιδευσία. The German word *Bildung* ["education," literally "formation"] comes closest to capturing the word παιδεία.[288]

---

[288] Heidegger, "Plato's Doctrine of Truth" in *Pathmarks*, 166; idem, *Vremia i bytie*, 350.

Here, "education" (*Bildung*) is understood in two senses: as "developing formation" and as "guidance in accordance with a certain model." Both *paideia* and *apaideusia* ("education"/"formedness" and "uneducatedness"/"unformedness") represent spheres of the unhiddenness of human Dasein on different stages of the path. Thus, *paideia* and "truth" turn out to be inseparably intertwined. Heidegger says even more:

> But if we are not satisfied with simply translating the words παιδεία and ἀλήθεια "literally," if instead we attempt to think through the issue according to the Greek way of knowing and to ponder the essential matter that is at stake in these translations, then straightaway "education" and "truth" come together into an essential unity.[289]

Instead of resorting to strong assertions, such as claiming an identity between the two, it would be more accurate to say that *paideia* combines two approaches to understanding "truth": the metaphysical one and the earlier one. However, it does not simply "combine" them, but rather describes their correlation within the scope of the whole process of "education" and, most importantly, leads to the conclusion of the priority of the metaphysical understanding of "truth" as "correspondence." The original understanding of truth as unconcealment, as we have already said, is present in *paideia* in the form of the alternating spheres of the "unhidden": the shadows in the cave, the reflections in the water, and, finally, the things themselves. In correspondence with this understanding of "truth," what is disclosed to man at each stage of "education" will be what is "true" to him at this stage, i.e., what is unhidden, what is truly a being to him, and so on — "true" in the full sense of the word, insofar as there can even be something of the sort. But the very presence of multiple stages, each with their own "unhiddennesses," already leads us to think of the limited nature of such an understanding of truth. Thus, there arises a readiness to

---

289 Ibid., 168; idem, *Vremia i bytie*, 351.

rethink truth, and Plato leads us to this rethinking: "And yet, even though ἀλήθεια is properly experienced in the 'allegory of the cave' and is mentioned in it at important points, nonetheless in place of unhiddenness another essence of truth pushes to the fore."[290] The very indication of the possibility of passing from one "sphere of the unhidden" to another was nothing new during the time the *Republic* was written. The sophists had developed subjectivist and skepticist views on the basis of this possibility. Of course, they did not recognize one "sphere of the unhidden" to be more true than another, but even if one permits the ascendant direction of *paideia*, then it still does not by any means follow that one determinate level of unconcealment will turn out to be the "final truth." Yet, according to Heidegger, it is for this sake that the tale of the cave was composed: to make glaringly obvious the premise that there is a *limited number* of rungs of "education." After man has beheld the things themselves, he gains the notion that the source of the visibility of forms, and the very capacity for sight, is the sun. The "Sun" in Plato's own interpretation of the image of the cave is the "idea of the good" (ἰδέα τοῦ ἀγαθοῦ). Heidegger translates this passage (*Republic* 517b8) thusly: "In the sphere of what can be known, the idea of the good is the power of visibility that accomplishes all shining forth and that therefore is properly seen only last, in fact it is hardly (only with great pains) really seen at all."[291] "Plato," Heidegger writes, "points to something unsaid, namely, that henceforth the essence of truth does not, as the essence of unhiddenness, unfold from its proper and essential fullness but rather shifts to the essence of the ἰδέα. The essence of truth gives up its fundamental trait of unhiddenness."[292] What is now foremost in the understanding of truth is "correctness of seeing." Heidegger translates Plato's words (*Republic* 515d3-4) as "and

---

290 Heidegger, "Plato's Doctrine of Truth," 172; idem, *Vremia i bytie*, 354.

291 Ibid., 174; idem, *Vremia i bytie*, 357.

292 Ibid., 176; idem, *Vremia i bytie*, 357.

thus turned to what is more in being, they should certainly see more correctly," and he turns to interpret:

> Nevertheless in a certain way Plato has to hold on to "truth" as still a characteristic of beings, because a being, as something present, has being precisely by appearing, and being brings unhiddenness with it. But at the same time, the inquiry into what is unhidden shifts in the direction of the appearing of the visible form, and consequently toward the act of seeing that is ordered to this visible form, and toward what is correct and toward the correctness of seeing. For this reason there is a necessary ambiguity in Plato's doctrine. This is precisely what attests to the heretofore unsaid but now sayable change in the essence of truth. The ambiguity is quite clearly manifested in the fact that whereas ἀλήθεια is what is named and discussed, it is ὀρθότης that is meant and that is posited as normative — and all this in a single train of thought.[293]

Heidegger sees in this "ambiguity" the "substitution of the essence of truth" that comes about in the "image of the cave." Of course, he does not pin the blame for this substitution on Plato himself: "Plato's thinking follows the change in the essence of truth, a change that becomes the history of metaphysics."[294] This "substitution" was only a consequence of the "event of the oblivion of Being" that came about at the time in the "onto-history" of Western European mankind.

It may still appear to be the case that Heidegger is "conditioned" by his "attitude" of "overcoming metaphysics" and therefore cannot see any positive, progressive moments in the metaphysical rethinking of "truth." But did this rethinking not make all of Western European history possible? Heidegger's philosophizing is historical and belongs to its epoch even when he is speaking of the ancient Greeks. Heidegger saw his own epoch as one of liberation from the metaphysical past, and it is in the context of this task that the Platonic "rethinking" of the essence of truth is spoken of as a departure from a more original, more truthful

---

293 Ibid., 177; idem, *Vremia i bytie*, 357.

294 Ibid., 181; idem, *Vremia i bytie*, 360.

understanding. Moreover, Heidegger's pointing to Plato's "image of the cave," and to Plato's philosophy as a whole, as a "turning point" in the understanding of truth, and thus as the "beginning of metaphysics," is not entirely accurate, for Heidegger himself first discovered the understanding of "truth" as "unconcealment" in Aristotle, who in logic is regarded as the author of the classical understanding of truth as correspondence. Yet, although the classical understanding of truth is indeed dominant in Aristotle, Heidegger's hermeneutic analysis revealed an "unreflected layer of terminology" in which "truth" is still understood in the sense of "unconcealment" (just as the metaphysical interpretation of "truth" as "correspondence," an inevitably legacy of tradition, might be revealed within Heidegger's own philosophizing). Before Plato, instances of the metaphysical understanding of truth might also be discerned in Socrates and in most of the Presocratics. Plato only expressed the transition from one understanding of truth to another in the most vivid and consistent way, which really does make his "image of the cave" the ideal object of interpretation.

In 1964, impressed by the substantive critique put forth by Ernst Tugendhat, Heidegger somewhat adjusted his understanding of truth as unconcealment, one of only a few of his views that did not undergo cardinal revision after the Turn. In the words of Karl-Otto Apel, Heidegger "admitted that he was wrong, before the 'Kehre' and after the 'Kehre', in identifying the disclosure or clearing of being with the original essence of truth. For, as Heidegger now declared, the clearing or uncovering of the meaning of being is 'not yet truth' but a condition of the possibility of true and of false propositions."[295] I think, however, that what is at stake

---

[295] Karl-Otto Apel, "My Intellectual Biography in the Context of Contemporary Philosophy" in idem, *Auf der Suche nach dem letzen Grund*, ed. Reinhard Hesse (Berlin: Lit Verlag, 2022), 101; idem, "*Moia intellektuel'naia biografiia v kontekste sovremennoi filosofii*" in V.V. Mironov (ed.), *Filosofiia bez granits* (Moscow: Vorob'ev AL, 2001), 35.

here is only a more adequate word usage. When it comes to the essence of understanding truth, nothing changed for Heidegger (otherwise he probably would not have made such a concession). Instead, the "clearing" is called "truth" because everything entering it and illuminated within it turns out to be "true," that is, it takes on the meaning of "existing" (or "essencing"). But for philosophers who are accustomed to thinking in metaphysical categories, it is absurd to call "truth" a "clearing" which in and of itself, seen apart from beings, is absolutely without content. But, according to Heidegger, the clearing cannot be torn away from beings, and thus beings always turn out as its "content." The clearing itself is both the truth of these beings in hermeneutic terms and, simultaneously, the "condition for the possibility of true and false propositions about beings" in metaphysical terms.

2. The Beginning of Modernity: The "Way"

The beginning of Modernity marks another one of the most important "events" in the onto-history of European mankind. Heidegger sees the essence of the "event" of Modernity in the establishment of the *dominance of method* in science, philosophy, and in all domains of spiritual life. Taking the metaphysical concept of "method" back to its "ontological ground," Heidegger thinks of method as a distorted form of the more primordial and profound principle of "way."

The term *Weg*, "way" or "path," can be encountered across Heidegger's works ever since his earliest period (for example, the section "Paths of Interpreting the Being-There of Dasein" in *Hermeneutics of Facticity*). It is possible that this word is encountered more often in Heidegger's works than in the works of many other authors, and this is to be expected, proceeding from the very problematic that his works treat. But Heidegger begins to obtain a philosophical substantiation of the term "way" within his hermeneutic framework only after his discovery of the "primordial" Greek understanding of truth and in connection with the task of gaining a non-conceptual experience of Being. In this experience, there can be no final clarity: Being always strives to evade, and the wayfarer must set off in its direction again and again. The principle of "way," of moving along, has an inner kinship with hermeneutics. Hermeneutics is a method, that is, a certain way — e.g., moving around the hermeneutic circle, the "way of questioning." But the sciences and "scientific philosophy" also have "method." Modernity as a whole maintains a holy faith in the potency of method. Already in the 17th century, Francis Bacon reflected the mood of the onsetting era when he praised method for allowing a scientist to achieve reliable results regardless of his personal abilities.[296] His was the age of the development of manufacturing and technology, the beginning of the mechanization of labor. Artisanal craft, where everything depended on the personal skill of the creator (the "demiurge") could not hold out against the competition posed by the technological development of manufacturing. From that point on, technology accomplished gigantic successes, and along with them our faith in method was ultimately strengthened.[297] Heidegger discusses the dominance of method in modern science by drawing on Nietzsche's testimony (in *The Will to Power* §466, §469): "It is not the victory of *science* that distinguishes our nineteenth

---

[296] "Our method of discovery in the sciences is designed not to leave much to the sharpness and strength of the individual talent; it more or less equalises talents and intellects. In drawing a straight line or a perfect circle, a good deal depends on the steadiness and practice of the hand, but little or nothing if a ruler or a compass is used. Our method is exactly the same." Francis Bacon, *The New Organon*, ed. Lisa Jardine and Michael Silverthorne (Cambridge: Cambridge University Press, 2000), I. LXI.

[297] "Method here does not signify the tool, with the aid of which scientific research elaborates the thematically delimited domain of its objects. Method rather means the manner in which any domain of objects to be researched has been delimited in advance according to its objectivity. The method is the anticipatory blueprint of the world... Method signifies the victorious challenging of the world for its thoroughgoing availability to mankind." Martin Heidegger, "The Provenance of Art and the Destination of Thought (1967)," trans. Dimitrios Latsis, ed. Ulrich Haase, *Journal of the British Society for Phenomenology* 44:2 (2013), 122-123; idem, *Raboty i razmyshleniia raznykh let*, 285.

century, but the victory of scientific *method* over science... The most valuable insights are gained last of all; but the most valuable insights are the *methods*."²⁹⁸ In the second of the three lectures that make up the work *On the Way to Language*, Heidegger thinks of the dominance of method in the terms of his philosophizing:

> The sciences know the way to knowledge by the term "method." Method, especially in today's modern scientific thought, is not a mere instrument serving the sciences; rather, it has pressed the sciences into its own service... In the sciences, not only is the theme drafted, called up by the method, it is also set up [*hereingestellt*] within the method and remains within the framework of the method, subordinated to it. The furious pace at which the sciences are swept along today — they themselves don't know whither — comes from the speed-up drive of method with all its potentialities, a speed-up that is more and more left to the mercy of technology.²⁹⁹

In modern European science, based as it is on metaphysics, method is part of the "fore-structure," the "projection" that determines the course and results of scientific cognition. In terms of practical results and the transformation of actuality, the possibilities afforded by method are enormous. However, the assessment of whether the achieved results are truly positive is still, to this day, carried out by society and by scientists themselves only "from the point of view of beings," that is, in the ontic rather than ontological sense, lacking a "preliminary grasp of Being." If we translate Heidegger into the language of contemporary global problems, then the greatest "successes" that science has achieved through method would, in the end, prove to be the most dangerous, due to the impossibility of foreseeing all the consequences of such "successes."'" As a result, "fate is left to the mercy of technology": the greatest possibilities offered by modern technology are not thought through in their "disposition-of-

---

298 Heidegger, *On the Way to Language*, 74; idem, GA 12, 168.
299 Ibid.

being," in their relation to the place that they should occupy in the life of the Earth, in terms of the end which they are meant to serve. Technology is increasingly spiraling out of control, generating unforeseen consequences.

But method is still a "way," and hermeneutics is, above all, a method, which confirms Nietzsche's words on the dominance of method. Therefore, Heidegger had to confront the task of distancing himself from the traditional, metaphysical understanding of "method" and provide a new interpretation of it as "way." "In thinking," Heidegger says, "the situation is different from that of scientific representation. In thinking there is neither method nor theme, but rather the region, so called because it gives its realm and free reign to what thinking is given to think. Thinking abides in that country, walking the ways of that country."[300] This "region" is one of the "poetico-philosophical" images that Heidegger uses in order to convey thoughts which are otherwise inexpressible in metaphysical "concepts." This "region" is such that being positioned within it constitutes a "disposition-of-being," and it is within this "region" that the "events" of "onto-history" occur. Traversing one or another path or "way" through this region means gaining a certain experience of Being. "To undergo an experience with something means that this something, which we reach along the way in order to attain it, itself pertains to us, meets and makes its appeal to us, in that it transforms us into itself."[301] Heidegger speaks in his style of "*Unterwegs-sein*," "being-on-the-way," "being-upon-a-path." This understanding of "way" obviously exhibits the influence of the image of *paideia* from Plato's tale of the cave, not in the "metaphysical" part of the dual meaning of this image in Heidegger's interpretation, but in the more original meaning, where *paideia* is understood as "leading man into changing his soul." Like Plato's *paideia*, Heidegger's "way" lies not in a simple passage from one place to another, but in the change

---

300 Ibid.

301 Ibid., 73-74; idem, GA 12, 167.

of the whole being of man with every step.³⁰² However, if Plato's *paideia* is directed from less true "regions" to more true ones, specifically in the original sense of truthfulness as *aletheia*, then Heidegger's "way" is more horizontal: what is important is not the result, not the region into which the path leads us, but the movement itself, as well as what is revealed in moving along the path. In Plato, the image of the "path" is the prisoners' rising up out of the cave of ignorance, whereas in Heidegger it is the country road along which the peasant farmer carries along his heavily loaded cart. In both cases, the image of the way is a reflection of a certain foundational trait of philosophizing: in the first case, it is striving beyond beings ("physics") towards the Absolute, that is, metaphysics; in the second case, it is philosophically thinking through what is most ordinary, everyday, and commonplace.

Furthermore, as Heidegger's hermeneutics underwent transformation from an auxiliary method into the foundation upon which philosophizing proper unfolds, the "way" ("method") gains an "ontological" meaning. Heidegger correlates his understanding of "way" with the Chinese *Tao*:

> All is way. These lectures make their way within the neighborhood of poetry and thinking, underway on the lookout for a possibility

---

302 In *Unterwegs zur Sprache*, in a passage omitted from the English edition (*On the Way to Language*, 92), we find a typical example of how Heidegger bases his interpretation in dialectal variations of the German language: "*Sonst verstehen wir bewegen im Sinne von: bewirken, daß etwas seinen Ort wechselt, zu- oder abnimmt, überhaupt sich ändert. Be-wëgen aber heißt: die Gegend mit Wegen versehen. Nach altem Sprachgebrauch der schwäbischalemannischen Mundart kann »wëgen« besagen: einen Weg bahnen, z. B. durch tief verschneites Land. Wëgen und Be-wëgen als Weg-bereiten und Weg als das Gelangenlassen gehören in denselben Quell- und Strombereich wie die Zeitwörter: wiegen und wägen und wogen.*": "We otherwise ordinarily understand moving [*bewegen*] in the following sense: to cause something to change its place, to rise or fall, or to generally change. However, 'to move' [*Be-wëgen*] also means to make a way through the region. According to the olden usage of the Swabian-Alemannic dialect, 'to move [along a path]' [*wegen*] means to make a way, i.e., to clear a path through land covered in deep snow. 'Moving' [*Wegen und Bewegen*] as 'preparing a way' [*Weg-bereiten*] and 'way' [*Weg*] as a 'letting pass' [*Gelangenlassen*] belong to the same root and stream [in the sense of 'language tradition'] as the verbs *wiegen* ['to sway'], *wagen* ['to dare'], and *wogen* ['to be worried']."

of undergoing an experience with language... The way allow us to reach what concerns us, in that domain where we are already staying... because where we already are, we are in such a way that at the same time we are not there, because we ourselves have not yet properly reached what concerns our being, not even approached it.[303]

The neighborhood that is spoken of here is nearness in a certain relation, that between poetry and thinking, as already discussed above, and the task of "undergoing an experience of language" corresponds to the earlier task of a "non-conceptual grasp of Being." But what is foremost that is said in this phrase about "way" concerns Being. Heidegger here affirms the two-fold, simultaneously immanent and transcendent character of Being. On the one hand, the being of beings, including the being of man as a "special kind of being," is inseparable from what "is." If Being is simply taken away from a being, everything would simply disappear. But we, in some sense, "are not" there, that is, we "are not" by Being, because we have not yet neared that which "concerns our being." In what sense are we alienated from our own being, and how can we come close to it? After all, according to Heidegger, this is the essence of the "way." Simply explaining everything in terms of the finitude of human cognitive capacity would be unjustified haste. Heidegger says that "at the same time we are not there," although he could have said that "even though we are always already there, we *do not know* that we are." This replacement of a cognitive relation, which has its own grounds, with an ontological one ("do not know" vs. "are not") is no merely deliberate contradiction (that we simultaneously "are" and "are not" near Being). Such a replacement has grounds in the logic of the development of Heidegger's thought, although this logic is hidden here. Let us recall that in *Being and Time*, similar expressions speak of Dasein in the existential of "projection": "It is existentially that which it is *not yet* in its potentiality of being." That is, the possibilities that Dasein constitutes in going beyond

---

[303] Heidegger, *On the Way to Language*, 92-93; idem, GA 12, 187.

its "actual" self into the world existentially belong to the essence of Dasein, i.e., Dasein "is" these possibilities. In *Being and Time*, these possibilities play an important role, but not the leading one. Over the course of developing this notion, Heidegger arrived at the thought of the "quiet *power of the possible*" and "being-possibility" (*Möglich-sein*), whereby the "ontological" examination of Dasein becomes more "existential." Thus, a change occurs, as always, without loud declarations, in the design of Heidegger's philosophizing: instead of Dasein constantly going beyond itself, to the forefront now emerges *Sein*, Being, in its twofold nature, which prevents any transcending. In the wake of the context of *Being and Time* and Heidegger's arrival at a new understanding of "Being as twofoldness," we can draw a tentative conclusion as to the character of how we both "are" and "are not" near Being: as finite human beings, we "are not" by Being *in actuality*; but *in possibility*, to the contrary, we "are" always there. We need only issue the caveat that "possibility" and "actuality" here are not ordinary modalities of judgements, but the "onto-characteristics of Dasein" ("the possibility of Dasein to be something or do something"). Against the ordinary understanding of the "actual" as something with more weight and significance than the "possible" which has yet to come about, Heidegger puts the "possible" in the first place: the "possible" is the source that grants or does not grant actuality to beings; it is not possibilities that are conditioned by a present state of affairs, but, to the contrary, everything that "is a being" is rooted in *Möglich-sein*, "being-possibility," at all times drawing only a small part of that which is already inlaid in the possible.

All of this defines the Heideggerian understanding of the essence of "way" as a "way towards Being": every step on the "way" is the "coming-to-be" of some possibility, and man himself, as an actual being, is the totality of such steps along the "way." With every step, man "nears" *Möglich-sein*, but the possible is inexhaustible, and therefore, the way to it can have no end. At the same time, the possible is the entire "region" which Dasein's way traverses. Thus, in some sense, man "is" not only "near" Being, but "is" also *in* Being."

3. The Event of the "Conclusion of Metaphysics"

"Being" is the main category (but not "concept") of the entirety of Heidegger's philosophizing. As we have seen, posing the problem of Being at the center of the problematic of hermeneutics appeared to Heidegger to be one of the consequences of rethinking "truth" from "correspondence" to "unconcealment": Being is that which is the ground of "unconcealment," but how this is so only became clearer to Heidegger later on. The question of "Being" is the main metaphysical question ("Why are there beings at all rather than Nothing?"), and "Being" is the most "metaphysical" of all metaphysical categories, bound up with metaphysics both in its origin and for all of history. From the very beginning, Heidegger makes "Being" the subject of hermeneutic consideration in order to communicate the hermeneutic status of his own philosophizing. But, as it turned out, overcoming the metaphysical heritage of this concept ("metaphysical" in the traditional sense) is practically impossible. Heidegger admitted that he tried to overcome metaphysics and the metaphysical legacy of the word — "neither a destruction nor even a denial of metaphysics" — but that he did not find it, for "how is one to give a name to what he is still searching for?"[304] In order to introduce an element of "liveliness" and "concreteness" into his doctrine of "Being," Heidegger often speaks of Dasein, life, and existence in the ontological context by analytically dividing the word into *Da*, "here," and *Sein*, "Being." Soon after *Being and Time*, Heidegger was inclined to call the main subject of hermeneutics "Nothing," and then, simultaneously in different contexts, he called such "language" (as the "house of Being"), "twofoldness," and "presencing." After the Turn, Heidegger distanced himself from the metaphysical tradition to so far of an extent that

---

304 Heidegger, *On the Way to Language*, 20; idem, GA 12, 105.

he once again considered it possible to use the metaphysical category of "Being," and he employed such as the object of altogether fruitful interpretation.

We have already characterized in broad strokes the interpretation of Being as simultaneously immanent and transcendent to human Dasein, as the "being-possibility" that "quietly reigns" in the domain of beings. Now, let us dwell on some important expressions for hermeneutic philosophy which contain the category of "Being."

"Being," Heidegger says, means "the presence of present beings, the two-fold of the two in virtue of their simple oneness."[305] Here "presence" corresponds to "Being" and along with "present beings" composes the "ontological difference," which is here called "the two-fold." "Presence" names the being of beings in their unconcealment and "unhiddenness" to man. "Presence" and "unhiddenness" are almost identical, as both are constituted by human Dasein and constitute the circle of its "lifeworld," its "reality." But "unhiddenness" names Being as that which should be "wrested out of concealment," in a sense "kidnapped," whereas the truth of Being tries to evade and conceal itself. Dasein figures here as the active subject of cognition, and Being as its object. "Presence" is interpreted by Heidegger in a completely different way: it is not that man strives to "grasp" Being, but Being that "needs" man. Why? For What?

> Man *is* really as man when needed and used by...what calls on man to preserve the two-fold...which, as far as I can see, cannot be explained in terms of presence, nor in terms of present beings, nor in terms of the relation of the two... Because it is only the two-fold itself which unfolds the clarity, that is, the clearing in which present beings as such, and presence, can be discerned by man... by man who by nature stands in relation to, that is, is being used by, the two-fold... for the two-fold is not an object of mental representations, but is the sway of usage.[306]

---

305 Ibid., 30; idem, GA 12, 116.

306 Ibid., 32-33; idem, GA 12, 119.

The "two-fold" of presence and presencing beings is at once the duality of Being and beings and, in some way, Being itself, as we have already heard that Being is "the presence of present beings, the two-fold of the two in virtue of their simple oneness." Giving a "clearly intelligible" interpretation of "the two-fold" is very difficult, since this term itself is the furthest removed from the "clarity" of metaphysical concepts. Such "unclear intelligibility" is originally inlaid in this term itself as a stimulus for the reader-listener's independent thinking. How can man "preserve the two-fold"? What endangers it, and how? What "clearing" (*Erlichtung*) opens up the two-fold so that man can first therein discern presence (Being) and what is presencing (beings)? Finally, what is the "sway of usage"?

According to Heidegger, the "human role" in ontology remains insufficiently studied to this day. The peculiarity of man as a being among other beings and yet as a "special kind" of being lies in that man alone is capable of "going out" in existing beyond beings as a whole towards Being, which is identical to Nothing. This is the "being held out into the Nothing" that is intrinsic to man, the experience of "primordial angst," etc. Evidently, it is thanks to this "twofoldness" that man stands in a special relation to Being: the twofoldness of Being and beings is upheld exclusively in the act of man's existing. Apart from man's existing, no other two-fold can be: all other beings are incapable of standing in relation to beings as whole, and Being itself is transcendent to human knowledge. The question as to why Being has any relation to beings is just as difficult as the tricky question of theology: Why did God create the world? Heidegger avoids this problem by attributing the twofoldness of Being and beings to Being itself. If this is the case, then Being (as twofoldness) is "founded" only by man in the act of transcending beings. Does this then mean that the pledge of the being of beings belongs to man? No: the twofold that man founds is what first makes man human, for Being and man are inseparably interconnected, almost identical, or, more accurately, are distinguishable "moments" of one and the same principle of "twofoldness."

What endangers this twofold? Obviously, the only danger is that man himself might "forget Being" and completely give himself up to beings. But does the two-fold thereby disappear? No, for man does not simply cease to be human, and this means that he is crucified between the poles of Being and beings. As has already been said, being-possibility does not depend on man and is beyond him, but man is also needed by Being so that he might go out on the "way" and, with each step, bring one or another possibility into being. To this end, man must constantly dwell in the "clearing of Being" (in its original meanings in the German language, *Erlichtung* also means "glade," that is, an actual "forest clearing"). The "clearing" of Being is the region in which the way of thinking traverses without "concepts"; at the same time, it is the state of man discerning Being and beings without being entirely submerged in beings. Only in this state does man "find his way," and only in this way can man take a beingful step.

But why such a narrow "clearing" of Being rather than a "sphere" or something else? Light can take on the form of a ray in two ways: either due to objective obstacles that redirect and focus it in a given direction, or due to the restricted vantage point of the viewer. The light of any star in the night sky can fill the entire dark space of the sky, but it might be visible to us only as a thin, needle-point beam. Clearly, this size does not reflect the breadth of the spread of light or the magnitude of its source; rather, it reflects only the narrowness of our sight and our distance from the light. Likewise, the "clearing of Being" opens up to us as a thin, subtle beam of light within the horizon of beings only on account of our extremely distant "thrownness," our far-flung a-partness from Being, yet this light fills and brings out all beings.

In the German language, "presence" sounds thusly: *Anwesenheit*. "*Anwesenheit*" contains "*Anwesen*," which means "small homestead," "allotment." Being as "presence" as such (*Anwesenheit*) "wants" to be presencing (*anwesen*) with-in man, to have in him a caretaker who can cultivate the "field of Being" and gather its fruits.

> Thinking is not a means to gain knowledge. Thinking cuts furrows into the soil of Being. About 1875, Nietzsche once wrote (*Grossoktav* WW XI, 20): "Our thinking should have a vigorous fragrance, like a wheatfield on a summer's night." How many of us today still have the senses for that fragrance?[307]

Yet, all the while as man remains overly subjected to the influence of beings and only in rare moments stands up into the "clearing of Being," Being still constantly turns and addresses its "call" to man.

§5. Interpreting Hölderlin's Poetry

In conclusion, for the sake of presenting an example of the "mytho-poetic" thinking in Heidegger's later works, let us examine his interpretations of several poetic fragments by Hölderlin, all of which are brought together by the search for the poetically thought and poetically expressed *essence of poetry*. Over the course of this interpreting, Heidegger makes a number of important philosophico-historical summations concerning the "conclusion of metaphysics."

Heidegger selects five "key verses" from among Hölderlin's poems, that is, five "keys" which most fully draw out the contours of the essence of poetry, and presents them in his lecture "Hölderlin and the Essence of Poetry."

1. Composing poems: "This most innocent of occupations." (Ill, 377)

---

307 Heidegger, *On the Way to Language*, 70; idem, GA 12, 163.

2. "That is why language, the most dangerous of goods, has been given to man... so that he may bear witness to what he is..." (IV, 246)
3. "Much has man experienced,
Named many of the heavenly ones,
Since we have been a conversation
And able to hear from one another." (IV, 343)
4. "But what remains is founded by the poets." (IV, 63)
5. "Full of merit, yet poetically, man dwells on this earth." (VI, 25)[308]

At the outset, a few words are in order regarding the new understanding of the hermeneutic method and the hermeneutic circle at which Heidegger has evidently arrived over the course of his deep meditations on Hölderlin's poetic works. The hermeneutic circle means that any text can be understood only on the basis of a pre-understanding. But *this pre-understanding is in no way bound to the text itself*; therefore, it cannot be evaluated as adequate or inadequate until the interpretation has produced some kind of results. Over the course of the interpreting, however, the pre-understanding changes, becomes understanding, and then it is already pointless to evaluate the pre-understanding, except perhaps retrospectively, as a case of reflecting on the history of the interpretation.

Pre-understanding is always subjective, always individual, and even personal. Its necessity for interpretation shows the need for "subjectivity," and hence a subject, for *beginning* the path of interpretation. But the latter is needed only as a "launch mechanism," only to then "die," "removing" oneself in the interpreting and passing from pre-understanding to understanding, giving birth to a new "subject."

Here it seems to me that Heidegger is overcoming metaphysics in a much deeper way than Foucault and Deleuze

---

308 Heidegger, *Elucidations of Hölderlin's Poetry*, 51; idem, *Raz'iasneniia k poezii Gel'derlina*, trans. G.B. Notkin (Saint Petersburg: Academic Project, 2003), 64-65.

with their "death of the subject." In the latter, the "death of the subject" is merely a polemically sharpened expression of the "relativization" of the subject, depriving it of the status of original principle and translating it into an array of derivative concepts.

The subject is nothing more than a point of view, one among infinitely many possible perspectives. Nevertheless, perhaps it is such precisely because it possesses an irreplaceable value. *Without a subject, without a point of view, there would be no seeing*, no experiencing, and hence no experience. A point of view not only constitutes the domain of what is discernible (cf. German *vernehmbar*, Russian *vniatnoe*) and unconcealed, but allows everything to *come about*, to be illuminated within this domain. *The unity of the Event is constituted by the point of view (the subject).*

The space which a path traverses, the "region of the poetic country," is a *space that consists of possible "points of view."* Traversing a path in this region means changing one's point of view, changing oneself.

A point of view does not simply establish a "horizon of visibility" for a given subject, as if it were a horizon of space visible to sight. Every point of view constitutes its own world, one that is infinite in its spatial, temporal, and semantic relations. It is an integral *Event of World*, in which there is room for all gods and demons, all people and all living things, even if this world is of the smallest essence (a "simple monad" per Leibniz). Changing a point of view always means founding a new world, a new Event of World.

Thus, once again, in following Heidegger around the "hermeneutic circle," we arrive at an awareness of the *kinship of thinking and poetry*. Just like the poet, the philosopher cannot produce any grounds for his "pre-understanding" or for the interpretation subsequently built thereupon. Thinking turns out to be just as (seemingly) *arbitrary* and just as (essentially) *unarbitrary* as poetry. In its essence, metaphysics harbors a fear of arbitrariness and has always tried to find a law and measure for it. Just like poetry, thinking finds grounds for its arbitrariness in "authenticity" (*Eigentlichkeit*) and "essentiality" (*Wesentlichkeit*), in the depths of the experience that is accessible in the Event of a given point of view and a given subject, in the clarity of "seeing" that illuminates the essence and meaning of that which is coming about. *Essence and meaning* alone are what can be conveyed from one point of view to another, from one subject to another. Neither the philosopher nor the poet, nor anyone else, can share the "matter" of their experience with a reader or listener. Even the most detailed and vivid story cannot attain this goal. But if an experience really did *come about*, and really did become "*my own*," and myself "its own," then the resounding of the Event alone is what can be *heard* by others.

Now let us move on to examining the five keys in the lecture on "Hölderlin and the Essence of Poetry."

1. "*Poetry is the most innocent of occupations*" — this is so, because poetry lives and has power only in the world of its own imagination. Although imagination turns out to be of far greater gravity than it ordinarily seems (cf. key 4), what could be safer than ordinary poetic language? This is an expression of a "non-reflective" point of view, analogous to the phenomenological "natural attitude" in relation to poetry and language in general. Hölderlin wrote this not in a poem, but in a letter to his mother, which lends ground to thinking that he probably simply wanted to assuage her, for mothers always deeply feel any danger that threatens their children. The ensuing poetic indications lead Heidegger from this "natural attitude" to a completely different, hermeneutic comprehension of the essence of language and poetry, their danger and safety. But a path that has been traversed remains only part of the way, like ascending a mountain — even beginning the ascent from the valley is part of the heights that we reach with our last step. Just like the mountain's inseparability from the valley, the "natural" understanding

281

of language always remains with the poet. Yet, in this twofoldness lies the source of the danger of the *fall*.

2. Hölderlin's second indication says that language is "the most dangerous of goods." Why? In order to understand the idea expressed by Hölderlin, we need to answer three questions:

(1). To whom does this good belong? That is: Who is man? "He is the one who must bear witness to what he is... Man is *he* who he is precisely in the attestation of his own existence."[309] This "bearing witness," "testifying," or "attesting" (*Bezeugung*) is what constitutes the essence of man. By his very way of being, man is a sign, a "bearing witness" or "signifying" (*Zeugesein*). In its essence, a sign is what sends attention to something other than itself, to what is being signified. This can be expressed in the formula: *Man is the generally significant being*. He is insofar as he participates in "drawing attention" between the earthly and the heavenly, the divine and the mortal (the Fourfold). According to Heidegger, "To bear witness can signify to testify, but it also means to be answerable for what one has testified in one's testimony."[310] According to Hölderlin, man testifies to his belonging to the earth.

It is interesting to compare Heidegger's thesis here to the views of the Postmodernists (such as Deleuze). They would agree that the being of man (like everything else) is akin to a sign, Heidegger's *Zeugesein*, but they would deny, firstly, that man is *answerable* for what he signifies. *Who* could answer for such? After all, there is no such subject that is itself subject to freedom and responsibility. Secondly, they would disagree that man testifies to *something,* much less to belonging to the earth. For them, there is only a network of signs and the thoughts flailing around therein, and the latter does not refer to anything — or, more precisely, it does not

---

309 Heidegger, *Elucidations of Hölderlin's Poetry*, 54.
310 Ibid.

refer (as a sign) to anything but other signs. Behind signs stand other signs and nothing else. The early Heidegger was close to this position. The *Verweisungszusammenhang*, the "context of references," and the being of signs themselves, without any presupposed signified, have now been replaced by the supra-human, supra-lingual, as well as pre-lingual being of "earth." Man's "attestation" refers to the earth and is answerable to the earth by its sign-being: if it fares poorly in drawing attention to Being, then it takes up different signs, and *man simply loses his individual being*.

(2). Why is language the most dangerous? Language by nature is common and manifold, but, according to Heidegger, this does not mean that it is a means for expressing and conveying thought. Language simply always exists in the form of one or another speech, and speech is audible to many others, but these "many others" are not always ready to hear the depth of meaning in speech, that is, the Event. Therefore, speech (language) is always a struggle, an effort, and essential thought insists on its right to being essential (*Wesentlichsein*), while superficial speaking opposes it to the extent of its power. Thus, Hölderlin was fully conscious of this eternal struggle and the danger bound up with it, as is reflected in his verses:

> For a fragile vessel is not always able to hold the divine gift,
> Only at times can man bear it.[311]

Already overtaken by madness, the poet wrote in a letter to a friend: "The mighty element, the fire of the heavens and the stillness of men, their life in nature, and their confinedness and their contentment, moved me continually, and as one says of heroes, I can well say of myself that Apollo has struck me."[312] Heidegger adds: "Excessive brightness drove the poet into darkness. Do we need any further testimony in regard

---

311 [Translated from the Russian edition: *Raz'iasneniia k poezii Gel'derlina*, 95-95. Cf. the alternative translation in Heidegger, *Elucidations of Hölderlin's Poetry*, 65].

312 Ibid., 62; idem, *Raz'iasneniia k poezii Gel'derlina*, 86-87.

to the extreme danger of his 'occupation'? The poet's own fate tells us everything."³¹³

Evidently, no single philosophical current can ever be regarded as superficial. Rather, any philosophical current might become superficial when the fire of creation, the effort and struggle over truth (the struggle with nature's striving to "hide itself"), leaves it. Superficial thinkers can be found among the followers of any philosophy.

(3). *Why is language a "good" that, as it were, has been "given" or "inherited"?* As we already saw in discussing the correlation between word and thing in the case of Stefan George's poem "The Word," it is the name alone that first lets the essence of a thing be rooted in Being. In this lies the "good" or "gift" of language: the founding of being(s) in the word. But man himself also exists "by way of the being of a sign," and he must testify to his belonging to the Fourfold — it is to this end that he is given language. That is, the second "gift" of language and the "good" gifted by it is what is properly human in man. Heidegger writes: "Language is a good in a more primordial sense. It holds good for the fact that man can *be* as historical, i.e., it guarantees that. Language is not a tool at man's disposal, but that primal event which disposes of the highest possibility of man's being."³¹⁴

3. *"Since we have been a conversation..."* Heidegger writes: "Man's being is grounded in language; but this actually occurs only in *conversation* [Gespräch]."³¹⁵ In this conversation, "being able to talk and being able to hear are co-original... We are a conversation, that always also signifies we are *one* conversation [*ein Gespräch*]."³¹⁶ For Heidegger, the lines "Much has man experienced, named many of the heavenly

---

313 Heidegger, *Elucidations of Hölderlin's Poetry*, 62; idem, *Raz'iasneniia k poezii Gel'derlina*, 86-87.

314 Ibid., 56; idem, *Raz'iasneniia k poezii Gel'derlina*, 74-75.

315 Ibid.

316 Ibid., 57; idem, *Raz'iasneniia k poezii Gel'derlina*, 75.

ones" mean that "it is precisely in the naming of the gods and in the world becoming word that authentic conversation, which we ourselves are, consists."[317] The gods ask for us and ask from us, claiming us: "A word which names the gods is always an answer to such a claim."[318] This is to say that the relation to the gods and naming them is in some essential way inlaid in the nature of man; it is the "human" in him.

But who are the gods? Has Heidegger given in to the temptation of his mythopoetic "tale-telling" to construct some kind of new theology in the spirit of neo-paganism? The word "gods" has a tradition of usage that is even more ancient and even more prevalent than the word "Being," and yet Heidegger resolves to bring it into his interpretation, evidently believing that it is utterly impossible to bypass it. Of course, based on what we already know of Heidegger's hermeneutics, we can confidently presume that these "gods" are not to be understood as "persons," "beings," or "substances," as anything "real in itself." Rather, the gods are part of that "magical country" of poetic reality. Strictly speaking, man himself, as a poet, creates the gods, but he is at the same time dependent upon them, for only in this creative naming of the gods does man become human.

The gods are the "rays of the light of Being" overflowing and pouring forth from the "Holy," *das Heilige*. "The Holy" is nature in its beingful dimension, and the gods are the bearers and expression of its power, *das Machtende selbst*, the "Self-Ruling." The gods are living, cheerful, joyful forces that inhabit the "clearing of Being," the personification of the creative, destructive, rhythmic movements of nature. But the "creation of their face," giving them a guise and a glorious name, is the work of the poet and of every human. It is the act of answering the gods' claim, becoming the conductors of their power in the world of beings. This participation in their divine game (which closely resembles the Hindu notion of

---

317 Ibid., 58; idem, *Raz'iasneniia k poezii Gel'derlina*, 78-79.
318 Ibid.

līlā) involves filling the vessel of the divine name with glory, dignity, and nobility, and taking communion from this vessel.

4. *"But what remains is founded by the poets."* Here, once again, the *significance of the imagination* is affirmed: Being and essence can never be derived from any available (superficial) phenomenon, for they must be freely co-created, founded, and offered up as a gift in poetic saying.

What was previously considered to be the "weakness" or frivolousness of poetry, i.e., its "restriction" to an imaginal world, now comes back around as its strength. Heidegger thereby indirectly confirms anew the conclusion he had drawn in his *Kant and the Problem of Metaphysics* lectures, namely, that Kant's main discovery, along with the thing-in-itself, was the power of the imagination. Only the imagination raises man above the level of phenomena and gives him access to "things-in-themselves."[319] Although it molds its images from the present material of sensibility according to the patterns of the categories of reason, the imagination is *completely free* in its combining of both of the latter and therefore presents the most direct of all the expressions of an *intelligible character* that are presently available to us, and it is therefore a bearer of freedom. Only from the noumenal freedom of the productive imagination can we glean the pre-understanding that is necessary for understanding the world *before* any contact with it — such is the measure, the essentiality, the "condensation points" around which sensuality as well as the forms of rational concepts "precipitate." Imagination is the "regal capacity" of the soul, for it is with the imagination that we create and destroy worlds — in fact and deed, not only in one thought alone. This is an immense freedom and responsibility, and it is not without reason that man avoids using this capacity too often. The flight from Being in metaphysics is a flight from freedom and, above all, from the freedom of the imagination.

---

[319] This is also how one of the Neo-Kantians, Friedrich Lange, interpreted Kant in his work *The History of Materialism.*

The world is also the human world, the world co-created by the human imagination of the "primal poets": we perceive the world as we do rather than in another way precisely because the poets (like the *kavih* in Indian tradition) have thought of it in such a way and have *proclaimed and raised up* each thing within it ("a thing [*veshch'*] is what is proclaimed [*vozveshcheno*])."

Being itself, prior to man, is one and indivisible. It has no ground to be many — Parmenides was right. That which first posits a limit within the One (the Father), thus making Two — the Word (the Son, the *Logos*) — is the fruit of the imagination, for there were no grounds whatsoever that determined that the primal limit be drawn in such a way rather than otherwise. Measure, law, and order are the domain of the freedom that founds them; the measureless, lawless, and chaos are the domain of necessity and coercion.

5. "*Full of merit, yet poetically, man dwells on this earth.*" Heidegger writes: "'To dwell poetically' means to stand in the presence of the gods and to be struck by the essential nearness of things. Existence is 'poetic' in its ground — which means, at the same time, as founded (grounded), it is not something earned, but is rather a gift."[320] Yet, in Hölderlin's poetic words, accepting this gift means

> To grasp the father's ray, itself, with our own hands,
> And to offer to the people
> The heavenly gift wrapt in song.[321]

And this is the dangerous affair of the poet. Only thanks to the poet can people become, without fear, involved with the gods, and accordingly, involved in their own essence:

> And hence the sons of the earth now drink
> Heavenly fire without danger.

---

320 Heidegger, *Elucidations of Hölderlin's Poetry*, 60; idem, *Raz'iasneniia k poezii Gel'derlina*, 82-83.

321 Ibid., 61.

And hence, however indirectly, the conclusion follows that poets are the only ones entrusted with the service of the priests who guard the connection between the human and the divine. Indeed, in the most ancient pagan cults, the priests were poets.

But what does it mean that the poets are exposed to the thunderstorms of the gods? What is this danger that struck Hölderlin and Nietzsche, Gogol and Dostoevsky? How can the "most innocent of occupations" — imagining aloud — turn around to be the greatest danger? Here is one more of Hölderlin's testimonies presented by Heidegger:

> For among all that I can see of God, this sign [the lightning of a thunderstorm] has become my chosen one. I used to be able to rejoice over a new truth, a better view of what is above us and around us, but now I fear that I shall end like old Tantalus, who received more from the gods than he could digest.[322]

In the past, the ones who could withstand this danger were the heroes — from Hercules and Odysseus to Arthur and Lancelot — because their hearts were sufficiently strong. Heidegger brings the reader to the conclusion that at the core of this danger lies *pure imagination*. This is the fiery breath of freedom that the poet breathes, but "only he is deserving of life and freedom who every day goes to battle for them" (Goethe). Ordinary, weak people "feed" themselves with necessity and subordinate themselves to exterior circumstances, to whatever is devised by a foreign imagination. Freedom is always a battle, and one can always lose this battle. Defeat in this battle is not simply death and not simply a return to necessity. Defeat means falling under the power of one's own images, whether positive or negative. The stronger the creator (the stronger his imagination), the mightier the image he creates, and hence the greater the risk of simply "going along with" this image and losing one's freedom — though in a different way than healthy people,

---

322 Heidegger, *Elucidations of Hölderlin's Poetry*, 61; idem, *Raz'iasneniia k poezii Gel'derlina*, 86-87.

yet with the same outcome. Madness or insanity, as in the cases of Hölderlin and Nietzsche, is only an expression of the contradiction between the imagined worlds of a fallen creator and the very same worlds of ordinary people. But the state of the former and the latter is the same: slavery in the kingdom of necessity.

In order for a creator to not fall, his imagination must always find sufficient material for his creativity — material of sensory and generally empirical diversity. The creator must have a strong sensory experience, rigid reason, and broad mind — and burn all of this within the fire of the imagination. If there is insufficient material, then this fire can burn man himself. Already aware that he had been struck by such a lot, Hölderlin wrote in his letter to a friend: "I can well say of myself that Apollo has struck me."[323]

In Hölderlin's poem "Remembrance" (*Andenken*), Heidegger finds a poetically expressed answer to one of the questions that remained open from *Being and Time*: Why is man's own being the most "propulsive," why does it "throw" Dasein into a world of beings?

> nemlich zu Hauß ist der Geist
> nicht im Anfang, nicht an der Quell.
> Ihn zehret die Heimath.
> Kolonie liebt, und tapfer Vergessen der
> Geist.
>
> For the spirit is not at home
> At the beginning, not at the source.
> The homeland preys upon it.
> The spirit loves the colony and valor forgotten.[324]

The spirit wandering far away from its native source, gaining invaluable experience and returning with it like a treasure back to the source, is an often repeated theme in Hölderlin

---

323 Ibid., 62; idem, *Raz'iasneniia k poezii Gel'derlina*, 87.
324 Ibid., 114. The poet's style of writing here differs from the standard in modern German.

as well as other poets (indeed, it is present in Stefan George's poem "The Word," which we examined above). The reason why such wanderings are necessary is expressed in the following words: "The homeland preys upon it." Heidegger clarifies: "Turned toward the homelike and wanting to find the homeland in it, at the beginning the spirit is expelled from the homeland and pushed into an always more fruitless search."[325] The spirit is by its nature a creator, and it is most difficult of all for it to remain eternally "with its own," for its creative power finds no outlet and no application "at home." In this lies the cause of the only *real* suffering that man as a creator shares with the gods: the state in which the gift of creative power is not in use, and creation cannot overflow and pour forth into the primal element of the Other so as to give itself up and thus come into being. All other sufferings are illusory and, as soon as the spirit awakens, dissipate like nighttime fog when the sun rises. This is why "the spirit loves the colony and valor forgotten." One could, of course, see this figure of the spirit's movement towards its source through a foreign land as analogous to the Hegelian triad of the "in itself," "for itself," and "in and for itself," but this very same principle of the spirit's self-knowledge through the image it creates, nature, has been known since deep antiquity, including in Europe and in the Platonic-Hermetic tradition. On the other hand, one could also draw a parallel with Taoist wisdom: "The best in life is wandering. The best in wandering is returning."

***

Thus, Heidegger's philosophy of history is fully based on the "Event" (*Ereignis*), which presents a vivid example of the "pre-reflective grasp" of Being: it is not a concept, nor is it

---

325 Heidegger, *Elucidations of Hölderlin's Poetry*, 116; idem, *Raz'iasneniia k poezii Gel'derlina*, 194-195.

even a symbol, at least in the traditional sense; rather, it is an indication of the "experience of time" that the philosopher undergoes prior to any concepts. The Event is the sphere of meaning within which time, space, and history are constituted. It is "events," and not mere "incidents" (*Geschehen*) or facts, that constitute the "substance" of history. The connection between events and history is semantic, not causal in nature: the impact of the future on the past is just as regular as the impact of the past on the present and the future. Any event is finite and has a timeframe.

The main object of interpretation in Heidegger's philosophy of history is the "event of Western European metaphysics," within which "history" in its modern understanding became possible. Heidegger analyzes the basic historical milestones of this event: the "change in the essence of truth" in antiquity with Parmenides and Plato, the victory of method in the science of Modernity, and the final "unbridling" of metaphysics in technocratic states, which devastates the world of beings as well as the inner world of man. The event of the "end of metaphysics" is also the "end of history" and the "end of Europe," whose fate is the fate of metaphysics. Heidegger directly associates his philosophy with this "end of history," but leaves the chronological scope of this "end event" open.

Conclusion:
The Outcomes of Heidegger's Hermeneutics

Finally, let us summarize some of the outcomes of our study. The starting point of Heidegger's philosophizing, like that of many other philosophers in the interlude between the two World Wars, was the event to which Nietzsche most vividly bore witness: "God is dead," "values have been devalued," and hence, man's life in the world, and the world itself, have lost meaning, as they had derived meaning from values whose ultimate pillar was God. The desolation of human existence became the defining trait of the epoch: besides the meaninglessness of life, this desolation was also expressed in the technological devastation of nature, in the "disposing expendability" of man as a resource needed for technological production, and in the culmination of this desolation, the World Wars, during which the "disposing expendability" of man reached terrifying scales.

One of the lessons that philosophy drew in the aftermath of the First World War was that reason and its role in the life of man had been overestimated. The epoch of "Modernity" created the cult of reason and granted it full authority to subject even the very grounds of the existence of man to transformative critique. However, as it turned out, there is much in human nature that is irrational, that is beyond the control of rational critique, and which even revolts against reason. Weapons of mass destruction and concentration camps became the last "arguments" of metaphysics in its attempts to suppress and reduce to naught everything that is irrational in man, everything that is not subject to calculation and planning.

As a result, the right of reason to critique actuality became disputed, and the very concepts of "pure reason" and the "epistemological subject" — in whose name both naturally and socially given mankind had been critiqued —

were themselves subjected to counter-critique and reintegrated into the irrational, primal element of human and natural existence. Across their diverse variations, phenomenology, existentialism, and hermeneutics proposed their own ways for solving the problem of the meaninglessness of the world. The hermeneutic response was that the source of meaning is Dasein, that is, human existence in the world as such. In order to deal with the world's meaninglessness, man himself must take responsibility ("care") and impart it with meaning through the creative act of interpretation. The source of meaning is not a sign or a text, nor is it interpretive consciousness or subjectivity, but the very event of interpreting. According to Heidegger, this event is none other than Dasein, human existence in the world.

But interpretation needs an object, a potentially inexhaustible one, and in the search for such an object, Heidegger first turned to human life in its "everydayness," then to the texts of historical philosophers, and finally to language itself. Language as such thus becomes an object of interpretation, first by way of "hearkening" into the resounding of meanings inlaid in the roots of the words of natural language, which keep the "memory" of the usage of words from before the enthronement of metaphysics, and secondly by turning to the poetry of the "essential poets," and above all Hölderlin, whose utterances most fully express the primordial experience of language as "Saying."

Can we judge the extent to which Heidegger's philosophizing has been overcome by subsequent critique, or the extent to which it retains its relevance today? If we take "relevance" to mean the capacity to generate meaning in the "event of interpretation," then Heidegger's "philosophizing" is perhaps even more "relevant" than the deliberations of most of his critics. Somewhat paraphrasing Heidegger himself, let us ask: Have many of these critics resolved — and managed — to go further than Heidegger himself went? This might very well be a rhetorical question. But it suggests that Heidegger's philosophizing retains no small amount of untapped possibilities to this day, and its transformative influence on the thinking and life of Europeans has by no means exhausted its potential.

In conclusion, I will only point out a few directions in which, in my view, this possible influence is relevant.

1. After Heidegger, it is no longer possible to separate the existence of philosophy, history, and the history of philosophy. Although the grounds of their unity were already established within Hegel's metaphysics, the course of the 19th century still saw philosophy, history, and the history of philosophy persist rather independently within separate disciplinary boundaries. Heidegger submerged all three into the "primal element of interpretation" to the point that none of these three "modes of interpretedness" can be regarded as primary or self-sufficient: history turns into "philosophy of history" and into the interpretation of "onto-historical events" through their manifestation on the surface of the historical phenomena of "everyday Dasein"; in merging together, philosophy and the history of philosophy interpret the very same onto-historical events on their own plane as "determinations of Being."

2. In Heidegger's wake, we cannot speak of any "self-evident" or linear-evolutionary character of the unfolding of the historical process as a whole and the historico-philosophical process in particular. Nor can we speak of any "singular ends" of historical progress: history consists of epochs, each of which bears its own ends, its own criteria of progress and decline, and in passing, it takes them with it. At the same time, possibilities open up for genuinely understanding distant epochs and cultures — not by forcing them into one or another corner of our own system of "historical coordinates," but by seeking the more universal "event" that encompasses all historical epochs.

History — and the history of philosophy — unfolds cyclically, not linearly, in accordance with the structure of the "hermeneutic circle," and therefore it cannot be claimed that the next philosopher who subjects the views of his predecessor to critical "annulment" has "risen above" him — to the contrary, he might be expressing a downward movement along the arc of the historical cycle.

Furthermore, history is not linear; it unfolds simultaneously in multiple directions, fully exhausting the space of the "horizon" of the corresponding onto-historical event. This is especially, distinctively manifest in the history of philosophy. As philosophers have long been aware, the Absolute, unconditioned Reality and Truth, is inexpressible in the non-contradictory categories of reason, and therefore, the fullness of Truth cannot find expression on the plane of rational notions or in any singular construct, but rather only in a whole system of teachings distributed across divergent axes in speculative space. The hermeneutic tradition, on the one hand, and transcendentalism from Plato to Kant and Husserl on the other, represent two divergent lines of thinking that fill in the intelligible "space of all possible points of view." They cannot be rationally reconciled or refuted by one another, but instead should be seen as complementary means of comprehending the one Truth.

3. As for the "end of metaphysics," Heidegger is, without a doubt, an heir to the European metaphysical tradition from Parmenides, Plato, and Aristotle to Hegel and Nietzsche, but the very course of the unfolding of his philosophizing led him — and in his guise, the entirety of European metaphysics — to the boundaries of this tradition. Completely rejecting metaphysics would mean denying Europe a place in the future global life of mankind, for metaphysics is the "essence of Europe" as an onto-historical phenomenon. But preserving that which is most valuable and common to all of mankind in the content of metaphysics is now possible only by pushing apart or stepping over its boundaries as designated by Heidegger.

This concerns, firstly, the boundaries between East and West. I do not dare to assert such unreservedly, but it is possible that Heidegger was the first of the Western metaphysicians to come close to and become understandable to Eastern thinking. Testimony to this can be seen in the stable interest, which arose quite early, shown towards Heidegger in Japan, particularly among Zen Buddhists. For many centuries, the East has been self-contained and has seen Western thinking, like all of Western civilization, as something barbaric. Heidegger's role in bringing the West and East closer together, a process that has rapidly developed through globalization since the late 20th century, remains to be assessed by future historians. Likewise, future philosophers will need to learn to think within a planetary context and dimension, one in which West and East meet and engage in a peaceful conversation about Being.

Secondly, Heidegger led metaphysical thinking to the borders where it neighbors poetry, and to this day, this direction remains the least developed in all of its potential consequences for the thinking and life of the West. The professional standards of philosophizing reject the late Heidegger's "mythopoetic" style of thinking along with all the outcomes to which the event of the meeting of thinking and poetry led him. I am confident that this event's possibilities for transforming human existence have been far from exhausted, and the conclusions at which Heidegger arrived over the course of interpreting works of poetry should be treated with all seriousness. This also concerns the essence of language, the relation between word and thing, and the fate of European and global mankind in the near future. The meeting of thinking and poetry was the final outcome of Heidegger's philosophizing, and the outcome of this meeting was a fully optimistic premonition of a new, luminous epoch to follow the "end of metaphysics," which is poetically experienced as "night":

> *Jetzt aber tagts! Ich harrt und sah es kommen,*
> *Und was ich sah, das Heilige sei mein Wort.*
>
> But now day breaks! I awaited and saw it come,
> And what I saw, may the holy be my word.[326]

Thus, "the poet sees the coming of... the holy."[327] Furthermore: "The holy... grounds another beginning of another history. The holy primordially decides in advance concerning men and gods, whether they are, and who they are, and how they are, and when they are."[328]

Let us end on this optimistic note and proceed to observe the signs of the new day being born.

---

326 Friedrich Hölderlin, "Wie wenn am Feiertage..." ("As when on a Holiday...") in Heidegger, *Elucidations of Hölderlin's Poetry*, 68-69.

327 Ibid., 127, 169; idem, *Raz'iasneniia k poezii Gel'derlina*, 216-217.

328 Ibid., 97-98; idem, *Raz'iasneniia k poezii Gel'derlina*, 158-159.

Bibliography

I. Works by Heidegger

Heidegger in German:

"*Der Zeitbegriff in der Geschichtswissenschaft.*" *Zeitschrift für Philosophie und philosophische Kritik* 16:1, 1916.

Gesamtausgabe [GA] (Frankfurt am Main: Vittorio Klostermann):

Abteilung I: Veröffentlichte Schriften 1910–1976:

GA 3: *Kant und das Problem der Metaphysik*. 1991.

GA 4: *Erläuterungen zu Hölderlins Dichtung*. 1981.

GA 5: *Holzwege*. 1977.

GA 12: *Unterwegs zur Sprache*. 1985.

Abteilung II: Vorlesungen 1919–1944:

GA 20: *Prolegomena zur Geschichte des Zeitbegriffs*. 1979.

GA 24: *Die Grundprobleme der Phänomenologie*. 1975.

GA 25: *Phänomenologische Interpretation von Kants Kritik der Reinen Vernunft*. 1977.

GA 29/30: *Die Grundbegriffe der Metaphysik: Welt - Endlichkeit - Einsamkeit*. 1983.

GA 34: *Vom Wesen der Wahrheit: Zu Platons Höhlengleichnis und Theätet*. 1988.

GA 40: *Einführung in die Metaphysik*. 1983.

GA 48: *Nietzsche: der europäische Nihilismus*. 1986.

GA 50: *1. Nietzsches Metaphysik; 2. Einleitung in die Philosophie. Denken und Dichten*. 1990.

GA 59: *Phänomenologie der Anschauung und des Ausdrucks. Theorie der philosophischen Begriffsbildung (1920)*. 1986.

GA 61: *Phänomenologische Interpretationen zu Aristoteles. Einführung in die phänomenologische Forschung*. 1985.

GA 63: *Ontologie (Hermeneutik der Faktizität)*. 1988.

Kant und das Problem der Metaphysik. Frankfurt am Main: Gerhard Schulte-Bulmke, 1934.

Martin Heidegger im Gespräch. Edited by Richard Wisser. Freiburg: K. Alber, 1970.

Sein und Zeit. 16th ed. Tübingen: Max Niemeyer, 1986.

Unterwegs zur Sprache. Pfullingen: Günther Neske, 1960.

Vorträge und Aufsätze. Pfullingen: Günther Neske, 1954.

Wegmarken. Frankfurt am Main: Vittorio Klostermann, 1967.

Zollikoner Seminare. Frankfurt am Main: Vittorio Klostermann, 1987.

Heidegger in English:

Being and Time. Translated by Joan Stambaugh, revised by Dennis J. Schmidt. Albany: State University of New York Press, 2010.

Elucidations of Hölderlin's Poetry. Translated by Keith Hoeller. Amherst: Humanity Books, 2000).

The End of Philosophy. Translated by Joan Stambaugh. New York: Harper & Row, 1973.

History of the Concept of Time: Prolegomena. Translated by Theodore Kisiel. Bloomington: Indiana University Press, 1985.

Kant and the Problem of Metaphysics. Translated by Richard Taft. Bloomington: Indiana University Press, 1997.

Logic: The Question of Truth. Translated by Thomas Sheehan. Bloomington: Indiana University Press, 2010.

Ontology — The Hermeneutics of Facticity. Translated by John van Buren. Bloomington: Indiana University Press, 2008.

Pathmarks. Edited by William McNeill. Cambridge: Cambridge University Press, 1998.

Poetry, Language, Thought. Translated by Albert Hofstadter. London: Harper Perennial, 2001.

Ponderings II-VI: Black Notebooks 1931-1938. Translated by Richard Rojcewicz. Bloomington: Indiana University Press, 2016.

Ponderings VII-XI: Black Notebooks 1938-1939. Translated by Richard Rojcewicz. Bloomington: Indiana University Press, 2017.

Ponderings XII-XV: Black Notebooks 1939-1941. Translated by Richard Rojcewicz. Bloomington: Indiana University Press, 2017.

"The Provenance of Art and the Destination of Thought (1967)." Translated by Dimitrios Latsis, edited by Ulrich Haase. *Journal of the British Society for Phenomenology* 44:2, 2013: 119-128.

The Question Concerning Technology and Other Essays. Translated by William Lovitt. New York: Harper Perennial, 2013.

On Time and Being. Translated by Joan Stambaugh. New York: Harper Torchbooks, 1972.

On the Way to Language. Translated by Peter D. Hertz and Joan Stambaugh. New York: Harper Collins, 1982.

"Why Do I Stay in the Provinces?" Translated by Thomas Sheehan. In: Sheehan, Thomas (ed.). *Heidegger: The Man and the Thinker*. Chicago: Precedent Publishing, 1981.

"Wilhelm Dilthey's Research and the Current Struggle for a Historical Worldview." Translated by Theodore Kisiel. In: Kisiel, Theodore and Thomas Sheehan (eds.). *Becoming Heidegger: On the Trail of his Early Occasional Writings, 1910-1927.* 2nd ed. London: Routledge, 2014.

Zollikon Seminars: Protocols — Conversations — Letters. Edited by Medard Boss, translated by Franz Mayr and Richard Askay. Evanston: Northwestern University Press, 2001.

Heidegger in Russian:

Bytie i vremia. Translated by Vladimir V. Bibikhin. Moscow: Ad Marginem, 1997.

Chto zovetsia myshleniem?. Translated by E. Sagetdinov. Moscow: Academic Project, 2006.

"Davosskaia diskussiia." In: *Issledovaniia po fenomenologii i filosofskoi germenevtike*, edited by E.B. Borisov, I. Inishev, and A. Lavrukhin. Minsk: European Humanities University, 2001.

"Gel'derlin i sushchnost' poezii." Translated by A.V. Chusov. Logos 1, 1991 [republished in *Kul'tury v dialoge*, ed. A.S. Gagarin. Ekaterinburg: Ural University, 1992].

"Issledovatel'skaia rabota Vil'gel'ma Dil'teia i bor'ba za istoricheskoe mirovozzrenie v nashi dni. Desiat' dokladov, prochitannykh v Kassele (1925 g.)." In: Shpet, G.G. and M. Khaidegger. *Dva teksta o Vil'gel'me Dil'tee.* Moscow: Gnozis, 1995.

Kant i problema metafiziki. Translated by O.V. Nikiforov. Moscow: Logos, 1997.

"Moi put' v fenomenologiiu." Translated with commentary by Igor Mikhailov. Logos 6, 1994.

"Nekotorye ukazania na osnovnye tochki zreniia dlia teologicheskogo kollokviuma po teme: Problema neob'ektiviruiushchego myshleniia i slovesnogo vyrazheniia v sovremennoi teologii." Translated by V.K. Zelensky. In: *M. Khaidegger i teologiia*. Moscow: Institute of Philosophy of the Academy of Sciences of the USSR, 1974: 23-35.

Nitsshe, vol. 1. Translated by A.P. Shurbelev. Saint Petersburg: Vladimir Dal', 2006.

Nitsshe i pustota. Edited by O.V. Selin. Moscow: Algoritm / Eksmo, 2006.

"O linii." In: *Sud'ba nigilizma. E. Iunger, M. Khaidegger, D. Kamper, G. Figal'*, edited by G. Khaidarova. Saint Petersburg: Saint Petersburg State University, 2006.

Osnovnye poniatiia metafiziki. Translated by V.V. Bibikhin and A.V. Akhutin. Voprosy filosofii 9, 1989.

Osnovnye problemy fenomenologii. Translated by A.G. Chernyakov. Saint Petersburg: Vysshaia religiozno-filosofskaia shkola, 2001.

O sushchestve i poniatii φύσις. Aristotel' Fizika B-1. Translated by V. Mikushevich. Moscow: Medium, 1995.

"O sushchnosti istiny." Translated by Z.N. Zaitseva. *Filosofskie nauki* 4, 1989.

"Pet' — dlia chego?." Translated by V.M. Bakusev. In: Ril'ke, R.M. *Prikosnovenie. Sonety k Orfeiu*. Moscow: Nauka, 2003.

Polozhenie ob osnovanii. Translated by O.A. Koval'. Saint Petersburg: Saint Petersburg State University, 1999.

Prolegomeny k istorii poniatiia vremeni. Translated by E. Borisov. Tomsk: Vodolei, 1998.

Raboty i razmyshleniia raznykh let. Translated and edited by A.V. Mikhailov. Moscow: Gnozis, 1993.

Razgovor na proselochnoi doroge. Izbrannye stat'i poslednego perioda tvorchestva. Edited by A.L. Dobrokhotov. Moscow: Vysshaia shkola, 1991.

Raz'iasneniia k poezii Gel'derlina. Translated by G.B. Notkin. Saint Petersburg: Academic Project, 2003.

Razmyshleniia II-VI. Chernyie tetradi 1931-1938. Translated by Aleksei Grigoryev, ed. Mikhail Maiatskii. Moscow: Izdatel'stvo Instituta Gaidara, 2016.

Razmyshleniia VII-XI. Chernyie tetradi 1938-1939. Translated by Aleksei Grigoryev, ed. Mikhail Maiatskii. Moscow: Izdatel'stvo Instituta Gaidara, 2018.

Razmyshleniia XII-XV. Chernyie tetradi 1939-1941. Translated by Aleksei Grigoryev, ed. Mikhail Maiatskii. Moscow: Izdatel'stvo Instituta Gaidara, 2020.

"*Seminar v Tseringene 1973 g.*" Translated by I.N. Inishev. In: *Issledovaniia po fenomenologii i filosofskoi germenevtike*, edited by E.B. Borisov, I. Inishev, and A. Lavrukhin. Minsk: European Humanities University, 2001: 108-123.

Vremia i bytie. Stat'i i vystupleniia. Translated and edited by Vladimir V. Bibikhin. Moscow: Respublika, 1993.

Vvedenie v metafiziku. Translated by N.O. Guchinskaia. Saint Petersburg: Vysshaia Religiozno-filosofskaia shkola, 1998.

II. Literature

In Russian:

Al'bert, Kh. "*Kritika chistoi germenevtiki.*" In: *Filosofiia bez granits*, edited by V.V. Mironov, 45–60. Moscow: Vorob'ev AL, 2001.

Altukhov, A.A. and I.S. Shern-Borisova (eds.). *Ontologicheskaia problematika iazyka v sovremennoi zapadnoi filosofii.* Moscow: Institute of Philosophy of the Academy of Sciences of the USSR, 1975.

Apel', K.-O. "*Bambergskie lektsii.*" In: *Filosofiia bez granits*, edited by V.V. Mironov, 75–90. Moscow: Vorob'ev AL, 2001.

Apel', K.-O. "*Moia intellektuel'naia biografiia v kontekste sovremennoi filosofii.*" In: *Filosofiia bez granits*, edited by V.V. Mironov, 61–74. Moscow: Vorob'ev AL, 2001.

Baranov, S.T. "*Germenevticheskaia struktura bytiia: iazyk — dom bytiia.*" In: *Iazykovaia deiatel'nost': perekhodnost' i sinkretizm*, 112–130. Moscow: Stavropol', 2001.

Bibikhin, V.V. "*Delo Khaideggera.*" In: *Filosofiia Martina Khaideggera i sovremennost'*, edited by N.V. Motroshilov, 34–50. Moscow: Nauka, 1991.

Bibikhin, V.V. "*K stoletiiu so dnia rozhdeniia M. Khaideggera.*" Istoriko-filosofskii ezhegodnik 89 (1989): 45–60.

Bimel', V. *Martin Khaidegger sam o sebe.* Cheliabinsk: Cheliabinsk University Press, 1998.

Binsvanger, L. *Bytie-v-mire.* Moscow: Progress, 1999.

Bol'nov, O. F. *Filosofiia ekzistentsializma.* Saint Petersburg: Saint Petersburg University Press, 1999.

Bonch-Bruevich, V.D., ed. *Voprosy istorii religii i ateizma. Sbornik statei.* Moscow: Academy of Sciences of the USSR, 1950.

Borisov, E.B., I. Inishev, and A. Lavrukhin, eds. *Issledovaniia po fenomenologii i filosofskoi germenevtike*. Moscow [Minsk?]: European Humanities University, 2001.

Brosova, N. Z. *Evoliutsiia ponimaniia predmeta filosofii v kontseptsii Khaideggera*. Moscow: Moscow University Press, 1988.

Brosova, N. Z. *Teologicheskie aspekty filozofii istorii M. Khaideggera*. Doctoral dissertation, Moscow: Institute of Philosophy of the Russian Academy of Sciences, 2008.

Bukreeva, N. P. *Filosofiia bytiia iskusstva M. Khaideggera*. Ekaterinburg: Ural University Press, 1995.

Cherniakov, A. "Samoprozhivanie i samosoznanie: Aristotel', Dil'tei, Khaidegger." In: *Germenevtika. Psikhologiia. Istoriia. Vil'gel'm Dil'tei i sovremennaia filosofiia*, edited by N.S. Plotnikov, 123–140. Moscow: Nauka, 2002.

Ershov, M. V. *Problema bytiia v filosofskoi evoliutsii Martina Khaideggera*. Petrozavodsk: Petrozavodsk University Press, 1982.

Fogeler, Ia. G. *Kritika ontologii nemetskogo ekzistentsializma*. Moscow: Progress, 1965.

Gadamer, Kh.-G. *Istina i metod. Osnovy filosofskoi germenevtiki*. Moscow: Progress, 1988.

Gaidenko, P. P. *Ekzistentsializm i problema kul'tury (kritika filosofii M. Khaideggera)*. Moscow: Nauka, 1969.

Gaidenko, P. P. *Filosofiia M. Khaideggera kak vyrazhenia krizisa sovremennoi burzhuaznoi kul'tury*. Moscow: Nauka, 1962.

Gaidenko, P. P. *Iskusstvo i bytie. M. Khaidegger o sushchnosti khudozhestvennogo proizvedeniia*. Moscow: Nauka, 1982.

Gaidenko, P. P. "Nauchnaia ratsional'nost' i filosofskii razum v interpretatsii Edmunda Gusserlia." *Voprosy filosofii* 7, 1992: 45–60.

Gaidenko, P. P. "Ot istoricheskoi germenevtiki k germenevtike bytiia (kriticheskii analiz evoliutsii M. Khaideggera)." Voprosy filosofii 10, 1987: 34–50.

Gaidenko, P. P. "Problema intentsional'nosti u Gusserlia. I ekzistentsialistskaia kontseptsiia transtsendentsii." In: Sovremennyi ekzistentsializm, edited by P.P. Gaidenko, 112–130. Moscow: Nauka, 1966.

Gafarov, Kh. S. Lingvo-filosofskaia kontseptsiia kak osnovanie germenevtiki G.-G. Gadamera. Saint Petersburg: Saint Petersburg University Press, 1993.

Gegel', G. V. F. Fenomenologiia dukha. Saint Petersburg: Nauka, 2002.

Gronden, Zh. Germenevtika faktichnosti kak ontologicheskaia destruktsiia i kritika ideologii. K aktual'nosti gremenevtiki Khaideggera. In: Issledovaniia po fenomenologii i filosofskoi germenevtike, edited by E.B. Borisov, I. Inishev, and A. Lavrukhin, 45–60. Moscow: European Humanities University, 2001.

Gordeziani, R. Sh. Problema sushchestvovaniia (Dasein) v ekzistentsializme (kritika fundamental'noi ontologii Khaideggera). Tbilisi: Tbilisi University Press, 1968.

Gumvol'dt, V. von. Iazyk i filosofiia kul'tury. Moscow: Progress, 1985.

Gurevich, P. S., ed. Novaia tekhnokraticheskaia volna na Zapade. Moscow: Progress, 1986.

Gurevich, P. S., and Iu. N. Popov, eds. Problema cheloveka v zapadnoi filosofii. Moscow: Progress, 1988.

Gusev, S. S., and G. L. Tul'chinskii. Problema ponimaniia v filosofii: Filosofsko-gnoseologicheskii analiz. Moscow: Nauka, 1985.

Gusserl', E. Idei k chisteoi fenomenologii i fenomenologicheskoi filosofii. Translated by A.V. Mikhailov. Moscow: DIK, 1999.

Gusserl', E. *Krizis evropeiskikh nauk i transtsendental'naia fenomenologiia.* Saint Petersburg: Nauka, 2004.

Gusserl', E. *Logicheskie issledovaniia. Kartezianskie razmyshleniia.* Moscow/Minsk: Nauka, 2000.

Gusserl', E. *Sobrannye sochineniia,* vol. 1: *Fenomenologiia vnutrennego soznaniia vremeni.* Moscow: Nauka, 1994.

Iates, F.A. *Dzhordano Bruno i germeticheskaia traditsiia.* Moscow: Novoe literaturnoe obozrenie, 2000.

Khaidarova, G., ed. *Sud'ba nigilizma. E. Iunger, M. Khaidegger, D. Kamper, G. Figal'.* Saint Petersburg: Saint Petersburg State University, 2006.

Konacheva, S.A. *Bog posle Boga. Puti postmetafizicheskogo myshleniia.* Moscow: Russian Sstate University for the Humanities, 2019.

Konacheva, S.A. *Khaidegger i filosofskaia teologiia XX veka.* Doctoral dissertation, Moscow: Russian State University for the Humanities, 2010.

Koval'chuk, S. M. *Perevod (s kommentariem) raboty M. Khaideggera "Vremia obraza mira."* Brest: Brest University Press, 1983.

Kosolapova, E.A. *Problema traditsii i istorichnosti v gremenevtike Kh.-G. Gadamera.* Moscow: Moscow University Press, 1989.

Kosharskii, S. A. *Kritika teoreticheskikh osnov sovremennoi filosofskoi germenevtiki (V. Dil'tei i E. Gusserl').* Kiev: Kiev University Press, 1988.

Lebedev, A.V., ed. *Fragmenty rannikh grecheskikh filosofov.* Moscow: Nauka, 1989.

Malakhov, V. S. *Problema traditsii v filosofskoi germenevtike G.G. Gadamera.* Moscow: Nauka, 1986.

Malakhov, V.S. "*Khaidegger, Derrida i granitsy filosofii u grekov.*" *Obshchestvennye nauki za rubezhom* 3: *Filosofiia i sotsiologiia RZH*, 2, 1987: 45–60.

Maliavin, V.V., trans. *Zhuangzi, Laozi*. Moscow: Mysl', 1995.

Markov, B. V. "*Bytie i iazyk (Khaidegger i Vittgenshtein).*" *Vestnik Sankt-Peterburgskogo universiteta* 6, no. 2 (1992): 34–50.

Mattske, A. I. *Kant i M. Khaidegger — opyt sravnitel'noi kharakteristiki*. Moscow: Nauka, 1986.

Mironov, V.V., ed. *Filosofiia bez granits*. Moscow: Vorob'ev AL, 2001.

Molchanov, V. I. *Vremia i soznanie. Kritika fenomenologicheskoi filosofii*. Moscow: Nauka, 1988.

Molchanov, V. I. "*Ontologiia i obosnovanie fenomenologii u Gusserlia i Khaideggera.*" In: *Problemy ontologii v sovremennoi burzhuaznoi filosofii*, edited by V.I. Molchanov, 112–130. Riga: Riga University Press, 1988.

Molchanov, V. I. "*Filosofiia M. Khaideggera i problema soznaniia.*" In: *Filosofiia Martina Khaideggera i sovremennost'*, edited by N.V. Motroshilov, 45–60. Moscow: Nauka, 1991.

Motroshilov, N.V., ed. *Filosofiia Martina Khaideggera i sovremennost'*. Moscow: Nauka, 1991.

Motroshilova, N. V. "*Drama zhizni, idei i grekhopadeniia Martina Khaideggera.*" In: *Filosofiia Martina Khaideggera i sovremennost'*, edited by N.V. Motroshilov, 61–74. Moscow: Nauka, 1991.

Motroshilova, N. V. "*Zachem nuzhen Gegel'? (K voprosu o tolkovanii Khaideggerom gegelevskoi filosofii).*" In: *Filosofiia Martina Khaideggera i sovremennost'*, edited by N.V. Motroshilov, 75–90. Moscow: Nauka, 1991.

Nikitin, S.A. "*Simvol Vostoka v uchenii M. Khaideggera.*" *Kul'tury v dialoge / Chelovek. Kul'tura. Filosofiia* 1, 1992: 45–60.

Nitsshe [Nietzsche], Fr. *Sobrannye sochineniia.* 2 vols. Moscow: Mysl', 1991.

Ozeirman, T.I., ed. *Filosofiia Kanta i sovremennost'.* Moscow: Mysl', 1974.

Oznobkina, E. V. "K khaideggerovskoi interpretatsii filosofii I. Kanta." *Istoriko-filosofskii ezhegodnik* 89, 1989: 34–50.

Oznobkina, E. V. *Sootnoshenie etiki i ontologii v klassicheskoi i sovremennoi burzhuaznoi filosofii (K voprosu o khaideggerovskoi interpretatsii filosofii I. Kanta).* Moscow: Nauka, 1990.

Patent, G.I. *Marksizm i apriorizm. Kritika irratsionalisticheskogo apriorizma M. Khaideggera.* Sverdlovsk: Sverdlovsk University Press, 1972.

Plotnikov, N. S., ed. *Germenevtika. Psikhologiia. Istoriia. Vil'gel'm Dil'tei i sovremennaia filosofiia.* Moscow: Nauka, 2002.

Pogorelyi, A. I. *Evoliutsiia ekzistentsializma M. Khaideggera i krizis sovremennoi burzhuaznoi filosofii.* Kiev: Kiev University Press, 1974.

Podoroga, V. A. "Erectio. Geo-logiia iazyka i filosofstvovanie M. Khaideggera." In: *Filosofiia Martina Khaideggera i sovremennost',* edited by N.V. Motroshilov, 112–130. Moscow: Nauka, 1991.

Postovalova, V. I. *Iazyk kak deiatel'nost': opyt interpretatsii kontseptsii V. Gumbol'dta.* Moscow: Nauka, 1982.

Potebnya, A.A. *Slovo i mif.* Moscow: Nauka, 1989.

Potebnya, A.A. *Teoreticheskaia poetika.* Moscow: Nauka, 1989.

Pushkin, V. G. *Sushchnost' metafiziki. Ot Fomy Akvinskogo cherez Gegelia i Nitsshe k Martinu Khaideggeru.* Saint Petersburg: Saint Petersburg University Press, 2003.

Pshigotizhev, I. Sh. *Kritika ucheniia M. Khaideggera o iazyke.* Nalchik: Nalchik University Press, 1974.

Raboty M. Khaideggera po kul'turologii i teorii ideologii. Moscow: Institute of Scientific Information on the Social Sciences, Academy of Sciences of the USSR, 1981.

Radkhakrishnan, S. *Indiiskaia filosofiia*, vol. 2. Moscow: Mysl', 1993.

Ril'ke, R.M. *Prikosnovenie. Sonety k Orfeiiu*. Translated by V.M. Bakusev. Moscow: Nauka, 2003.

Rtishchev, V. I. *Kritika nemetskogo pozitivnogo ekzistentsializma*. Moscow: Nauka, 1969.

Rutkevich, A. M. *Ot Freida k Khaideggeru*. Moscow: Nauka, 1985.

Safranski, R. *Khaidegger*. Moscow: Molodaia Gvardiia, 2005.

Sivertsev, E. Iu. *M. Khaidegger i filosofiia dosokratikov. Problema bytiia*. Saint Petersburg: Saint Petersburg University Press, 1991.

Sivertsev, E. Iu. *Religiia i iskusstvo v filosofii M. Khaideggera*. Saint Petersburg: Saint Petersburg University Press, 1992.

Solov'ev, E. Iu. "Popytka obosnovaniia novoi filosofii istorii v fundamental'noi ontologii M. Khaideggera." In *Novye tendentsii v zapadnoi sotsial'noi filosofii*, edited by E.Iu. Solov'ev, 45–60. Moscow: Nauka, 1988.

Stavtsev, S. N. *Vvedenie v filosofiiu Khaideggera*. Saint Petersburg: Saint Petersburg University Press, 2000.

Stepin, V. S. *Teoreticheskoi znanie*. Moscow: Progress-Traditsiia, 1999.

Tavzadze, G. G. *Obosnovanie fenomena istorii v filosofii M. Khaideggera*. Tbilisi: Tbilisi University Press, 1991.

Trukhina, A. A. *Kritika ekzistentsialistskoi kontseptsii poznaniia*. Moscow: Nauka, 1974.

Tugendkhat, E. "Khaideggerovskaia ideia istiny." In: *Issledovaniia po fenomenologii i filosofskoi germenevtike*, edited by E.B. Borisov, I. Inishev, and A. Lavrukhin. Minsk: European Humanities University, 2001.

In German:

Adorno, Theodor. *Jargon der Eigentlichkeit. Zur deutschen Ideologie.* 3rd ed. Frankfurt am Main: Suhrkamp, 1967.

Allemann, Beda. *Hölderlin und Heidegger.* Zürich: Atlantis, 1954.

Apel, Karl-Otto. "Die beiden Phasen der Phänomenologie in ihrer Auswirkung auf das philosophische Vorverständnis von Sprache und Dichtung in der Gegenwart." *Jahrbuch für Ästhetik und allgemeine Kunstwissenschaft* 3, 1958.

――――――― "Heideggers philosophische Radikalisierung der 'Hermeneutik' und die Frage nach den Sinnkriterien der Sprache." In: *Schriften zum Weltgespräch,* vol. 3: *die hermeneutische Frage in der Theologie,* edited by Oswald Loretz und Walter Strolz. Freiburg: Herder, 1968.

Axelos, Kostas. *Einführung in ein künftiges Denken. Über Marx und Heidegger.* Tübingen: Max Niemeyer, 1966.

Ballmer, Karl. *Aber Herr Heidegger!* Basel: Rudolf Geering, 1933.

Beaufret, Jean, Hans-Georg Gadamer, Karl Löwith, and Karl-Heinz Volkmann-Schluck (eds.). *Die Frage Martin Heideggers. Beiträge zu einem Kolloquium mit Heidegger aus Anlass seines 80. Geburtstages.* Heidelberg: Carl Winter, Universitätsverlag 1969.

Bernet, Rudolf (ed.). *Zeit und Zeitlichkeit bei Husserl und Heidegger.* Freiburg/Munich: K. Alber, 1983.

Beydoun, Afaf. *Das vergessene Geheimnis des Daseins nach Heidegger.* Munich: 1974.

Biemel, Walter. *Martin Heidegger.* Hamburg: Rowohlt, 1975.

――――――― *Martin Heidegger in Selbstzeugnissen und Bilddokumenten.* Hamburg: Rowohlt, 1973.

Blust, Franz-Karl. *Selbstheit und Zeitlichkeit. Heideggers neuer Denkansatz zur Selbstbestimmung des Ich*. Würzburg: Königshausen & Neumann, 1987.

Bochenski, J. M. *Europäische Philosophie der Gegenwart*. Munich/Bern: Francke, 1947.

Bohrmann, Katharina. *Die Welt als Verhältnis: Untersuchung zu einem Grundgedanken in den späten Schriften Martin Heideggers*. Frankfurt am Main: Peter Lang, 1983.

Bock, Irmgard. *Heideggers Sprachdenken*. Meisenheim am Glan: A. Hain, 1966.

Bollnow, Otto Friedrich. *Deutsche Existenzphilosophie*. Bern: Francke 1953.

_____ *Existenzphilosophie*. Stuttgart: Kohlhammer 1949.

_____ *Studien zur Hermeneutik*, vol. 1. Frankfurt am Main/Munich: Königshausen & Neumann, 1982.

Brecht, Franz Josef. *Heidegger und Jaspers. Die beiden Grundformen der Existenzphilosophie*. Wuppertal: Marees-Verlag, 1948.

Bretschneider, Willy. *Sein und Wahrheit. Über die Zusammengehörigkeit von Sein und Wahrheit im Denken Martin Heideggers*. Meisenheim am Glan: A. Hain, 1965.

Bubner, Rudiger, Konrad Cramer, and Reiner Wiehl (eds.). *Hermeneutik und Dialektik*. 2 vols. Tübingen: Mohr, 1970.

Dilthey, Wilhelm. *Briefwechsel zwischen Wilhelm Dilthey und dem Grafen Paul Yorck von Wartenburg: 1877-1897*. Hildesheim: Niemeyer, 1974.

Bröcker, Walter. "Rückblick auf die Existenzphilosophie." *Philosophische Perspektiven* 4, 1972.

Bücher, Alexius J. "*Martin Heidegger. Metaphysikkritik als Begriffsproblematik.*" *Meinzer philosophische Forschungen* 14, 1983.

Del-Negro, Walter. "*Von Brentano über Husserl zu Heidegger — Eine vergleichende Betrachtung.*" *Zeitschrift für philosophische Forschung* 7:4, 1953.

Demske, James M. *Sein, Mensch und Tod. Das Todesproblem bei Martin Heidegger.* Freiburg/Munich: K. Alber, 1953.

Diehl, Otto Siegfried. *Sprache als Schicksalgestaltung: Essay.* Frankfurt am Main: 1980.

Dilthey, Wilhelm. *Einleitung in die Geisteswissenschaften. Versuch einer Grundlegung für das Studium der Gesellschaft und der Geschichte.* Berlin: 1933.

Feick, Hildegard. *Index zu Heideggers Sein und Zeit.* Tübingen: Max Niemeyer, 1968.

Fischer, Alois. *Die Existenzphilosophie Martin Heideggers.* Leipzig: Meiner, 1935.

Flashar, Hellmut, Karlfried Gründer, and Axel Horstmann (eds.). *Philologie und Hermeneutik in 19. Jahrhundert: zur Geschichte und Methodologie der Geisteswissenschaften.* Göttingen: Vandenhoeck & Ruprecht, 1979.

Franzen, Winfried. *Martin Heidegger.* Stuttgart: J.B. Metzler, 1976.

Gadamer, Hans-Georg. *Heideggers Wege.* Tübingen: Max Niemeyer, 1986.

_____(ed.). *Anteile: Martin Heidegger zum 60. Geburtstag.* Frankfurt am Main: Vittorio Klostermann, 1950.

Gerlach, Hans-Martin. *Martin Heidegger: Denk- und Irrwege eines spät-bürgerlichen Philosophen.* Berlin: Akademie-Verlag, 1982.

Görland, Ingtraud. *Transzendenz und Selbst: Eine Phase in Heideggers Denkens*. Frankfurt am Main: Vittorio Klostermann, 1981.

Gruber, Wilfried. *Vom Wesen des Kunstwerkes nach Martin Heidegger: eine Untersuchung über die Möglichkeit und Notwendigkeit der Kunst*. Frankfurt am Main: 1956.

Gudopp, Wolf-Dieter. *Der junge Heidegger. Realität und Wahrheit in der Vorgeschichte von Sein und Zeit*. Frankfurt am Main: Verlag Marxistische Blätter, 1983.

Hamann, Johann Georg. *Sämtliche Werke, Historisch-kritische Ausgabe*. 6 vols. Edited by Josef Nadler. 1946-1957.

Hessen, Johannes. *Existenzphilosophie. Grundlinien einer Philosophie des menschlichen Daseins*. Essen: Chamier, 1948.

Hollenbach, Johannes Michael. *Sein und Gewissen. Über den Ursprung der Gewissensregung; eine Begegnung zwischen Martin Heidegger und thomistischer Philosophie*. Baden-Baden: B. Grimm, 1954.

Hornstein, Norbert. "Das Haus des Seins: zu Heideggers Sprachphilosophie." Neues Abendland, 10:7, 1955.

Hufnagel, Erwin. *Einführung in die Hermeneutik*. Stuttgart: Kohlhammer, 1976.

Hühnerfeld, Paul. *In Sachen Heidegger*. Hamburg: Hoffmann & Campe, 1959.

Humboldt, Wilhelm von. *Werke in fünf Bänden*, vol. 3: *Sprachphilosophische Schriften*. Edited by Andreas Flitner and Klaus Giel. Stuttgart: J.G. Cotta, 1963.

Husserl, Edmund. *Cartesianische Meditationen*. Munich: 1950.

Ipsen, Gunther. *Sprachphilosophie der Gegenwart*. [Philosophische Forschungsberichte 5]. Berlin: Junker u. Dünnhaupt, 1930.

Jaeger, Petra. *Heideggers Ansatz zur Verwindung der Metaphysik in der Epoche von Sein und Zeit.* Frankfurt am Main: Peter Lang, 1976.

Kraft, Julius. *Von Husserl zu Heidegger. Kritik der Phänomenologischen Philosophie.* Leipzig: Hans Buske, 1932.

Kraft, Peter. *Das anfängliche Wesen der Kunst: zur Bedeutung von Kunstwerk, Dichtung und Sprache im Denken Martin Heideggers.* Frankfurt am Main: Peter Lang, 1984.

Krong, Wolfgang. "Das Sein zum Tode bei Heidegger." *Zeitschrift für philosophische Forschung,* 7:3, 1953.

Küchler, Hans. *Der innere Bezug von Anthropologie und Ontologie (Das Problem der Anthropologie im Denken M. Heideggers).* Meisenheim am Glan: A. Hain, 1974.

Kuhn, Helmut. *Begegnung mit dem Nichts. Ein Versuch über die Existenzphilosophie.* Tübingen: Mohr, 1950.

_____"Heideggers Holzwege." *Archiv für Philosophie* (Stuttgart) 4:3, 1952.

Lang, Peter. *Hermeneutik, Ideologiekritik, Ästhetik: Über Gadamer und Adorno sowie Fragen einer aktuellen Ästhetik.* Königstein: Forum Academicum, 1981.

Lohmann, Johannes. "Martin Heideggers ontologische Differenz und die Sprache." *Lexis* 1, 1948.

Löwith, Karl. *Heidegger. Denker in dürftiger Zeit.* Frankfurt am Main: S. Fischer, 1953.

Maraldo, John C. *Der hermeneutische Zirkel. Untersuchungen zu Schleiermacher, Dilthey und Heidegger.* Freiburg/Munich: K. Alber, 1974.

Marx, Werner. *Absolute Reflexion und Sprache.* Frankfurt am Main: Vittorio Klostermann, 1967.

_____*Heidegger und die Tradition*. Stuttgart: Kohlhammer, 1961.

Meulen, Jan van der. *Heidegger und Hegel oder Widerstreit und Widerspruch*. Meisenheim am Glan: A. Hain, 1954.

Misch, Georg. *Lebensphilosophie und Phänomenologie*. Leipzig/Berlin: Teubner, 1933.

Mörchen, H. *Macht und Herrschaft im Denken von Heidegger und Adorno*. Stuttgart: K. Cotta 1980.

Neske, Günther (ed.). *Martin Heidegger zum siebzigsten Geburtstag*. Pfullingen: Günther Neske, 1959.

Neunheuser, K. H. "Heidegger und die Sprache." *Wirkendes Wort, Deutsches Sprachschaffen in Lehre und Leben* 8, 1957-1958.

Orth, Ernst Wolfgang. *Bedeutung, Sinn, Gegenstand. Studien zur Sprachphilosophie Edmund Husserls und Richard Hönigswalds*. Bonn: Bouvier, 1967.

Ott, Heinrich. *Denken und Sein. Der Weg Martin Heideggers und der Weg der Theologie*. Zollikon: Evangelischer Verlag, 1959.

Passweg, Salcia. *Phänomenologie und Ontologie. Husserl - Scheler - Heidegger*. Leipzig: Heitz, 1931.

Pfeiffer, Johannes. *Existenzphilosophie. Eine Einführung in Heidegger und Jaspers*. Leipzig: Meiner, 1933.

Picotti, Dina V. *Die Überwindung der Metaphysik als geschichtliche Aufgabe bei M. Heidegger*. Munich: 1959.

Pöggeler, Otto. *Der Denkweg Martin Heideggers*. Frankfurt am Main: Günther Neske, 1963.

_____*Heidegger und hermeneutische Philosophie*. Freiburg/Munich: K. Alber, 1983.

_____(ed.). *Heidegger: Perspektiven zur Deutung seines Werkes*. Cologne/Berlin: Beltz-Athenäum, 1994.

Presas, Mario A. *"Von der Phänomenologie zum Denken des Sein."* Zeitschrift für philosophische Forschung 28:2, 1974.

Rainer, Marten. *Heidegger Lesen.* Munich: Fink, 1991.

Riedel, Manfred. *Verstehen oder Erklären? Zur Theorie und Geschichte der herme- neutische Wissenschaften.* Stuttgart: K. Cotta, 1974.

Rodi, Frtihjof. *Erkenntnis des Erkannten. Zur Hermeneutik des 19 und 20 Jahrhundert.* Frankfurt am Main: Suhrkamp, 1990.

_____(ed.). *Dilthey-Jahrbuch für Philosophie und Geschichte der Geisteswissenschaften.* Göttingen: Vandenhoeck & Ruprecht, 1988.

Rolf, Bernd. *Die Destruktion der Substanzionalität in der Analitik des Daseins (Untersuchungen zum Verhältnis von Subjektivität und Existenz).* Frankfurt am Main: 1975.

Rosales, Alberto. *"Zum Problem der Kehre im Denken Heideggers."* Zeitschrift für philosophische Forschung 38:2, 1984.

Sass, Hans-Martin. *Heidegger — Bibliographie.* Meisenheim am Glan: A. Hain, 1968.

Schmidt, Raymund (ed.). *Die Deutsche Philosophie der Gegenwart in Selbstdarstellungen,* vol. 1. Leipzig: Felix Meiner, 1921.

Schöfer, Erasmus. *Die Sprache Heideggers.* Pfellingen: Günther Neske, 1962.

Schulz, Walter. *"Über die philosophiegeschichten Ort Martin Heideggers."* Philosophische Rundschau 1:4, 1953.

Schwan, Alexander. *"Martin Heidegger, Politik und praktischer Philosophie. Zur Problematik neuerer Heidegger-Literatur."* Philosophisches Jahrbuch 81:1, 1974.

Schweppenhäuser, Hermann. *"Studien über die Heideggerische Sprachtheorie."* Archiv für Philosophie 7:1-2. 1955; 8:1-2, 1958.

Seebohm, Thomas. *Zur Kritik der hermeneutische Vernunft.* Bonn: Bouvier, 1972.

Siebers, Georg. *Die Krisis des Existenzialismus.* Hamburg: Stromverlag, 1949.

Simon, Josef. *Problem der Sprache bei Hegel.* Munich: Kohlhammer, 1958.

Spranger, Eduard. "Rickerts System." *Logos* 12, 1923/24.

Stenzel, Julius. *Dilthey und die deutsche Philosophie der Gegenwart.* Berlin: Pan-Verlagsgesellschaft, 1934.

Szilasi, Wilhelm et al. (eds.). *Heideggers Einfluss auf die Wissenschaften.* Bern: Francke, 1949.

Thomä, Dieter. *Die Zeit des Selbst und die Zeit danach. Zur Kritik der Textgeschichte Martin Heideggers.* Frankfurt am Main: Suhrkamp, 1990.

Tugendhat, Ernst. *Der Wahrheitsbegriff bei Husserl und Heidegger.* Berlin: De Gruyet, 1967.

Vietta, Egon. *Die Seinsfrage bei M. Heidegger.* Stuttgart: Schwab, 1950.

Wagner, Hans. "Weltenwurf und Sprache." *Zeitschrift für philosophische Forschung* 16, 1962.

Weier, Winfried. "Existenz und Sinn." *Zeitschrift für philosophische Forschung* 26:3, 1972.

Wilhelm, Anz. "*Die Stellung der Sprache bei Heidegger.*" In: *Heidegger: Perspektiven zur Deutung seines Werkes,* edited by Otto Pöggeler. Cologne/Berlin: Beltz-Athenäum, 1994.

Wiplinger, Fridolin. "*Sein in der Sprache.*" *Wissenschaft und Weltbild* 12:1, 1959.

Zöckler, Christofer. *Dilthey und die Hermeneutik: Diltheys Begründung der Hermeneutik als Praxiswissenschaft und die Geschichte ihrer Rezeption.* Stuttgart: Metzlersche, 1975.

In English:

Apel, Karl-Otto. "My Intellectual Biography in the Context of Contemporary Philosophy." In: Apel, Karl-Otto. *Auf der Suche nach dem letzten Grund*. Edited by Reinhard Hesse. Berlin: Lit Verlag, 2022.

Bacon, Francis. *The New Organon*. Edited by Lisa Jardine and Michael Silverthorne. Cambridge: Cambridge University Press, 2000.

Ballard, Edward G. and Charles E. Scott (eds.). *Martin Heidegger in Europe and America*. The Hague: Martinus Nijhoff, 1973.

Barrett, William. *What is Existentialism?*. New York: Evergreen-Grove Press, 1965.

Bauman, Zygmunt. *Hermeneutics and Social Science*. New York: Columbia University Press, 1978.

Betti, Emilio. "Hermeneutics as the General Methodology of the Geisteswissenschaften." In: Bleicker, Josef (ed.). *Contemporary Hermeneutics: Hermeneutics as Method, Philosophy, and Critique*. London: Routledge & Kegan Paul, 1980.

Bubner, Rudiger. "Is Transcendental Hermeneutics Possible?" In: Manninen, Juha and Raimo Tuomela (eds.). *Essays on Explanation and Understanding: Studies in the Foundations of Humanities and Social Studies*. Dordrecht/Boston: D. Reidel Publishing Company, 1976.

Cerf, Walter H. "An Approach to Heidegger's Ontology." *Philosophy and Phenomenological Research* 1-2, 1940.

Gray, J. Glenn. "Heidegger's Being." *Journal of Philosophy* 49:19, 1952.

Grene, Marjorie. *Martin Heidegger*. New York: Hillary House, 1957.

Halliburton, David. *Poetic Thinking: An Approach to Heidegger*. Chicago: University of Chicago Press, 1981.

Hegel, G.W.F. *Phenomenology of Spirit*. Translated by A.V. Miller. Oxford: Oxford University Press, 1977.

Husserl, Edmund. *Ideas Pertaining to a Pure Phenomenology and to a Phenomenological Philosophy, Book 1: General Introduction to a Pure Phenomenology*. Translated by F. Kersten. The Hague: Martinus Nijhoff Publishers, 1983.

Kean, Charles D. *The Meaning of Existence*. New York: Harper & Brothers, 1947.

Langan, Thomas. *The Meaning of Heidegger: A Critical Study of an Existentialist Phenomenology*. New York: Columbia University Press, 1959.

Löwith, Karl. "Heidegger: The Problem and Background of Existentialism." *Social Research* 15:3, 1948.

Nietzsche, Friedrich. *The Gay Science*. Translated by Josefine Nauckhoff and Adrian del Caro, edited by Bernard Williams. Cambridge: Cambridge University Press, 2001.

_____ *Twilight of the Idols or How to Philosophize with a Hammer*. Translated by Duncan Large. Oxford: Oxford University Press, 1998.

Palmer, Richard E. *Hermeneutics: Interpretation Theory in Schleiermacher, Dilthey, Heidegger, and Gadamer*. Evanston: Northwestern University Press, 1969.

Radhakrishnan. *Indian Philosophy*, vol. II. New York: Macmillan Company, 1958.

Richardson, S.J., William J. *Heidegger: Through Phenomenology to Thought*. The Hague: Martinus Nijhoff, 1963.

Rodi, Frithjof. "Dilthey, Gadamer and 'Traditional' Hermeneutics." *Reports on Philosophy* 7, 1983.

Rickman, H.P. "Hermeneutics." *Journal of the British Society for Phenomenology* 7:3, 1976.

Ricoeur, Paul. *The Conflict of Interpretations: Essays in Hermeneutics.* Edited by Don Ihde. Evanston: Northwestern University Press, 1974.

Savile, Anthony. "Historicity and the Hermeneutic Circle." *New Literary History* 10, 1978.

Weiss, Helene. "The Greek Conceptions of Time and Being in the Light of Heidegger's Philosophy." *Philosophy and Phenomenological Research* 2:2, 1941.

Werkmeister, William H. "An Introduction to Heidegger's Essential Philosophy." *Philosophy and Phenomenological Research* 2:1, 1941.

Yates, Frances A. *Giordano Bruno and the Hermetic Tradition.* London: Routledge and Kegan Paul, 1964.

www.ingramcontent.com/pod-product-compliance
Lightning Source LLC
Chambersburg PA
CBHW070048080526
44586CB00013B/955